THE NEXT
REFORMATION

THE NEXT REFORMATION

Why Evangelicals Must Embrace Postmodernity

CARL RASCHKE

Baker Academic

Grand Rapids, Michigan

© 2004 by Carl Raschke

Published by Baker Academic
a division of Baker Publishing Group
P.O. Box 6287, Grand Rapids, MI 49516-6287
www.bakeracademic.com

Printed in the United States of America

Library of Congress Cataloging-in-Publication Data
Raschke, Carl A.
    The next reformation : why evangelicals must embrace postmodernity / Carl Raschke.
        p.   cm.
    Includes bibliographical references and index.
    ISBN 0-8010-2751-9 (pbk.)
    1. Theology—History—20th century. 2. Postmodernism—Religious aspects—
Christianity. 3. Evangelicalism. I. Title.
BT28.R35 2004
261.5′1—dc22   2004012193

CONTENTS

PREFACE

THE CURIOUS THING ABOUT WRITING prefaces is that one always accomplishes the task *after* writing the book. Thus, a preface is really an afterword, or at least a thoughtful survey and careful reflection concerning what one has actually accomplished with the text. This preface is no different, but it provokes some considerations that were definitely not apparent in the first conception of the project.

In many ways this book was not really conceived. It was laid upon me in quite a few circumstantial ways, though undertakings of this sort are never accidental. They appear to have been God-intended. In the late summer of 2001, only a few weeks before the momentous day of September 11 (which happens to be my birthday), I honored a request to attend the annual meeting of the Evangelical Theological Society in Colorado Springs, Colorado, in November of that year—something I had never done before. I was asked to appear on a panel to discuss postmodernism and give a brief paper. Countless times over the years I had appeared on similar panels outside the evangelical setting, and my initial instincts were to honor the request merely out of a sense of obligation to the one making the request. Nothing elaborate was involved. The meeting was only seventy miles away from my office at the University of Denver. I thought of the assignment as nothing more important than preparing another hour of graduate lectures.

But on that day in November "something funny happened on the way" to the Broadmoor Hotel, where the meeting was held. The idea came to me that I needed to evangelize a group of evangelicals. That comment should not be taken wrongly. Throughout my own odyssey of personal doubt and faith, I have always considered myself an evangelical in the biblical sense of the term.

7

Baptized a Lutheran in a very German Lutheran church in Philadelphia, I was raised a Presbyterian and almost ordained a Presbyterian minister in the 1960s until, as I am fond of saying, "God called me out of the Presbyterian ministry" to be an academician. I taught for years in a Methodist school (my mother had been raised a Methodist), but in the early 1980s I joined the Christian Reformed Church in an effort to recapture my Calvinistic faith, because the Methodists I was familiar with, who were historically always trying to get right with God, did not seem to get it very well.

Several years later a move to a small mountain community in Colorado, where there are no Christian Reformed churches, led me to join a community church, which hired an evangelical Methodist minister, which resulted in a split in the church, mainly over the style of music. It is ironic that these days music splits churches more than doctrine. I followed half of the split church to a new storefront praise-and-worship ministry—the forerunner of what we are now calling postmodern ministry—which lasted as long as the pastor, who left to go to a larger church. When I moved to Texas a year or so later, I became a Methodist again for a while, then totally unexpectedly became involved in the charismatic movement, where I stayed for about four years. Then in Dallas I joined an urban, truly postmodern, noncharismatic Generation-X church with a Baptist and dispensationalist background. I am currently a member of a nondenominational—or perhaps postdenominational, the new nomenclature—Bible church in North Texas that defines itself officially as noncharismatic, but not anticharismatic. It has the postmodern format of worship. This Bible church is next door to the Methodist church to which I once belonged. The long and short of it is that I have been around.

The Lord seems to have given me a tour of much of the entire evangelical spectrum, preparing me to write a book such as this one. I have been confident of my postmodernism, into which I stumbled philosophically in the 1970s, longer than my evangelicalism, mainly because I assumed wrongly that one could not be simultaneously an evangelical and a postmodernist. I had the wrong notion of evangelicalism, even though I really was evangelical, because I thought the word really meant what the people who bashed postmodernists said it meant. We all were wrong. God had a plan.

When I gave my little talk in Colorado Springs, I expected people to throw stones at me. The opposite was the case. God was working. I met my current publisher a few days later at the American Academy of Religion meeting in Denver. I had walked into the wrong reception, started stuffing myself with hot hors d'oeuvres, realized I was not where I thought I was, and sheepishly headed out the door. Then an editor for Baker Books accosted me. He said he had heard me in Colorado Springs: "Would you write a book?" I said yes.

The purpose of this book is threefold: (1) To acquaint evangelical thinkers and ministers with what postmodernism really is and what postmodernist thinkers—especially philosophers—have really said, as opposed to what the polemicists are telling us too glibly it is and says. (2) To offer a historical analysis concerning how evangelical Christianity made its own unholy alliance with Cartesian rationalism and British evidentialism as far back as the seventeenth century, taking the wrong turn at a decisive juncture and thereby compromising the original spirit of the Reformation. And (3) to explore and suggest how embracing, rather than simply villifying, the postmodern turn in Western thought widens the prospects for evangelical Christianity to flourish once again as a progressive rather than reactionary force in the present-day world.

The prospects are staggering and the vision is breathtaking. I have summed up these prospects with the label "the Next Reformation," which is admittedly more a slogan than an incisive caption. On the other hand, reformations are historically propelled by slogans. For the Next Reformation I have appropriated two that are just as valid in this new, postmodern reformation as they were in the Reformation of the sixteenth century. Those slogans are *sola fide* and *sola scriptura*—"by faith alone" and "by Scripture alone." The postmodernist turn in thought is an opportunity for Christian thinkers to claim and seize these slogans at this revolutionary moment in history. It allows us finally to wrest thought away from all those surly habits of reasoning that Francis Schaeffer, in his passionate but fruitless diatribes, contended were eroding the Christian worldview. It is time for Christian intellectuals to regain the offensive after more than three hundred years of cravenly throwing incense before the statue of the modernist intellectual Caesar. It is time to say confidently, "Back to the Bible, back to the Mount of Olives, back to Sinai!"

Books, like lives, are impossible without submitting oneself to the direction of the God whom we always meet, not only as the postmodern philosopher Jacques Derrida says, "at the end of the book," but also at the end of our lives. This book is really about theology, or what in 1979 I called "the end of theology." It is also about ministry, which requires theology, or the end of theology. But my book on the end of theology was only a beginning. When we are in the living presence of the Lord of history, there is really no end. In the doxology we say "world without end. Amen." That is what this book is really about.

Books, like wives, are impossible without love and patience. My first acknowledgment of thanks is to my wonderful wife, Sunny, who took care of five cats and four dogs—which she loves to do—while I finished this manuscript in the summer of 2003. When I first met her, I wrote her a poem that said, "You have more faith than in a thousand anthems." My thanks to my partner, a woman of deep and abiding faith and love for the Lord.

I want also to thank my son Erik, a writer with talents of his own, for doing some crucial, early research on this book to motivate me to get it going. Finally, I wish to acknowledge a debt of thanks to the following: my comrade in spiritual arms and postmodern thinker extraordinaire David Hale for many useful conversations about postmodernism and evangelicalism and for inadvertently steering me to the wrong reception at the American Academy of Religion (AAR) meeting, which turned out to be the right one; to Dan Allender, Christy Lynk, Kirk Webb, Heather Webb, and the whole gang at Mars Hill Graduate School in Seattle, who showed me that evangelical believers can be not only fun but also "wild"; to Don Hudson, for his inspiration and friendship as I was going through one of the darkest periods of my life on the way to learning what I needed for this text; to Giles and Connie Hudson, for their discipleship and deep friendship; to pastors Robert Heidler, David Anderson, Gary Roe, and Claude Webb, who have taught me, amid the varieties of evangelical faith, what it means to "keep the main thing the main thing," that is, Jesus Christ; to Pastor King, Brother Danny, Brother Gene, Sister Rosemarie, T., and others at the "Eagles' Wings" Church, who introduced me to the awesome power of the Holy Spirit in the most incredible situation, and from whom I learned what the Next Reformation is ultimately all about—unlimited, undeserved, *amazing grace*.

1

POSTMODERNISM AND THE CRISIS OF EVANGELICAL THOUGHT

THE CHALLENGE OF POSTMODERNISM

It is no secret that evangelical thought today is in crisis. The crisis has blown up from within as well as from without. Just about the time international communism collapsed at the start of the 1990s, evangelical Christianity in the West began eyeballing an intellectual challenge of a magnitude it had never before confronted. The challenge was protean and elusive. It was neither a heresy that undermined the essentials of the faith, nor an obvious new style of paganism in competition with classical Christianity. It could not be strictly or reliably characterized, but at least it had a name: *postmodernism.*

During the past several decades, while postmodernism has altered the face of academic culture, particularly in the arts and humanities, it has only recently begun to pound at the door of evangelical thought and faith. Although "postmodern ministry" has become something of a buzz term among new urban evangelicals, it denotes more cultural style than theoretical weight. Overall, postmodern theology and philosophy have been reviled in the evangelical community as a kind of *agent provocateur*—an outlook and habit of thinking that fosters nihilism, moral relativism, as well as emotionalism and irrationalism.

Interestingly, these accusations are the same sorts of calumny that liberal theology brought against postmodernism over a decade ago. The caricatures are symptomatic of the breakdown of the modernist paradigm of rationality and religious discourse that has reigned since at least the seventeenth century and has powerfully influenced evangelical Protestantism. The malaise of modernism has grown profound as we enter the third millennium. The efforts of evangelical theology to shore up its fundamental commitment to scriptural authority have been damaged by its own dependence on various sorts of metaphysical theories of truth, such as inerrancy, which are neither truly biblical in origin nor persuasive to nonbelievers.

Postmodernism—or "pomo," if one wants to be colloquial—was already stirring up dust in both popular and academic literature long before it became a bone of contention in the evangelical world. The locution had even entered the American political lexicon, largely as a shibboleth of the culture wars that were then raging in the university and gaining rapt attention in the media. Social conservatives—or neoconservatives, as they are called—roundly condemned postmodernism. They deployed many of the same terms old liberals had drawn upon during the 1960s to condemn the campus protests and the arguments of what was known in those days as the New Left. They cited a familiar syllabus of dangerous and erroneous isms—anarchism, relativism, and nihilism.

Mainline liberals, called neoliberals, were equally and instinctively suspicious as well. But they had slightly different cause for anxiety. They despised postmodernists as incurably narcissistic and individualistic.

Political liberals feared they were rendering an entire generation of political activists apolitical. Theological liberals were aghast that the postmodernists seemed to be erasing their long and hard-won success in making Christianity socially relevant and scientifically acceptable. They regarded religious postmodernism *tout suite* as a kind of scholarly spiritualism, as a sophisticated subterfuge for speaking in tongues, where obscure and baffling pronouncements by the gurus of the movement were adulated, validated, and circulated with little shame, only to corrode the critical and moral armor of the greater populace.

At the center of the cyclone was Jacques Derrida, an Algerian Jew from France who had scorned protocol not merely by accenting the last syllable of his surname, but also by making himself into an intellectual celebrity without leaving himself beholden to any academic institution or constituency. Not only did he write book after book that was translated from French into English for the leading university publishers; he also became the darling of both the

Parisian café scene and the American bicoastal media culture. And he did so with a panache that even the most astute academic entrepreneurs in this country could barely imagine, let alone bring off. A philosopher by training and temperament, Derrida gained fame initially, and in the beginning almost exclusively, within the literary set. Though he did not actually coin the word, Derrida became known almost singularly in the 1970s and early 1980s for having invented a new, and disarming, method for reading literary texts: deconstruction. The expression alone was unsettling, especially to those who were unable to follow his seemingly ad-libbed style of composition that came across as a curious combination of anthropological obiter dicta, couch confessions, notebook jottings, and tedious exposition of passages from ancient sources in their original languages. It was often daunting to understand what Derrida was actually saying. One had simply to follow along and try to catch the drift, which often required reading him as rapidly as he could churn out one book after another.

Because Derrida in both profile and profession shattered every conceivable mold, he became an object of both reverence and derision. He was the quintessential Frenchman, which was bad enough. A joke that made all the rounds during the early Reagan years (at a time when the *Godfather* movies created a mystique for the Italian Mafia) summed up all the primal fear and fascination that America's learned elites had toward the Derridean phenomenon. Question: "What happens when you meet a deconstructionist in a dark alley?" Answer: "He offers you a deal you can't understand." Though Americans feared they couldn't understand postmodernism at all, they knew they had to deal with it and to take it seriously—very seriously.

By the late 1980s postmodernism and deconstruction fortunately were no longer identified in the public mind as one and the same. In a relentless effort to communicate Gallic sensibility to America's barbaric soul, the French ministry of culture began subsidizing a stream of English translations of many of Derrida's own intellectual contemporaries. Derrida himself had never had the pride of place in Paris that he was enjoying in New York, Boston, San Francisco, and southern California. Because he was a philosopher and not one of the abundant cultural theorists of his day who spoke almost exclusively to French concerns and French dissatisfactions, his reputation in the United States far surpassed his influence on the Continent. Derrida was an exotic attraction to which American arts and letters, chafing from years of dowdy academicism, were drawn like a moth to the flame. But his popularity also whetted the American appetite for everything French and trendy. A motley assortment of postwar figures—such as Giles Deleuze, Jean Baudrillard,

Emmanuel Lévinas, and Maurice Blanchot—well known for years among the Parisian set, began to see their works increasingly appear in translation. Soon the concept of postmodernism increasingly came to mean everything and anything that was au courant among the intelligentsia.

In another brief interval the phrase came to be applied to thinkers, writers, and forms of writing that were not distinctive in any sense other than they were novel and perchance controversial. Not too many years later, Marxists in both the English-speaking world and on the European continent began to speak out against the Derridean phenomenon as self-indulgent and injurious to the mobilization of the masses. Ironically, neoconservatives in this country had at the same time been making the opposite point. Deconstruction was no different than Marxism, they harangued, because it weakened cultural backbone and the norms of truth and authority. Neoconservatives, of course, had been training their assaults on the tenured radicals in academia who had gone from revolution in the streets of the 1960s to renovation of the curriculum in the 1980s, replacing Shakespeare with contemporary feminist novelists, the speeches of Lincoln with the biographies of black slaves, Plato and Aristotle with the *Little Red Book* of Mao-Tse Tung, and so forth. These people were Marxists, or at least Marxists of the more rarefied variety, and the fact that they also read and talked about Derrida was sufficient proof that deconstruction had been cut from precisely the same cloth.

With the fall of the Berlin Wall in 1989 and the collapse of the Soviet Union two years later, on the other hand, the Marxists received their comeuppance. Suddenly and spectacularly, the allure of free markets and open societies in the former Soviet client states made Marxism seem economically irrelevant. "Cultural Marxism"—an expression invented again by conservative critics of what was going on in colleges and universities—had already captured the flag during the curriculum wars of the previous decade. And these unreformed detractors now began to sneer publicly at the emergent global consumer civilization with the same verve as conservatives once had attacked the Marxists themselves. Frederic Jameson, one of America's leading cultural Marxists, referred to postmodernism as the "cultural logic of late capitalism."[1] Updating Marxism, which for a century and a half had regularly predicted the culminating crisis of capitalism, Jameson construed postmodernism as a true sign of the end. The worldwide span of capitalism no longer depended on the accumulation and control of capital in the financial sense. Yet, Jameson insisted, it had now spread its tentacles even across former Communist societies. Through mass media and pop culture it was enchaining them not through outright poverty, but by stuffing their heads with name brands and celebrity puffery, alchemizing them into mindless consumers.

A similar, but more idiosyncratic, interpretation citing the rise of cyberculture was proffered by Jean Baudrillard, who talked about something called hyperreality. Hyperreality was "more real than real," Baudrillard crooned. It was an unreal reality where effigies produced by dancing electrons on television and computer screens were no longer distinguishable from real places and real things. Baudrillard's philosophy, which had always been mildly Marxist and was now at its height of popularity in France, inspired the groundbreaking motion picture *The Matrix*, released in 1999. The cultural Marxists succeeded in doing in reverse what their conservative opponents had also done ten years before. They popularized the concept of postmodernism even more by virulently attacking it. Now postmodernism was becoming something of a bon mot among conservatives, even religious conservatives. Malls and megachurches were now labeled postmodern, along with the new hip, informal fashions of so-called Generation X, which was amassing publicity. When evangelical Christianity began adapting its message and ministerial modus operandi to the new cultural landscape, particularly with music and styles of worship, all at once something recognizable as the postmodern church flashed onto the screen. But past controversies continued to haunt the environs.

EVANGELICAL BROADSIDES

In his book *Truth Decay: Defending Christianity against the Challenges of Postmodernism*, Doug Groothuis, professor of apologetics at Denver Seminary in Colorado, launched the same vicious volley of imprecations against "postmodern Christianity" that neoconservatives had hurled against cultural Marxists a decade earlier. The "postmodern temptation," Groothuis asserted, "is to entice souls to create a self-styled spirituality of one's own, or to revert to the spiritual tradition of one's ethnic or racial group without a concern for objective truth or rationality." Furthermore, said Groothuis, postmodernism is the same as "nihilism," the fashionable view, emerging in the late-nineteenth century, that there is no supreme or enduring truth other than what anyone arbitrarily wills or chooses that truth to be. "Truth decay is a cultural condition in which the very idea of absolute, objective, and universal truth is considered implausible, held in open contempt, or not even seriously considered."[2] The fault is wholly that of postmodernism. For "postmodernist thinkers," according to Groothuis, "the very idea of truth has decayed and disintegrated. It is no longer something knowable by anyone who engages in the proper forms of investigation and study. Truth is not over and above us, something that can be conveyed across cultures and over time. It is inseparable from our cultural conditioning, our psychology, our race, and our gender. At the end of the day, truth is simply what we, as individuals and as communities, make it to be—and nothing more. Truth dissolves into a host of disconnected 'truths.'"[3]

The value of Groothuis's book was not that it had anything of substance to say, philosophically or theologically, against postmodernism. Groothuis rarely cited or presented the offending texts of postmodernist writers, preferring instead to use the familiar rhetorical device of associating the term "postmodernist" with every avant-garde intellectual trend that has come down the pike since the Vietnam era. Postmodernism thus was equivalent to virtually all the isms of the twentieth century that traditionalists had been pounding against for more than a hundred years—libertarianism, subjectivism, feminism, relativism, sociologism, psychologism, Marxism, social constructivism, fascism, and so forth. In an interview with the online magazine *Antithesis,* Groothuis went so far as to identify postmodernism with everything (wrong) about American culture itself.

> If you think critically, in terms of either/or or antithesis, then you can't hold contradictory beliefs, and your goal—your ideal—as a thoughtful being is to have a consistent and coherent set of beliefs that matches reality, that corresponds to fact. And I'm afraid that many Americans, in their sense of spirituality, have lost that as an intellectual ideal. It's like a smorgasbord: take a little of this and a little of that. As long as you don't get indigestion—"What's the problem!? A little bit of Buddhism, a little bit of Taoism. . . . Oh, Jesus was a wonderful spiritual figure. . . . I go to church—sometimes I go to New Age seminars—and I find they all help me. It's not what is true, what is rational, but what feels right—what seems right, what helps me and gives me a sense of community and solidarity and so forth."[4]

Of course, Groothuis found himself making many of the same arguments against postmodernists that American and British philosophers had been making against the claims of Christianity for generations. Oddly enough, Groothuis sounded a lot like Bertrand Russell in his famous, or infamous, essay *Why I Am Not a Christian.* In that essay, delivered in 1927 to the National Secular Society in London, Russell lambasted the history of the church as a record of "irrational" enthusiasms. Christians are silly and stupid people because they base their beliefs on emotion rather than "argumentation," Russell huffed. Christian beliefs are nonnegotiable when it comes to the use of logical analysis and scientific evidence. The basic quarrel science has with Christianity concerns the doctrine of divine revelation, which reason finds repugnant. Russell put forth as an alternative to Christianity the method of scientific experiment and the rational sifting of details and data which, he opined, allows us to "conquer the world by intelligence."[5] If the world is not as reason would have us envision it, then "we ought to make the best we can of the world, and if it is not so good as we wish, after all it will still be better than what these others [such as Christians] have made of it in all these ages." But now Christianity itself can play the role that Russell envisioned for science, according to Groothuis, as a "cogent explanation for a whole range of facts in accordance with the essential tenets of logic and criteria for evidence that are required for all critical thinking." Christianity must aggressively challenge "the postmodernist worldview," which "collapses in on itself." Postmodernism "is ultimately a house of cards," the same sort of metaphor Russell used for his attack on the "Christian" worldview.

Evangelical Counterpunches

In a little essay simply entitled "Postmodernism," Graeme Codrington points out that postmodernism has carried the day because the kind of rationalism both Russell and Groothuis commend has failed miserably to slake the spiritual hunger in today's world. "Postmodernism is a reaction to the rationalistic outlook of modernism," Codrington writes, "specifically a reaction to the concept that truth can be discovered by simple rationalistic induction. The most common caricature of postmodernism is that it is a complete denial of truth, thus relativizing everything. Postmodern people, however, do not deny that there is truth and objective reality. What they question is our ability to distinguish truth from nontruth."[6] Codrington further suggests that this inability to draw such a distinction is what makes postmodernism attractive to believers. Christians, he maintains, do not, and cannot, make judgments concerning truth in accord with their own capacity for systematic thought. The truth that makes us free as Christians comes to us as direct dispensation from Christ. It is a result of our encounter with him. It is not the product of some convoluted, or clever, Aristotelian syllogism.

Stan Wallace adopts much the same approach. Postmodernism redresses many of the intellectual imbalances that modernist thinking, sustaining a siege over many centuries against basic Christian beliefs, left with Western civilization. Culminating in the European Enlightenment of the eighteenth century, modernism exalted the independent rational subject over the Deity himself in a quest for scientific certainty. It substituted the hypothesis of human progress and social control for God's providential direction and ordering of history. "Concerning reason," Wallace asserts, "postmodernists shun modernist views which inflate reason to the status of an entirely independent, neutral, unbiased and objective instrument with which truth can and will be found." On the subject of historical progress, "postmodernists are quick to point out that, contrary to the optimistic outlook of modernity, we are not 'every day, in every way, getting better and better' [Émile Coué], but rather, in some cases we are creating survival-threatening conditions by the unbridled rush toward technological 'progress.'" It is the same with the premium modernism places on individual autonomy and freedom. "Modernity placed freedom and human autonomy as one of the highest values to be embraced," while the postmodernist suggests our freedom is an illusion.[7]

Wallace, however, concurs with Groothuis that the postmodernist critique of scientific rationality does not necessarily mean the partisans of postmodernism are dependable allies of Christianity. The postmodernist metaphysic, or theory of ultimate reality, is what Wallace calls nominalistic. Nominalism was a movement in European philosophy that began during the late Middle Ages and challenged the classical view, typically called realism, that knowledge mirrors the world as it actually is. Concepts are not "things," the nominalists proposed. They are merely tags, labels, or "names" that we attach to the specific and discrete phenomena we encounter. Postmodernism, so far as Wallace is concerned, follows the nominalist route of rendering the relationship between cognition and reality. Postmodernism is "the rejection of truth as correspondence to an objective, mind-independent world." The truths of postmodernism, or nominalism for that matter, cannot be considered truths at all, because the notion of truth implies universal validity. Postmodern statements of truth "are not objective and absolute, but subjective, bound to the individual and/or culture for their existence and validity."

Wallace, like Groothuis and many contemporary evangelical scholars, tends to confuse a supposedly Christian theory of truth with a narrow philosophical mind-set that is not indigenous, but rather only incidental, to the broader history of Christian reflection down through the ages. Realism and the "correspondence theory of truth" were the mainstay of Christian orthodoxy only during the Constantinian period of the church and the High Middle Ages (ca. 1175–1375), and they were often used as armaments of the Papacy to suppress dissent, especially among those reformers who might invoke Scripture. Martin Luther himself was hardly influenced by nominalism and constantly referred to the "bitch goddess Reason" as the most tawdry of pagan idols to which a Christian theologian might inadvertently pay homage. Very few of the church fathers were realists in the sense Groothuis and Wallace would presume. Tertullian, one of the greatest among the fathers, vowed that faith itself hinged not on any kind of rational consistency in propounding what Groothuis terms the "propositional truth" of Christianity, but was founded on a fundamental "absurdity"—that the infinite Creator took on the form of a finite creature. "What does Athens have to do with Jerusalem?" Tertullian sneered in dismissing the implication that there could be a Christian philosophy of any serious stature.

The theme of subjective truth, properly understood, has been far more congenial to the expansion of the gospel throughout the ages than any canon of propositional certitude. When evangelical believers undergo conversion by responding to an altar call and offer their own lives to Christ in a personal profession of faith, it is rarely the result of anyone having convinced them through careful and flawless reasoning that Jesus is their Savior. It is usually because God ministering as the Holy Spirit has grappled with them in their private depths of confusion and doubt and given them a whole new inner lease on life. Paul may have convinced a few Athenian citizens that the "Unknown God" they were worshipping was in fact the living Creator. But Paul himself was not drawn to Christianity because some philosopher offered a better argument than the Stoics, Cynics, or Epicureans of his time. Saul of Tarsus became Paul the apostle because the resurrected Lord encountered him on the road to Damascus, said only a few soul-wrenching words to him, and left him speechless and dumbstruck.

The early church, of course, did have its share of stalwart intellectual defenders of what many today would designate "the Christian worldview." But they tended to have an arrogant and exclusivist attitude toward those who were not as enlightened as they were. They were called gnostics—from the Greek word *gnōsis,* meaning a special kind of illuminated knowledge. While the writings of the ancient Christian gnostics are somewhat strange and difficult to unravel, a common thread running through all of them is that one must be truly mentally adept to know who Jesus really is. The curious notion that the truths of the Christian faith can, and should, be argued in much the same way as one would prove a mathematical theorem—a notion that has gained momentum in evangelical circles in recent decades—reeks of Gnosticism. Like the ancient gnostics, the new antipomo apologists measure themselves by a false standard and try to be something they are not—*secular philosophers*—when they should instead be communicating and sharing the heart of Jesus. Much of the current evangelical polemics against postmodernism also has a gnostic edge to it, inasmuch as postmodernists, whoever they might be, are generally accused of being shallow, stupid, excessively emotional or touchy-feely, and uncritical.

But that of course is the same as what the gnostics had in mind when they divided the world between those who truly knew who Jesus was in a philosophical and sophisticated way, and the blind masses, who clung to popular prejudices and superstition. The postmodernist preoccupation with popular culture, which many evangelical theologians disdain, is not necessarily an unchristian fascination with sex and celebrities, but a form of cultural sensitivity and intellectual humility that ultimately offers an evangelical opportunity that hard-core Christian rationalists overlook. Jesus targeted his ministry toward social misfits as well as the intellectually and morally challenged—called "sinners" in the Gospels—rather than to those who held out the greatest promise of becoming theologically correct. It was the Pharisees, not Jesus, who were constantly attempting to rationalize the message of God's kingdom and break it down into conceptually compact segments that made good, philosophical sense. Jesus' preference for speaking in parables surely would have evoked the same kind of clucking about nonsensical rhetoric for which postmodernist thinkers are regularly indicted. It would be gratuitous to call Jesus a postmodernist (throughout the ages he has been identified as the champion of virtually every cause by virtually every advocate of that cause); but it should give us pause that his contemporaries put him down for many of the same grievances for which some attack postmodernists today.

POSTMODERNISM IS CONGENIAL WITH EVANGELICALISM

The bottom line is that postmodernism is neither an amoral and anti-Christian movement, as familiar hyperbole would have it, nor any kind of movement at all. It is simply a descriptor or locator for the Zeitgeist, the spirit of the times, for better or for worse. As Lord Chesterton reminded us, we marry ourselves to the spirit of the times at the risk of widowhood, but we cannot refuse to consort with it either. The sorts of philosophical trends known as postmodernism have their own genesis and cachet. We need to evaluate them on their own terms, not by hastily lumping them together with anything and everything that disturbs the Christian intellectual and seems to be the common denominator in all manifestations of moral and cultural "decay." Indeed, as we shall see, the postmodernist revolution in philosophy—as opposed to the general usage of the term "postmodernism" in contemporary culture—has tendered an environment where the Christian gospel can at last be disentangled from the centuries-long, modernist gnarl of scientism, rationalism, secularism, humanism, and skepticism.

Daniel Ryan Street offers a trenchant rationale for this sort of revisionary reading of postmodernism. He notes that ever since the arrival of modernism, which historians tend to correlate with the work of René Descartes, Christian theology has been in a sort of self-protective funk. Descartes, of course, laid down the philosophical pylons for what has come to be known as foundationalism—the view that all sure knowledge must rest on those clear and indubitable premises that human thought is capable of ferreting out. Descartes is considered a classical, or metaphysical, rationalist; but foundationalism truly took wing in the seventeenth century with the rise of British empiricism, and soared to glory in the early twentieth century with the development of logical positivism. The latter school of philosophy sought to model all cogent propositions, or statements of truth, on what it termed the "verification principle"—the rule that all claims about this world, or the supernatural world, must go before the bar of experiment, observation, and the evidence of the senses. Foundationalism, like communism, all at once collapsed, according to Street, because of its "referential incoherence." It demanded a foundation upon which to assert that foundations were needed. "The statement that all knowledge must be either indubitable, incorrigible, or inferred from indubitable or incorrigible beliefs, is itself not indubitable or incorrigible, or inferred from one of these classes of beliefs. Therefore, it cannot constitute knowledge."[8]

Ironically, during the modern era the mainstream of evangelical theology acquired the habit of defending the truths of faith and the authority of the Bible in terms of the foundationalist argument. The discussion went something like the following: God, the Scriptures tell us, is absolute and sovereign. If we are authentic in our faith, we cannot allow any loose ends or ragged edges to how we conceptualize God's essence and authority. Groothuis lays out what he himself calls a "minimal foundationalism." The kind of foundationalism necessary to apologetics need not be Cartesian through and through. Groothuis asserts:

> There is no reason to claim that all our beliefs can be deductively proven from indubitable first principles, or that all our beliefs must be of necessary truths (a triangle has three sides) or be based on empirical evidence (the earth is round). Some beliefs are "properly basic," in that they are not logical necessities, but neither are they proven on the basis of other things more certainly known. One candidate for a properly basic belief is "there is a real past." One cannot marshal evidence for this; it is a presupposition of normal thought.[9]

Groothuis goes on to say that "what is essential to foundationalism is simply that some core of beliefs do serve as first principles; they are not derived from other beliefs, and they are not relative to cultures or individuals." He further contends that Christian beliefs can somehow be defended in this fashion. "There are essential truths of logic that are necessary for all intelligible thought and rational discourse, Christian or otherwise." When Paul confronted the Athenian philosophers at Mars' Hill as narrated in the book of Acts, he utilized these same protocols of reasoning and logic to which Christian apologetics should be attentive, according to Groothuis. Postmodernism rejects these protocols. Thus, within the parameters of foundationalism, "the best way to defend the truth of Christ is by presenting the Christian vision as the most cogent explanation for a whole range of facts in accordance with the essential tenets of logic and criteria for evidence that are required for all critical thinking."[10]

THE FOUNDATIONALIST PREMISE

What Groothuis terms "minimal foundationalism," however, is actually an updated version of what the Western philosophical tradition has dubbed "commonsense empiricism," which has prevailed in various guises in English and American thought for centuries. Commonsense empiricism was initially a response to the extreme skepticism of David Hume in the eighteenth century. Hume came up with ingenious arguments to demonstrate that we cannot be certain that even the sun will rise tomorrow, or that the ground on which we are standing is the same terra firma on which we rested even a moment ago. The German thinker Immanuel Kant reacted to Hume by elaborating what came to be known as the "critical philosophy," which overshadowed Western thought for the entire next century. Kant's critical philosophy was one comprehensive variant of minimal foundationalism. Kant maintained that we do indeed have a certain basic understanding of the world we experience because our minds are somehow hardwired, if we may employ a contemporary metaphor, to see and interpret things in certain ways. Kant referred to these tendencies toward a universal and common human experience as "a priori (prior to all experience)" concepts of "understanding." The commonsense features of knowledge that Hume with his extreme skepticism sought to doubt away were what Kant restored as a priori "categories" of cognition. Because of Kant's heavy and not easily translatable Teutonic style, Anglo-American philosophers adopted their own grammar and rhetoric for embroidering many of the exact same themes.

Most of the evangelical broadsides against postmodernism, therefore, have been couched as an indictment of the moral relativism allegedly inherent in it. But these critiques have masked what is perhaps the real animus—*the centuries-old hostility between the Anglo-American and European Continental traditions of philosophy*. The fact that most attacks on postmodernism have been aimed at either generalities or caricatures of the movement, rather than at specific writers or the texts representing their arguments and positions, suggests that the clash is far more one of apparel than of substance. At the same time, character and style may not be easily disentangled. The view that nowadays in the English-speaking world of philosophy is termed "foundationalism" derives from more ponderous intellectual premises put forth during the seventeenth century. The foundationalist outlook propelled the scientific revolution and ultimately led to the secularist mugging of Christianity.

Faith and philosophy have largely remained compatible in Continental thought, notwithstanding the kind of atheistic materialism that gained a foothold during the French Revolution. But in Anglo-American thought around 1900 under the progressive influence of such figures as Rudolf Carnap, Karl Popper, Ludwig Wittgenstein, Anthony Flew, and of course Bertrand Russell himself, the mood turned antireligious. The positivist principle that for any statement to be meaningful it must be subject to the possibility of empirical verification quickly came to dominate the new approach in Anglo-American circles known as "analytical philosophy." The positivist attitude served as a convenient truncheon to beat down the significance of all theological concerns and what came to be somewhat contemptuously labeled "God talk." Foundationalism was riding high in the saddle, but it was in no way sympathetic to the defense of the Christian faith. Quite the opposite was taking place.

The antifoundationalist tack of postmodernism, as evangelical philosopher Bruce Ellis Benson has pointed out, is actually more Christian in many senses of the term than foundationalism itself. In his *Graven Ideologies: Nietzsche, Derrida and Marion on Modern Idolatry*, Benson argues that postmodernism challenges evangelical thought to acknowledge that it is guilty of what from the biblical perspective is considered the greatest of sins—the sin of idol-worship. Because evangelical thinking has adopted by its own means and measure the criteria for conceptual adequacy that were put forth centuries ago by modern philosophy, it has ingested that unique fashion of idolatry. Modernist idolatry, according to Benson, encompasses three main characteristics: (1) a critical stress on the autonomy of the individual, (2) "a strong confidence in the powers of human reason in general and the rationality of the individual," and (3) the pure "objective" character of reason itself.[11] All these three commitments are interrelated and tend to emphasize the priority of the human or subjective stance, even when people employ that stance to underwrite the "objective" reality of God or Scripture.

The point was made repeatedly and with a broad brush by Martin Heidegger, who more than Derrida or Nietzsche should be considered the precursor of postmodernism. For Heidegger, the genesis of modernism as a philosophical movement occurs with René Descartes's *Meditations,* first published in 1641 as *Méditationes métaphysiques.* Descartes sought to replace medieval ecclesiastical authority, based on dogma and tradition, with the primacy of unaided human reason. In the *Meditations* Descartes employs the method of radical skepticism, or "hyperbolic doubt," in questioning whether there are any genuine philosophical foundations upon which clear and firm knowledge can be constructed. After he has doubted away even what would appear to be the most commonsense assumptions about how things are—for instance, the existence of a world external to the mind—Descartes concludes that there is one fact of experience that is truly indubitable, the "I," or self, that performs the doubting.

Although this insight was originally set forth by Augustine in the fifth century, Descartes adjusted it to the problem of modern epistemology. If the one thing that thought can think without doubt is the "I" that performs the thinking, then the possibility of thought must arise from that self-certifying reality, ego as a "thinking entity *(res cogitans).*" The true foundation of truth is the "I" that authenticates the truth. According to Heidegger, the Cartesian insurgency in thought occasions a usurping of the throne of the infinite God and his replacement with the human subject. Cartesianism is the beginning of what Nietzsche terms "the death of God," as we shall show. Modern evangelical thought has unwittingly bought into the Cartesian assumption about the nature of truth. Foundationalism is simply a less tendentious term for modernism. Even a minimal foundationalism, however, does not mitigate the idolatrous predisposition of all modernism. The kings of ancient Israel would not acknowledge the prophetic claim that, even though they gave lip service to Yahweh, they had actually profaned the temple with the images of the gods of foreign nations. So also, contemporary evangelical theologians have not realized that, although they rhetorically maintain God's unshakable power and presence, they do so by following modern philosophy to midnight worship on the high places.

The Reformation Context

In order to understand why modernism and bona fide evangelical faith are mismatched with each other, we need a quick refresher course on what happened intellectually in the West during the two centuries that followed the Protestant Reformation of the sixteenth century. In 1517 Martin Luther, an Augustinian monk from the eastern part of Germany, posted his famous 95 Theses on Halloween, the eve of All Saints' Day. The event sparked a theological and political upheaval throughout Europe that would not abate for at least the next hundred and fifty years. In the 95 Theses Luther mainly challenged the claim of the Pope in Rome to have absolute authority over the souls of individual Christian believers. No church or church prelate can remit sins and grant assurance of salvation, Luther insisted. God alone is the final arbiter of each human being's eternal destiny. Each position Luther took implied a further, and more radical, formulation of what historians have termed the "Protestant principle." The Protestant principle consists in the general rule that there can be no confusion at any level between divine and human prerogatives. During the sixteenth century it could be summarized in the Latin maxim of *"finitus non capax infiniti* (the finite is incapable of [expressing] the infinite)." Luther's attack on the Pope called to task the long-standing Catholic view that God's fellowship with humanity requires both priestly mediators and learned theologians to interpret the divine will and message. There can be no go-between, according to Luther, when it comes to matters of conscience. God speaks immediately to the believer in prayer, worship, and the reading of Scripture. The Bible, in particular, which the Catholic Church had heretofore regarded as opaque in its meaning to the untutored layperson, is God's holy Word. Even the uneducated plowman, if he can read at all, must read the Bible in order to comprehend the whole of God's will and plan for his life.

The notion that one cannot attain heaven without an intimate, personal relationship between the believer and the God in whom he believes is the first of three crucial Reformation tenets. Luther came to this position gradually in his young manhood as he agonized over what seemed to him the impossible task of doing enough good works to obtain favor with God. In a moment of both desperation and clarity, Luther made a discovery about the meaning of Scripture that both turned his conventional world upside down and precipitated a revolution in Western thought itself. Luther had been struggling all his life with a Catholic theology that treated salvation much like a double-entry bookkeeping system. Entry into heaven depended mostly on the balance of good and bad deeds in this life, which could be affected as well by certain "excess" merits contributed by departed saints, or by "infusions" of divine grace. Prayers for dead relatives, and even certain financial fillips known as "indulgences," could also make a difference. It was the practice of granting indulgences, of course, that specifically kindled Luther's ire and spurred him to challenge the Catholic prelates to debate by posting the 95 Theses. But Luther's opposition to indulgences rested squarely on his realization that no effort of a mere mortal to make restitution for sin could possibly meet the standards of an infinite and most holy God. One cannot achieve human "righteousness" even by the most passionate and pious works. The only real righteousness, as Paul tells us in Romans, is attained "through the righteousness that came from faith."[12]

The *first tenet* was captured in a slogan that became the very watchword of the Reformation—"*sola fide* (by faith alone)." The *second tenet* was its necessary corollary—"*sola scriptura* (by Scripture alone)." The unconditional authority of Scripture, in contrast with the Roman pontiff's pretense to absolute authority, secured what Luther termed the "freedom of a Christian" in relationship to Christ. Through this relationship the Christian learns to trust in what God is saying to him or her through his revealed Word. It is the Holy Spirit who illumines the conscience of the Christian reading the Scripture and discloses the unmistakable meaning of the text. The Christian is subject to no other human being in construing that meaning, or in securing one's own eternal salvation. At the same time, Luther insisted, each is subject to every other believer in Christian love.

Nonetheless, it is the relationship of the believer to Christ, and to Christ only, that matters in the final consideration. Thus we can adduce the *third tenet* of the Reformation, known as the "priesthood of all believers," which roughly corresponds to the Latin "*communio sanctorum*." The term "priest" was intended in both an ironic and a literal sense. Moses had called the nation of Israel to be a nation of priests. Luther understood the church in the same manner. But for Luther the term "priest" referred to the faithful and sanctified believer, not to a special office or function. Hence, the "priesthood of all believers" signified the flattening of all ecclesiastical hierarchies in the administration of God's grace. In the grand summation the believer must stand before God and come to a reckoning with him, and him alone.

The singularity of personal belief and the sovereignty of individual conscience were construed almost exclusively as religious considerations during the sixteenth century. Yet by the early-seventeenth century they had been rationalized as well as secularized. The Reformation principle of Christian liberty gradually morphed into the modern idea of political liberty and what Thomas Jefferson dubbed the right to the "pursuit of happiness." The consequence of this transformation was staggering. If the individual is accountable both to God in the religious sphere and to one's fellow citizens in the political arena (just as one is responsible to all other believers within Christ's kingdom), then God's revealed Word cannot be regarded as some kind of privileged truth accessible to only the cadre of believers. It must be commensurate somehow with our own natural knowledge.

Reformation thought had drawn an unmitigated distinction between "natural" and "supernatural" knowledge of God. This distinction was drawn from the first chapter of Paul's Epistle to the Romans, the same book of the Bible that had provoked Luther to change his mind on the means of salvation. Although "what can be known about God is plain" to all humanity (Rom. 1:19 NRSV), Paul writes, original sin and the corruption of mind and the will have led them to "futility" in their thinking, "exchanging the splendour of immortal God" and the "truth" concerning the divine for an idolatrous "lie."[13] The Reformation theology of Luther, Calvin, and their confreres had stressed the unqualified necessity of approaching God through faith and surrendering the intellect. Luther himself had regarded the preference for rational examination in coming to conclusions about God as a profound sort of spiritual prostitution. He referred to reason itself as "that bitch goddess." Yet by the turn of the eighteenth century the distinction between the natural and revealed truth about God had been fatefully blurred. Modernist rationalism was triumphant, and leading-edge philosophers such as John Locke in England began to speak routinely of the inherent "reasonableness of Christianity."

EMPIRICISM AND RATIONALISM

In Locke's view, and in most of modern philosophy in England and America, the criterion of reasonableness was the natural intellect. Locke's philosophy, which had evolved from the so-called scientific experimentalism of Francis Bacon a century earlier, centered on the contention that all our ideas come directly from sense experience. "Let us then," Locke wrote, "suppose the mind to be, as we say, white paper, void of all characters, without any ideas:—How comes it to be furnished? Whence comes it by that vast store which the busy and boundless fancy of man has painted on it with an almost endless variety? Whence has it all the *materials* of reason and knowledge? To this I answer, in one word, from EXPERIENCE. In that all our knowledge is founded; and from that it ultimately derives itself."[14] Although this outlook came to be known as "empiricism," it can be better characterized in terms of what philosophers nowadays term "physical realism." All symbolic representations are not, as

German philosophy would later hold, merely subjective constructs of the mind. They signify real things that exist in the external world of matter.

Locke was the first Western thinker to advocate religious toleration, chiefly because he maintained there is no way that the natural knowledge can be reconciled effectively with revealed truth. The only consistent and dependable claims we can make are scientific ones, which have their own kind of "self-evidence." Biblical claims are beyond the ken of natural reason and are not open to theoretical dispute. What makes Christianity reasonable and persuasive is not its account of God's miraculous and supernatural effects, but its ethical effect on each one of us. Christianity, in short, has a pragmatic purpose; it serves as the moral guarantor of democratic politics. Since revealed truth cannot be adjudicated by the fallible intellect, it must be either discarded as a serious prospect for thought and reflection, or left as an item of private conviction. The charge that postmodernism is the source of contemporary subjectivism and relativism, therefore, turns out to be historically inaccurate. *The pathology is implanted in the marrow of modernism itself.*

Because of his emphasis on the priority of sense knowledge and the liberty of the individual to know and understand God in accordance with his or her own natural intellect, Locke is generally considered the father of modern theological, as well as political, liberalism. The term "liberal" has its etymology in the Latin word *liber,* which means "[free] will." Locke's philosophical and theological notions, however, were not thoroughly developed or completely consistent. Throughout the eighteenth century—the so-called age of reason—Lockean empiricism functioned more as a cultural sentiment than as a tradition of thought. By the same token, it was not Locke per se, but a Scotsman by the name of Thomas Reid, who had the most forceful and long-standing impact on the theory of knowledge in both a philosophical and theological context.

Reid, at one time a member of the Presbyterian clergy, died in 1796 at the age of eighty-six. His lifetime coincides almost precisely with the time interval that historians mark as the epoch of the Enlightenment. Reid founded what came to be designated the Scottish "commonsense school of philosophy," sometimes identified as "commonsense realism." Rejecting all forms of rationalism and idealism that had preceded him, Reid argued that the objects we experience through the senses are not ideas or representations, but the things themselves. All human beings are capable, according to Reid, of knowing these objects, which he simply dubbed "facts." One does not need a complicated philosophical prospectus concerning how mental phenomena conform to physical events, or entities. What you see, literally, is what you get. In expatiating on this view of knowledge, Reid appealed to universal common sense, the *consensus gentium* of antiquity, which all human beings possess. Reason is not some abstruse faculty of a highly trained savant. The philosopher himself merely clarifies at a conceptual level what the average untutored person already knows for certain.

Thus Reid gave voice in a philosophical idiom to the anticlerical and egalitarian sympathies of the Reformers, who had demanded a level playing field for simple believers and theologians alike. The upshot, however, was that Reid's commonsense (or what might be described merely as a no-nonsense) approach to philosophy served, if only inadvertently, to deny any special authority to a theology of the revealed word. The natural light of reason, which Reid identified with the evidence of the senses, is sufficient. Indeed, common sense itself is the foundation of our knowledge of God. Common sense is "the inspiration of the Almighty." Reid argued, not inconsistently, that if God had wanted us to know him in any way other than through common sense, he would have endowed all human beings at birth with different habits of cognition. That common sense itself could be a darkened species of intelligence resulting from the fall, as Paul had suggested, did not occur to Reid. In many ways Reid's thinking was the purest expression of the age of reason, which the twentieth-century philosopher Alfred North Whitehead quipped was actually, as in medieval times, a grand "age of faith"—faith in the power of rationality alone, unaided by the means of grace. Reid indeed held that our own intelligence points to a divine intelligence. In a curious way he also seemed to be saying that the "fact" that ordinary believers experience the reality of God points to the fact of God himself. There is no perceptible difference between the rationality of common sense and the alleged irrationality of simple faith. The difference presupposes a philosophical view of reason that is incompatible with our ordinary human intelligence, which is nonetheless divinely endowed.

Reid's influence was felt in England, but it was most pronounced in America. And it was the marriage of Reid's commonsense philosophy with evangelical Methodism and Calvinism along the American frontier during the nineteenth century that gave rise to what a century later came to be labeled by critics of Christian evangelicalism, usually disparagingly, as fundamentalism. Reid's ideas early found a home at Princeton Seminary in the early 1800s and served as the academic infrastructure for the articulation of the fundamentalist standpoint a century later. Of course, the disparaging term "fundamentalist" was originally appropriated by particular evangelicals themselves in the early 1900s. They used it to tell themselves apart from modernists, particularly in defending the traditional story of creation as compared with evolutionary biology, and in insisting on the veracity of the biblical text as opposed to the new historical criticism imported from German universities.

While German philosophy seemed to encourage subjectivistic and relativistic readings of the Bible, Reid's commonsense method could easily be deployed to further the position that the authority of the Bible is indisputable and that Scripture means exactly what it says. According to Harriet Harris, a historian of theology, Reid's commonsense realism appealed strongly to the evangelical mind of the nineteenth and early-twentieth centuries because it could easily be conscripted to "defend the perspicuity of Scripture." Moreover, "as new interpretative methods emerged, evangelicals protected the beliefs of the common man against the learned judgments of the scholar and biblical critic."[15] Evangelicals asserted the truth of the "plain sense" of any given biblical passage, which was at the same time the inference of the "plain man." The plain sense of the text, therefore, was tantamount to common sense. Because nature never "lies," said Reid, God hence cannot confuse or mislead when he offers to even the most abject sinner his redeeming and holy Word, according to these early fundamentalists. Scripture is lucid and obvious on its own terms. It does not demand any sophisticated hermeneutic concocted by trained theologians and philosophers. Just as the natural mind presents us with "facts" of experience that cannot be explained away by any skeptical or convoluted strategy of analysis, so the Bible is a collection of facts about God and his workings in human history. When we believe what the Bible says, we are merely affirming what the human mind in a sense already apprehends. The implication of this view, as it was for Reid, is that atheism, or unbelief, is actually ignorance and stupidity. Conversion to the Christian faith could not be construed strictly as the acceptance of a superior truth disclosed to those who set aside reason and take the "leap of faith," as was the opinion of most religious thinkers before and throughout the Reformation.

In consequence, evangelicalism unwittingly succumbed to the kind of facile and expedient rationalism that the Reformers had valiantly exposed in Catholic doctrine and sought to expunge from the practice of the Christian faith. As Harris notes, evangelical apologetics from the nineteenth century onward impaled itself on the same sort of philosophical contradictions that the Reformers had detected in both Scholasticism and the Christian humanism of the Renaissance, wherein "Scripture is defended rationally even while reason is to submit to it." Over the long haul the commonsense hermeneutic has "undermined the inner testimony of the Holy Spirit" while contributing to a "preoccupation with a factually inerrant Bible."[16] The Reformation principle of *sola fide* was fatefully and coyly distorted. The Reformers had never intended that what Reid's critics called the "judgment of the crowd" should somehow become the touchstone for biblical authority. But that is exactly what transpired. The fundamentalist-modernist controversy was in many ways an intellectual variant of the gangs-of-New-York saga, where two hostile crowds from similar stock for generations were locked in bloody combat over what was by and large the same, paltry piece of territory.

The End of the Enlightenment Project

Unlike modernism and contemporary evangelicalism, both of which are blue-blooded heirs of the age of reason, postmodernism sets its face against what it denotes as "the Enlightenment project." By the mid-seventeenth century this project arose with the failure of the Reformation amid sectarian anarchy and Europe's debilitating wars of religion. It was in every respect the antithesis of the Reformation project, which sought to purify Christianity of its tendency to compromise the glory and majesty of God with human conceits and agendas. The Reformers' distinction between the natural knowledge of God and supernatural revelation was not a mere conceptual courtesy. It served as the underwriter of faith in the genuine, biblical sense. When Luther admonished us to "let God be God," he was expressing the Protestant principle to the fullest. Any effort to make God a plain item of common sense is both gratuitous and idolatrous. But evangelicalism in its century-long flirtation with commonsense philosophy, pseudoscientific rationalism, and the defense of theological "evidence" and biblical "facts" has sunk deeply into the type of anthropocentrism that the founders of the Protestant faith condemned. The peril does not reside in the relativizing propensities of postmodernism. Those tendencies can be found in modernism from its very inception.

What postmodernism as a philosophical movement has accomplished to date is to show up the idolatrous and relativistic proclivities of modernism as a whole. When postmodernism attacks the correspondence theory of truth, or the view of thought that the American philosopher Richard Rorty portrays as a "mirror of nature," it is not relegating knowledge, like Cain, to exile in some distant land of Nod. It is calling attention to the finite boundaries of human knowledge and meaning so that God can continue to speak and disclose himself from his infinite throne on high. We must, of course, admit that the preponderance of present-day thinking that fashions itself as postmodern is not concerned at all with either the claims or demands of classic faith. And we must also concede that there remains within certain strains of contemporary cultural theory a celebration of the turbulent flux of signs, which the nineteenth-century philosopher Friedrich Nietzsche, considered by many as the prophet of postmodernism, heralded "the death of God."

The destruction of the Jewish temple at Jerusalem in 70 by Roman armies created the climate for the rapid spread of Christianity throughout the empire. Thus likewise, the slow dissolution of the old familiar pieties and sureties among the emerging generation prepares a path for the coming of a strong and dynamic new relational faith, which Jesus himself required of his followers. Postmodernism may not be redemptive of its own accord, but it can be rightfully considered as a kind of reveille for evangelicalism. Taken as a whole, postmodernism is neither a social (anti-)morality nor an assault on the citadels of knowledge. Postmodernism cannot, and should not, be equated at all with relativism and skepticism, which for the most part are modernist ideologies. Postmodernism is *au fond* (at base) a theory of language that lays bare what the Danish philosopher Søren Kierkegaard called the "infinite qualitative difference" between the exhibitions of human intellect and the splendor of our eternal maker. By relativizing language and the theories of signification, postmodernism makes it possible to honor *the immeasurable holiness of God* in a manner that modern philosophy never could countenance. It also allows for a visionary critique of the myopia and idolatry into which biblical Christianity over the past two centuries has lapsed.

In the succeeding chapters we shall explore the ways in which the postmodernist challenge foreshadows what might be designated as the Next Reformation in the history of the Christian church. As Harris points out, "The roots of the fundamentalist mentality are not the same as the roots of evangelicalism,"[17] even though evangelicalism and fundamentalism have been ineradicably intertwined since the start of the nineteenth century. The roots of evangelicalism can be found in the historic Reformation tradition, which itself consisted of a quest to rediscover the prephilosophical core of Christian experience. One does not need to resort to such tendentious terms as "postevangelical," as writers such as David Tomlinson do, to wrest faith away from the idolatry of fundamentalism.[18] To stand up to both liberalism and fundamentalism we need merely to overcome modernism. If by evangelicalism we mean a commitment in every generation to the perennially saving message and person of Jesus himself, then we do not have to depend on a historically conditioned and beguiling epistemology that sprang largely out of the social and political ruins of England in the mid-seventeenth century after a disastrous civil war.

The Next Reformation will be one that, like the Reformation of the sixteenth century, does not leave any stone unturned in the unremitting pursuit of a compelling vision of the transcendent and mighty God. Along with the Reformers of the sixteenth century we must again exclaim, "Back to the Bible!" But we must insist, as the Reformers themselves did, on a hermeneutic of Scripture and a habit of theological thinking that truly allows God to be God, that does not box him in with some comfortable but subtly irreverent reliance on our own natural intellect. The next generation of reformers will also cry, "Back to the righteousness that comes through faith alone." Back to the Word not as a logical construct, but as the living power and presence, as the testament of the One who gave his life for us! Back to the revelation of the Spirit that searches our hearts and forces us to our knees in repentance for our intellectual pride and arrogance! Forward to the time when we must meet him face to face!

2

THE NEW FRENCH REVOLUTION

Derrida and the Origins of Postmodernism

POST-STRUCTURALISM AND POSTMODERNISM

When the term "postmodernism" first emerged in academic literature of the late 1970s, it had nothing to do with any of the things for which it is now routinely accused or commended. Though the word can be found in desultory use as far back as the 1920s, it did not acquire any sort of theoretical cachet until architect Charles Jencks began to use the term in the 1970s to typify what he termed the new "pluralism" in building styles emerging in the new planetary civilization. "Postmodernism" signified, as far as Jencks was concerned, a rampant eclecticism that melded the Oriental with the classical, modern functionality with playfulness.[1] How the locution became a general tag for nascent philosophical and theological thought of that period is not entirely clear. But the most plausible explanation is that it came to be used as a surrogate for the more technical expression "post-structuralism," which referred to the new intellectual stir that originated in France during the late 1960s and was just then reaching English-speaking lands. To understand what post-structuralism implied, it is incumbent on us to have some sense of the larger structuralist bequest that preceded it. To this day the vast majority of English and American thinkers have little idea what structuralism is, or was, all about. Structuralism is hazily associated in their minds with Claude Levi-Strauss's "structural anthropology," but that was a strange French sort of enterprise comparable to Sartrean existentialism, which certainly did not need to be expanded with a grand hyphen. "Post-structuralism" was a meaningful notion only if one had studied in Paris for a decade or more, becoming conversant with what appeared in French newspapers and was bruited about and discussed in cafés and coffeehouses on the Left Bank. One had to feel somehow the onerous presence of the postwar Parisian academy and its now-fading luminaries.

The presumption that we were now entering a new postmodern age, however, resonated with American ears. The prefix "post" had already been cast about promiscuously by American writers bent on either analyzing or celebrating the cultural changes that had been under way since the era of the Vietnam War. Social theorists had been saying that America was now in a "postindustrial" economy. The so-called radical theologians of the same period had been chattering for some years about the advent of the "post-Christian" era. If anything remains memorable about the 1960s, it was the rife and cocksure belief among commentators and pundits that virtually all of the historic past, including things most recent, had been suddenly superseded. That was the very condition best-selling author Alvin Toffler termed "future shock." Speaking of the present as postlude to everything else seemed altogether fitting. The concept of postmodernism was appealing as well, because it lent the impression that current events were already creating a chasm between nowadays and yesterdays. Until recently the term "modern" had been sufficiently catchall for what was trendy and au courant. Modern art was not yet historic art; it was contemporary art. "Thoroughly modern Millie," as the title of a popular Hollywood film suggested, was indeed still modern. If the culture of that generation had to imagine itself as pulling away with lightning speed from the already-vertiginous pace of postwar social change, it had to come up with slightly different nomenclature. "Ultramodern" would not stick. "Postmodernism" became all the rage.

Unfortunately for cultural conservatives who were already aghast at what the 1960s had wrought, postmodernism had come to connote a breezy and naive fascination with the savaging of traditions and standards that had come about in less than a decade. But just as a house is not a home, so the proverb goes, post-structuralism was really not postmodernism in the broader extension of the term. Post-structuralism was a serious philosophical initiative that would have caught fire regardless of whether the insanity of the 1960s had ever spread its shadow. From an epistemological perspective, post-structuralism in effect offered what evangelical theology had been clambering toward for almost a century. It routed all the claims amassed by the various forms of scientism since the eighteenth century, claims for the superiority of reason and logic over mere faith. So-called post-structuralism derived from the insight of the great linguist Ferdinand de Saussure and other structuralists that signs are not "duplicates" of things, but tiny particles of meaning arising from a process of differentiation between the many terms. Therefore, as a philosophy it was capable—in contrast to religion or theology—of effectively countering the argument of logical positivism and other types of pure scientism that reality could be simply mapped, cognized, and described.

In relativizing the hard sciences themselves by its own "scientific" method of linguistic analysis, post-structuralism delivered a stunning, if not a mortal, blow to the arrogant immanentism that had prevailed in both European and American thought since the nineteenth century. Postmodernism in this sense was nothing more or less than a theory of language that served to demystify previous theories of language routinely utilized to undercut the language of belief. But it was also a linguistic theory with momentous consequences. Just as Luther had turned to the Bible itself and promulgated the Reformation doctrine of *sola scriptura* to confound the Roman church's pretension to unassailable authority, so post-structuralism stressed the independence of the linguistic sign from any priestly posturing on the part of secular rationalists.

ORIGINS IN KANT

The post-structuralist slogan could have been summed up as "*sola significatione* (by signification alone)." But this innovation did not come easily. It took the genius and, in certain respects, the gall of a philosopher named Jacques Derrida, who had already made a name for himself in American literary circles. Derrida, however, has not been as much of an innovator as his reputation has led us to suppose. Derrida simply carried through to its inevitable climax a relentless critique of Western philosophy that had been underway in Germany since the late-eighteenth century. The process had begun with Kant, whose so-called critical philosophy undertook to sketch the limits of human reason and disclose the ways in which our knowledge of the world is construed in terms of prior "subjective" structures of understanding. In exploiting the term "subjective" Kant was not plumping for what today we would call relativism. He was not seeking to shrink truth to the idiosyncratic viewpoint of the solo individual, as is common nowadays. Kant was very much a child of the Enlightenment, with a heady conviction that reason held sway over all matters and could make definitive judgments that were "universally" valid. Furthermore, Kant held that even theological beliefs and religious sentiments could be justified in a philosophically coherent fashion. Yet this method of justification bears no connection with our attempts to "read off" the universe as we encounter and perceive it. Our perceptions, Kant insisted, are extrapolated from peculiar concepts inherent in the human mind, and those perceptions therefore remain prior to experience. The technical philosophical phrase Kant used is "a priori." Although we can never directly know things as they are "in themselves *(an sich)*," we can have an "objective" and reliable picture of the way the world actually is, inasmuch as our "subjective" concepts, or "categories of understanding," yield the exact same outlook for every "rational being." Although knowledge is subjective, or conditioned by the human observer, it is ultimately "objective" by dint of the universally consistent structure of rational thought and knowledge.

What Kant held in common with Derrida and the deconstructionists was a simple side-glance that perceived reality not as we naively see it, but as a system of signs and sign-relations and part of a rational architecture serving somehow to explain everything we know and see. Kant termed this system the "transcendental concepts" that make knowledge possible. Derrida identifies this system simply as "writing"—an idea we will investigate more thoroughly in a little while. This principle can be stated very elegantly. Things are not merely as they appear to us; things are as we comprehend the factors and functions that enable them to *appear* in the first place. The same principle ironically underlies most worldviews we designate as modern, including modern art, modern science, and even modern theology—liberal as well as conservative. When science in the sixteenth and seventeenth centuries invented mathematical equations—as opposed to the propositions of classical philosophers and the church fathers—to describe the natural realm, they were introducing such an approach.

When artists such as Cezanne, Picasso, and Mondrian in the late-nineteenth and early-twentieth centuries abandoned the practice of visually representing the order of things and began investigating through their paintings the conditions and circumstances of painting itself, they were tracing the same historical arc on an aesthetic plane. Even the efforts of fundamentalist theologians to explicate the sovereign nature of God by concentrating on the systematic and interlocking scaffolding of relations that constitute the Bible as the Word of God betray this inimitably modernist trait. Because it has always been concerned with structures as opposed to substances, modern thought is inextricably structuralist in its way of going about things. Post-structuralism was never intended to be anti-structuralist, or irrationalist, or—even worse—nihilistic. Like all the various modernisms that had preceded it, post-structuralism undertook to "see through" the structures that claimed to be pure substance, to flush out the structures of structuralism itself. The intellectual climate in postwar France had elevated structuralist thinking in its various guises to such a science that it had lost sight of the introspective tendency of modernism. In the spirit of radical critique that characterized the 1960s in both Europe and America, post-structuralism, later to be known as deconstruction, largely sought to finish the precise agenda Kant had inaugurated generations earlier.

This practice of seeing through, or looking inward at, all forms and structures, even the form and structures of language, ran counter to the foundationalist program. However, it can be readily said that structuralism was also its own kind of foundationalism. Kant routinely used the words "structure" and "foundation" interchangeably. Modernist structuralism sought to ground truth in some clear consensus about the intelligible structure of truth rather than in any doctrine of truth itself. The old custom of claiming that true statements constitute true "copies" of the real universe gradually gave place to the tendency to characterize truth as the absolutely incontrovertible starting point from which particular truths could be explored and confirmed. Descartes himself had dubbed this standpoint the "Archimedean point" of philosophy. It was named after the legend of the Greek mathematician Archimedes, who envisioned what he believed was a position of leverage whereby he could "move the world." Starting with the Archimedean point instead of with the things themselves that philosophy might leverage is what Kant called the Copernican revolution of thought. Copernicus was the sixteenth-century astronomer who hypothesized that the earth moves around the sun rather than the sun around the earth, as had been previously held. Generally speaking, we call such a move perspectivalism, which is not necessarily the same as relativism. Perspectivalism merely maintains that when we say we know something, we have to take into account the factors and circumstances under which that knowledge can be known. On a grand theoretical level Kant identified this approach as "critical philosophy," or "critical metaphysics."

The problem of metaphysics has been the preoccupation of modern, and postmodern, philosophy ever since Kant. He launched his critical philosophy by posing what he took as the most fundamental query: "How is metaphysics possible?" Ever since Aristotle, and especially during and after the heyday of medieval Scholasticism, metaphysics and theology had evolved hand in glove with each other. Metaphysics, as defined by Aristotle, asked what is meant by "Being" in general, or "Being as Being." Christian thought construed the metaphysical question of Being as essentially cognate with the issue of God, a fusion of terminology that later philosophers such as Heidegger and Derrida named "ontotheology." But Kant deliberately sought to separate the issues of God and Being—or thinking and Being—by arguing along the lines of his Enlightenment contemporaries that what we experience cannot be automatically taken as equivalent to what is. We cannot experience Being in the abstract. And if we cannot experience Being in this fashion, we must seek the true source of the "form" of our logical judgments or acts of predication, a source appropriate to our talk about "what is." Kant asserted that our deductive apparatus is "transcendental"; it does not inhere in the world, but in the events of reasoning and extrapolation themselves. Metaphysics as a "positive science" is completely meaningless. The very idea of metaphysical thinking only makes sense if we understand its task to be the mapping of the basic conditions of thinking itself. Philosophy is not concerned with Being; it is devoted to comprehending the internal relations of the mind that engender the very thought of Being. Thus, metaphysics is "critical" rather than descriptive. Metaphysics remains a "science," but strictly as the "pure" science of scientific experience, using the rules of evidence and inference.

THE INFLUENCE OF HEGEL

Later philosophy, especially in Germany, took as its task the ongoing dismantling of metaphysics. On the main, philosophy developed the routine of answering Kant's question about whether metaphysics is possible as "no, not really." After Kant, G. W. F. Hegel embroidered his system of "dialectical" or "speculative" philosophy. Speculative philosophy was the high point of a more expansive movement known as German idealism, which proceeded in the opposite direction from Kant. German idealism aimed to show how metaphysical or "absolute" thought can be reconstituted by unfolding the more profound and limitless capabilities of reason itself. Speculative philosophy has sometimes been regarded as the apotheosis of the thinking subject, the realization within finite language and reflection of the infinite "Spirit," to which religion has deferred under the name of God. Speculative philosophy did not have the humility of Kant's "critical" metaphysics. Quite the contrary! For a time it transformed the critique of metaphysics into a metaphysics of the self, where the divine is intimately and triumphantly posited as human thought thinking upon itself. The idea of Being as thought thinking upon itself, of course, was Aristotle's original notion of how one comprehends God. But Hegel took the exceptional step of identifying God as Being with the philosophical possibilities of human thought. Hence, Hegel also represents the apotheosis of the modernist subjectivism that first saw the light of day with Descartes. For Hegel, thought and being are one and the same, and being cannot be thought in any connection or by any variant apart from thought.

According to Hegel, every contradiction in metaphysical thought—for instance, the difference between Being and individual beings, or between Being and nothing—is absorbed and "taken up *(aufgehoben)*" into a progressive elevation of subjective consciousness. The evolution of human consciousness is fundamentally this self-unfolding of God or Spirit, which ultimately thinks all opposites and therefore becomes the thinking of Being as true being of the thinking subject. Metaphysics no longer has to be "critiqued." It has to be understood as a nominal means of characterizing the infinite capacity of all thinking. To understand human history is to chart the trajectory for the self-revelation of subjective thought in itself *(an sich)* to itself *(für sich)* as thought "in and for itself *(an und für sich)."* History is what Hegel designated the "march" of Spirit, or as he put it in an oft-quoted aphorism, "The philosophy of history is the history of philosophy." If we discern how philosophy itself has expanded in its range of comprehension over historical time, we grasp how metaphysics and psychology, or what today we would term spirituality, are inseparable from each other. We discover the modality in which Being has become "present" to itself as thought, or how God has become incarnate in self-reflective humanity.

The Hegelian solution to the problem of metaphysics left an impressive and disquieting legacy. It was the conceptual impetus not only for Marxism, but also for diverse modes of what Hegel's critics have labeled "totalistic" thinking. If God can be thought of metaphysically in terms of the progressive self-revelation of thought to itself, then the greatest of thinkers or leaders can be respected as the self-embodiment of divine thinking in a political or social setting. Such an attitude lay behind Hitler's pronouncement of the "*Führer-Prinzip* (leader principle)."

NIETZSCHE AND METAPHYSICS

The absorption of the Being into thought by nineteenth-century philosophy is the tactical key to extracting meaning from Nietzsche's infamous saying that "God is dead," which hovered over Western thought for more than a century. The saying actually occurs in Hegel's major work *The Phenomenology of Spirit*. Nietzsche merely developed and promulgated such an outlandish proposition with his wild and provocative Dionysian style of writing. Nietzsche's intent all along was not to convince his readers that God did not exist, or that we shall all cease on naturalistic or atheistic grounds to believe in, and worship, God. Nietzsche regarded himself as a seer who was simply proclaiming a historical "fact" that philosophy itself had established. God is "dead," Nietzsche implied, because there is no longer any need to interpret God as anything apart from our self-awareness. Nietzsche announced the death of God through the parable of a madman who comes into the marketplace, signifying of course the social world. We will quote most of the parable because it loses its impact if shortened too much:

> *The madman*—Have you not heard of that madman who lit a lantern in the bright morning hours, ran to the marketplace, and cried incessantly: "I seek God! I seek God!"—As many of those who did not believe in God were standing around just then, he provoked much laughter. "Has he got lost?" asked one. "Did he lose his way like a child?" asked another. "Or is he hiding? Is he afraid of us? Has he gone on a voyage? Emigrated?"—Thus they yelled and laughed.
>
> The madman jumped into their midst and pierced them with his eyes. "Whither is God?" he cried; "I will tell you. *We have killed him*—you and I. All of us are his murderers. But how did we do this? How could we drink up the sea? Who gave us the sponge to wipe away the entire horizon? What were we doing when we unchained this earth from its sun? Whither is it moving now? Whither are we moving? Away from all suns? Are we not plunging continually? Backward, sideward, forward, in all directions? Is there still any up or down? Are we not straying as through an infinite nothing? Do we not feel the breath of empty space? Has it not become colder? Is not night continually closing in on us? Do we not need to light lanterns in the morning? Do we hear nothing as yet of the noise of the gravediggers who are burying God? Do we smell nothing as yet of the divine decomposition? Gods, too, decompose. God is dead. God remains dead. And we have killed him. . . ."
>
> Here the madman fell silent and looked again at his listeners; and they, too, were silent and stared at him in astonishment. At last he threw his lantern on the ground, and it broke into pieces and went out. "I have come too early," he said then; "my time is not yet. This tremendous event is still on its way, still wandering; it has still not yet reached the ears of men. Lightning and thunder require time; the light of the stars requires time; deeds, though done, still require

time to be seen and heard. This deed is still more distant from them than the most distant stars—*and yet they have done it themselves.*"

It has been related further that on the same day the madman forced his way into several churches and there struck up his *requiem aeternam dei.* Led out and called to account, he is said always to have replied nothing but: "What after all are these churches now if they are not the tombs and sepulchers of God?"[2]

By acceding to the new metaphysical model of the divine as immanent spirit, or as Being as thought thinking itself, we have literally "killed" God. "All of us are his murderers." In the murder of God metaphysics abolishes itself. Modern thought can be intimated as Luciferian thought, insofar as it launches a kind of angelic rebellion against God as the infinite Other in relation to what at a historical level metaphysical thinking has considered itself incapable of compassing. Nietzsche was not casting an argument for nihilism. He was diagnosing what he viewed as the monstrous secret of modernity—the concealed and ubiquitous nihilism of the times, in consequence of modern civilization slaying God.[3]

In his posthumous aggregation of notes and scribblings from the 1880s published under the title *The Will to Power,* Nietzsche sketched out a somber vision of the twentieth century. "What I relate is the history of the next two centuries. I describe what is coming, what can no longer come differently: the advent of nihilism. This history can be related even now; for necessity itself is at work here. This future speaks even now in a hundred signs, this destiny announces itself everywhere."[4] In present-day discussions nihilism is for the most part explicated as a kind of social and cultural malady that is somehow carried and spread by freethinkers and various intellectual extremists. It is often associated with sundry experiments in unreason, especially in the arts and in the realm of moral behavior. The vague assumption is that some strand of philosophical radicalism is itself to blame. Hence, if the felonious cause of nihilism could be eliminated and intellectual hygiene applied, the trouble would evaporate. Nietzsche, however, denied that there was any means of warding off nihilism. "Nihilism stands at the door: whence comes this uncanniest of all guests? Point of departure: it is an error to consider 'social distress' or 'physiological degeneration' or, worse, corruption as the cause of nihilism. Ours is the most decent and compassionate age. Distress, whether of the soul, body, or intellect, cannot of itself give birth to nihilism (i.e., the radical repudiation of value, meaning, and desirability). Such distress always permits a variety of interpretations. Rather: it is in one particular interpretation, the Christian-moral one, that nihilism is rooted."[5]

NIHILISM AND THE MORAL VIEW OF THE WORLD

In other words, it is the Christian worldview that is responsible for nihilism. This pronouncement obviously will strike the ordinary person as both preposterous and odious. After all, is not Christianity the antidote to nihilism? Are not Nietzsche's philosophy, and its postmodernist progeny, themselves the source of these nihilistic tendencies? Our customary answer would be yes. But Nietzsche's seemingly paradoxical presentiment has been the basis not only for the struggle between modernism and postmodernism but also the tension between a modern and a genuinely postmodern evangelicalism. It should be noted that Nietzsche was the son of a Lutheran pastor and during his early years had imbibed the Christian-moral worldview. The hyphen is not capriciously inserted. In the aftermath of Kant much of popular Christianity in the Germany of the nineteenth century had reduced the gospel to the moral law. Kant himself had fostered this idea by effectively assimilating the transcendence of God to "transcendental" morality, thereby making the historical Jesus and the divine incarnation itself inconsequential.

More than any other historical factor, Kant's moralizing of Christian revelation is behind what today we consider theological liberalism. But it gradually had a closet impact on the formation of evangelical interpretations as well. The current fixation of the American evangelical movement on so-called social issues, or the relationship between public institutions and private moral conduct, is part and parcel of the Kantian legacy. The Kantian heritage has been the progressive amalgamation of the Christian tradition into a Christian-moral view of the world. Kantianism took up the cudgel of the age of reason and transformed the Reformation focus on Christian liberty and the assurance of personal salvation through faith into a rational certainty of the truths of doctrine as warranted by the precepts of universal morality. Kant did away with the Reformation theme of personal trust in a personal God and replaced it with what he alternately dubbed "moral faith," "rational faith," or the "metaphysics of morals." Completing the Enlightenment project inaugurated by Descartes, Kant's critical philosophy rendered the transcendent God superfluous. The truth of God was the truth of reason. Religion must be circumscribed "within the limits of reason alone."

The grounding of faith in reason, however, empties faith of its content. The incorporation of faith into sets of moral imperatives and propositions "kills" God. When Nietzsche declared that "all of us" are God's murderers, he was professing his own culpability as a modern person. The personal presence of God had become the Christian-moral view of the world. Modern moral rationalism has domesticated God to the point that the awesomeness of an infinite God become fully human—an illogicality that Kantian thought cannot countenance—is no longer comprehended. Christian belief was always by virtue of "absurdity." In *Beyond Good and Evil* Nietzsche directly fingers modernism itself as the culprit in the death of God and the commencement of nihilism. "Modern men, obtuse to all Christian nomenclature, no longer feel the gruesome superlative that struck a classical taste in the paradoxical formula 'god on the cross.' Never yet and nowhere has there been an equal boldness in inversion: it promised a revaluation of the values of antiquity."[6]

Nietzsche, of course, was not a Christian in any overt sense, nor was he sympathetic to the values of historical Christianity. It was not merely as burlesque that he fashioned himself in the last segment of his life as "the anti-Christ." But his criticisms concerning what had happened to Christianity over two millennia were telling. The triumph of a European "Christian" civilization in the nineteenth century had reduced revelation to reason and faith to morality—the self-idolization of a dominant middle-class culture. The ancient *credo* had been hollowed out and traded for a self-congratulatory Western provincialism that no longer feared nor respected God. Western humanity had made an idol of God, and all idols, as the biblical prophets thundered, are dead matter, not the living God. It was the so-called believers taunting the madman in the marketplace who were the bona fide unbelievers. "The faith in the categories of reason is the cause of nihilism."[7] In its inexorable campaign to rationalize and exonerate Christian "values" instead of allowing for mere faith, modern thought has allowed no room for faith, contrary to Kant. While Kant was sincerely convinced that he was "making room" for faith by making reason moral or practical, he was in fact undermining faith, insofar as he was converting faith into an analysis of values. This ongoing process of becoming self-conscious about our "moral grounds" for faith has been the self-destructive engine of modernity. As in an autoimmune disease, Christian theology has slowly atrophied because in attacking the "enemies" of faith, it has been attacking faith itself. The history of modern Christianity is a tale of its own self-devaluation. "What does nihilism mean? That the highest values devaluate themselves." Furthermore, "this realization is a consequence of the cultivation of 'truthfulness'—thus itself a consequence of the faith in morality."[8]

Nietzsche was ambivalent about the word "faith" because of the very way in which it had come to be used, or misused. He was also ambivalent about Christianity, which he concluded was really Greek metaphysics in disguise—"Platonism for the masses." The quip is worthy of reflection, because the "Christian-moral view of the world," identifiable with modernism, was really ancient Greek metaphysics in its senescence. As Heidegger in his detailed readings of Nietzsche underscored, nihilism begins with Plato. So-called Hellenic dualism—the distinction between the real and the ideal, between this world and the other world, between being and becoming, between time and eternity, between the "physical" and the metaphysical—is the constitutive moment of nihilism. According to Nietzsche, the beginning of nihilism is the valuation of the ideal over the real. Greek idealism, by identifying the "real" world with the realm of pure "ideas" was the consummation of world-weariness and world-denial. Greek metaphysics is a countervailing of the "natural" valuing of this world, an inversion of the desire to affirm the world as we know it. Greek thought, unlike its Hebraic counterpart, was unable to say that God made the world good. Plato made the "idea" of the good into the supreme reality. But if this supreme reality is indeed a moral negation of the world camouflaged as a metaphysical necessity or first principle, then idealism makes valuation a godlike principle. Idealism, and hence what today we call rationalism, is driven by a life-suppressing impulse and in the final analysis a "God-denying" spirit, if by God we mean that creative power that brought the world into existence and transcends even the summum bonum, the highest good. Underneath its silky skin *pure rationalism is disclosed as pure nihilism.* It seeks to negate the life that Christians proclaim has been conferred by the Creator. Metaphysical rationalism is a suave version of the ancient gnostic heresy, which has always sought to snare the soul of Christianity.

Nietzsche was not conversant with Gnosticism, nor did he seem interested in the topic. But what distinguished both Gnosticism and Nietzsche's portrait of Christianity was a metaphysical dualism that divided the world into what was "true" and what was merely illusory or "apparent." Gnostic dualism had its genesis in Persian thinking as well as in Neoplatonism, and most scholars agree that it manifested the more extreme proclivities of ancient Mediterranean thought, blending the esotericism of the Greek mysteries with the rococo mythologies of the ancient Near East. Nietzsche was preoccupied with the problem of dualism, which he alleged had been the Trojan horse of Western civilization. The origins of mythological dualism can be traced back to the Iranian religious teacher Zarathustra, who lived during the early half of the first millennium B.C. In his most famous and most baffling work, *Thus Spoke Zarathustra,* Nietzsche reinvented the legend of the Persian prophet to challenge the dualistic world picture and substitute for it his own revisionary, and "counter-Christian," philosophy, which he thought corresponded to the outlook of the pre-Platonic Greeks.

A classical philologist by training, Nietzsche was fascinated with the early Greek "tragic age" that antedated the rise of academic philosophy. The Greek poets and playwrights had an "innocent" intuition of the universe, Nietzsche submitted. They lived life to the fullest in this world and did not speculate about another world. They experienced the "divine" directly and sensibly, as early Greek art portrays. Furthermore, their sense of time was critically different from ours. They did not make the mistake of the dualists in segregating the timeless from the time-bound, the "eternity" of being in itself from the sphere of becoming. The "death of God" was the long-term historical result, according to Nietzsche, of locating God in this unchanging and eternal realm. Because we live in time and not "eternity," we cannot really comprehend anything but a God who is subject to change. We fool ourselves if we are persuaded otherwise. Hence, even though we have spoken reverently, religiously, and "metaphysically" for two thousand years of the eternal Deity, our God has been slowly "dying." We have increasingly held fast to formalized proofs and conjectures concerning who God is, while our raw "sense" of divinity has been diminishing.

It is clear from Nietzsche's writings that he did not share the Reformation preference for an "innocent" early version of Christianity. Born more than three hundred years after the Reformation, Nietzsche did not discern much difference between Protestantism and Catholicism. Hellenism and rationalism had commandeered both. It did not matter whether clerical authority resided in the Pope, or the cultural minister of the Prussian state. All of Western Christianity had surrendered to the dominance of the democratic state and thereby the values and mentality of the common man, what Nietzsche contemptuously called "the herd." The herd craves the metaphysical comfort of God and the moral certainty of theology all bundled up in the popular Platonic fiction of the hereafter. The banalization of faith went hand in glove with the nihilism and the death of God. Modernity has replaced the "tragic" and "heroic" sense of existence, celebrated by the ancient Greeks, with the "scholarly," "priestly," and metaphysical concept of God as eternal being (what Nietzsche contemptuously termed "immaculate knowledge"). The ancient Greeks, for Nietzsche, were not metaphysicians. For them, the world was theater, what Nietzsche's mentor Wagner had called the *Gesamtkunstwerk,* the complete art work. But the theater had given place to the metaphysical marketplace, in which cheap intellectual commodities are incessantly hawked and sold. The most banal commodity was the idea of God as eternal being, or substance—the key constituent in the "Christian-moral view of the world."

Nietzsche regarded his own thoughts as "unseasonal," or ahead of his time. For the most part he was correct. For well beyond the next half century, Nietzsche was roundly misread, misdiagnosed, and misused. The exploitation of his work by his sister Elizabeth immediately after his death is a case in point. Nietzsche's sister, married to one of the most famous anti-Semites of the day, sought to have his work published for the benefit of German nationalism and racism, which eventually fed into the propaganda machinery of the Third Reich. This mishandling of Nietzsche's ideas clouded his reputation outside Germany until well after the Second World War. In England and America both philosophy and theology all went along their merry way, oblivious to the kind of critique that Nietzsche had invested in. The turnabout came initially with Walter Kaufmann's translation of Nietzsche's major works during the 1950s and 1960s into English, and next with a collection of reinterpretative essays by leading intellectual figures, first published by Dell in 1977 and edited by American philosopher David Allison under the heading of *The New Nietzsche*.[9] Among the names included in the volume were Alphonso Lingis, Martin Heidegger, Gilles Deleuze, Maurice Blanchot, Jacques Derrida, and Thomas J. J. Altizer—all of whom later became identified in some decisive context with postmodernism. The fact that they all wrote about Nietzsche from a religious as much as a philosophical perspective supplies insight into the etiology of postmodernism.

The philosophical trends now decipherable as postmodernism have rested on the premise that metaphysics must not be condoned, but must be "overcome" in order to contend with the inherent nihilism of the metaphysical enterprise itself. Postmodern philosophy has served very much like the surgeon who tells the patient that his cancerous liver is going to have to be removed. The patient passionately does not want any vital organs excised and refuses to believe that he is in imminent peril of dying. Instead, he denounces the surgeon and calls him by various epithets. The attitude of much contemporary philosophy, and evangelical theology, toward postmodernism is analogous to the patient. Postmodernism is saying what we really do not want to hear. So we pummel the messenger and deny the message.

DERRIDA AND *DIFFÉRANCE*

Starting with Heidegger, postmodernist thought has endeavored to find a new avenue for thinking the Being of metaphysical thinking without becoming snagged in the nihilist birdlime. In thinking Being without resort to metaphysics—what Heidegger referred to as the "overcoming *(Überwindung)*" of metaphysics—postmodernism has in the same breath endeavored to go beyond the identification of God with Being; it has positioned itself to transcend the metaphysical, or rationalist, conception of God, which belongs to what it calls ontotheology. Jean-Luc Marion, one of today's most prominent postmodernist theologians, who comes out of the Roman Catholic tradition, has coined the phrase "God without Being." If we are truly to "let God be God," as Luther put it, we must not enclose God within even the most elegant architecture of reason, even the kind of thinking that portrays the Deity as the highest or supreme Being above all beings. Postmodernists such as the Jewish philosopher Emmanuel Lévinas have taken the prophetic cry against the idolatry of rationalist foundationalism even further. Only a God without Being, or who in Lévinas's phraseology is "otherwise *(autrement)*" than Being, can be a God who corresponds to the God of Abraham, Isaac, and Jacob. Such a God is a person and not a metaphysical principle. Foundationalism has confused metaphysics with faith, writers like Lévinas impress upon us. It has attempted to "ground" God in the logic of reflection and supposition while scanting the biblical experience of the relationship-seeking, covenant-making, most high and holy God who first reveals himself to Moses on Mount Sinai and demands, "You shall have no other god to set against me."[10]

In *God without Being* Marion seeks to capture this thoroughly iconoclastic vision of a nonmetaphysical standpoint for faith by crossing out the word "God" with an X. Marion designates this move the "crossing of Being." Heidegger, of course, had already contrived this notation during the transition from his early existentialism in *Being and Time* to what would later be known as "fundamental ontology"—the thinking of Being in terms of the difference between Being and beings. Heidegger's effort to "overcome" metaphysics as the science of Being, by stressing what he called the "ontological difference" between Being and beings, is the inaugural insight of postmodernist thought.

> The ontotheological constitution of metaphysics hails from the pervasive influence of difference which joins and separates as ground and Existence, both authenticating and understanding, and is sustained by the issue in carrying the action through. . . .
>
> Insight into the ontotheological constitution of metaphysics shows a possible way of answering the question as to how God entered philosophy by going to the essence of metaphysics. God entered philosophy through the issue which we think first of all as being the advance point in the essence of the difference between Being and Existence. Difference represents the ground plan in the essential structure of metaphysics. . . . The appropriate understanding is equivalent

to causation by the ultimate and original reality. This is the cause as *causa sui,* and this is the just and proper name for God in philosophy. Man may neither pray to this God, nor may he sacrifice to him. Confronted by *causa sui,* man may neither sink onto his knees, nor could he sing and dance.[11]

Derrida's orchestration of the theme of difference throughout his writings consists in a kind of arabesque embroidering of Heidegger's point. Marion, a Christian "theologian," however, is even more radical than Heidegger, and goes after the idolatry of all instances of Being-speak, even those that claim to have surpassed the false consciousness of metaphysics. "The God who reveals himself has nothing in common (at least in principle, and provided that he not condescend to it) with the 'God' of the philosophers, of the learned, and, eventually, of the poet."[12]

There is a major difference, however, between Heidegger and Derrida. The distinction between the two can be found in Derrida's unwillingness to countenance any kind of talk about Being, even if Being is crossed out or spoken about as if it were not an entity, but a limiting term. For Heidegger, the "difference" between metaphysical discourse and the new nonmetaphysical language of fundamental ontology can be gauged by the recognition that Being is only revealed in its concealment. Its presence is in its absence. The metaphor of "horizon" figures prominently in both Heidegger and in the whole tradition of modern phenomenology, in which his work performs a leading role. A horizon is a dividing line of sight between what we can see and what cannot—yet—be seen. When we say something lies, or is coming, over the horizon, we know what is there only in terms of what remains to be seen. Or, as in an iceberg, what is visible hides much of what continues to be invisible.

Similarly, the thought of Being contains much that is yet unthought. Derrida dismisses this mystifying give-and-take in Heidegger between a sense of Being-as-present and Being-as-absent as the last, lingering ghost of metaphysical philosophy. In his later writings Heidegger employs the trope of philosophical inquiry as a "dialogue" between thought and Being. Heidegger spoke regularly about listening for the "voice of Being." In its concealment Being presents itself, as in the spoken utterance, but then "withdraws" into silence, or absence.

Instead of belaboring the enigmatic image of a head-to-head encounter between the thinker and Being, Derrida contests the very idea of a "voice" from which meaning somehow stems. From a religious perspective one can always ask if the voice of Being is the same as the *vox Dei,* or whether it is something else. After all, not just saints but also the insane and demon-possessed hear voices. Heidegger was maddeningly elusive on this issue. But in place of the relic of metaphysics that Heidegger portrays as an ontological voice, Derrida proffers the idea of writing—in this situation, the writing of philosophy—as all we really have to start with when we ponder the nature of "what is." All ontology, for Derrida, must become "grammatology"—the science of inscription, the theory of writing. Whereas metaphysics and ontotheology are preoccupied with Being as "presence" (or in the case of speculative idealism, "self-presence"), grammatology is concerned with what is "left over" as the "supplement" of writing, what Derrida terms the "trace."

In the second chapter concerning linguistics in his early book *Of Grammatology*, Derrida writes about the trace as "the disappearance of origin—within the discourse that we sustain and according to the path that we follow, it means that the origin did not even disappear, that it was never constituted except reciprocally by a nonorigin, the trace which thus becomes the origin of origin."[13] Derrida can be incredibly difficult to understand until one acquires the general picture of what he is saying, and the angle of vision from which he is forcing us to take a careful look. It is comparable to studying cubist painting in a museum for the first time. The nonrepresentational portraiture is baffling until a docent explains that the artist is seeking to convey a full perspective, front and backside, on a two-dimensional plane. Then it becomes a straightforward matter of seeing what one was unable to see before.

In Derrida's case the objective is to recognize that writing is not "representational"—it does not duplicate the presence of something else. Writing is not a proxy for what is not writing. It is not the same as a sketch or a caricature. The different versions of hieroglyphic or pictographic writing, such as ancient Egyptian and Chinese, could be taken as representational in a primitive sense. But linguists tell us that the abstract and nonrepresentational usages of these languages have predominated almost from the start. When we go back to the "origin" of writing, we discover that the origin has already been superseded by more writing. The illusion of an "origin" in writing is fomented by the natural, though specious, analogy of writing as depiction. Just as we seek a "referent" or exterior meaning for each word in our language, so we desire a corresponding "objective" basis for writing itself. But that basis eludes us. Even the concept of "origin," Derrida intimates in the above citation, is extruded from the pictographic metaphor. The written word is prima facie a constellation of marks on a page, a dislodgment of paper fibers by an ink-saturated stylus or a phantasmagoria of electrical charges on a screen.

It "appears," but it does not appear from anywhere. It is a "trace." There is no "original" writing. "The pure trace is *différance.*"[14]

Derrida is most famous for introducing the word *différance,* a deliberate misspelling of the French and the English words. Derrida's illustration, nonetheless, becomes clearer when we recur to the French. In French *différance* sounds the same as the usual *différence*. It is only the writing, the marking, the trace, that makes the difference. Phonologically, there is no distinction between the two locutions. When we write "différance," we inscribe a microcosmic void, a space, between what is written and what was written before. The space makes all the difference in espousing the meaning. The meaning is not a presence, but a discontinuity, an absence. Rather than mimicking what is outside writing, writing begets writing. And through this constant begetting, which is at the same time a transgression or disruption of the syntax of meaning that preceded it, meaning unfurls.

> I will speak, therefore, of the letter *a,* this initial letter which it apparently has been necessary to insinuate, here and there, into the writing of the word *différence;* and to do so in the course of a writing on writing, and also of a writing within writing whose different trajectories thereby find themselves, at certain very determined points, intersecting with a kind of gross spelling mistake, a lapse in the discipline and law which regulate writing and keep it seemly. . . .[15]
>
> [Furthermore,] the signified concept is never present in and of itself, in a sufficient presence that would refer only to itself. Essentially and lawfully, every concept is inscribed in a system within which it refers to the other, to other concepts, by means of the systematic play of differences. Such a play, *différance,* is thus no longer simply a concept, but rather the possibility of conceptuality, of a conceptual process and system in general. For the same reason, difference, which is not a concept, is not simply a word, that is, what is generally represented as the calm, present and self-referential unity of concept and phonic material. . . . *Différance* is the nonfull, nonsimple, structured and differentiating origin of differences. Thus, the name "origin" no longer suits it.[16]

The difference of *différance* is but a difference of representation, or inscription.

> Such a difference would at once . . . give us to think a writing without a presence and without absence, without history, without cause, without *archē* (beginning), without *telos,* a writing that absolutely upsets all dialectics, all theology, all teleology, all ontology. A writing exceeding everything that the history of metaphysics has comprehended in the form of the Aristotelian *grammē,* in its point, in its line, in its circle, in its time, and in its space.[17]

Representational or "correspondence" theories of meaning, which have inhabited philosophy for millennia while fostering the foundationalist prejudice, obscure the fact that meaning and signification are not vertical connections between words and things. In the Middle Ages the theory of meaning was based on a representational model known as the "semantic triangle." Words referred to ideas, which referred to things. Later the triangle became a straight line. The word *(verbum)* signified the thing *(res)*. But in the theory of *différance* the connections become horizontal. One letter replaces the other, which changes the meaning. Meaning is in the "dislocation" of one portion of the text by the next, by ongoing sequences of inscription.

Derrida insists that this "diachronic" view of meaning—the necessity of going back over the terrain of language in order to ascertain what is signified in the present tense—is the key to both writing and the "deconstruction" of texts, which have linear architectures. Meaning can only emerge as we review the spaces between words, a process grammarians call the achievement of syntax. Every word or phrase thus disrupts the immediate meaning, or identity, of every word or phrase that preceded it. In addition, it decrypts it. Our success in cognizing this disruption is what Derrida means when he talks about "deconstructing" works of writing. Deconstruction is not a new metaphysics, let alone a metaphysics of "nothingness." It is a radical new theory of meaning, a groundbreaking semantics.

THE SIGNIFICANCE OF DECONSTRUCTION

Writing erases the meaning of what is written. All words and units of significance are, in Derrida's turn of phrase, "*sous rature* (under erasure)." Although the myth of presence ascribes meaning to some original speech or "phonological" purity, the deconstruction of texts shows that what is signified is never immediate to us. On the contrary, when we go back to find it, we discover that it has evaporated. As Derrida puts it, the only true paradise is a lost paradise. The Greek philosophical ideal of meaning as presence is founded on the metaphor of "truth as the unity of *logos* and *phonē*"—what Derrida dubs "logo-phonocentrism."[18] This logo-phonocentrism must give way to the new Hebraic understanding of meaning as textuality, as grammatology. In fact, the Christian conviction that the Bible is the Word of God is quite congenial to Derrida, an Algerian Jew, if we do not take the divine word as some kind of metaphysical entity in its own right but as the signature of the infinite God that is constantly being "written on our hearts," in Jeremiah's phrase, as we read and study Scripture. "Writing," Derrida asserts in *Writing and Difference*, "is the anguish of the Hebraic *ruakh* [spirit]." [19] Or elsewhere he quotes the Jewish author Edmund Jabès: "If God is, it is because He is in the book."[20] Derrida is closer to the Protestant Reformers than many contemporary theologians who subscribe to what Derrida dismisses as a "pagan" *logocentrism,* or metaphysical foundationalism. Logocentrism is the obsession of metaphysics with the logical, or representational, side of language. It is the distinguishing trait of Western metaphysical thought and what deconstruction sets about to unravel.

Further, according to Derrida, writing serves to bring forth an "eschatology" of language. The term "eschatology," of course, is built on a theological root word lifted from the reading of Scripture and connotes "the end of all things," the realization within time of God's eternal purpose, for souls, nations, and the human race as a whole. Derrida borrows the concept of eschatology from Hegel and Heidegger as well as Lévinas. Hegelian eschatology is the self-realization of the thinking self as Spirit. In his program of "overcoming metaphysics," however, Heidegger construes this eschatology as a thinking of Being in a way that has not hitherto been thought. The "eschatology of Being" is the consummation of philosophical—and hence ontotheological—thinking within the tradition of the West. Heideggerian thinking takes itself as the "second coming" (*parousia* in the Greek New Testament) of Being, inasmuch as Heidegger holds that fundamental ontology constitutes a thinking of the history of metaphysics as the "destiny" of Being in a manner that philosophy in its infancy, youth, and senility was never able to think whatsoever. It is in fundamental ontology that the *parousia* (literally, "fullness of presence") of Being becomes manifest.

But the eschatology of language in Derrida has nothing to do with the thought of Being as full presence. *Writing alone is present.* Before us in an "ontological" sense, we do not have the history of philosophy, or of theology, or even of God's acts. We have the texts, and nothing but the texts. Because of Derrida's textualism he has been relentlessly accused of taking the "nihilistic" stance that there really is no "meaning" in the text. But that is exactly the point. The meaning is not in the text. The text itself is the fullness of presence. When theologians and preachers from the pulpit exhort members of their congregation to read their Bible daily in order to know truly God's nature and will, they are saying for the most part what Derrida has all along been saying. God is in the Word of God. But the Word of God is not a mute idol, an idol not of stone but of vellum and leather. To hear God's Word the text must be read, and reread, and reread. The text "convicts" us of our self-constructed heathenism; our false anticipations and premises about what we believe are eminently real and certain.

The reading of the text thrusts us in the direction of a "meaningfull-ness" that cannot be attributed to any metaphysical object of prior meaning, any antecedent totality, or iterative presence. In the biblical idiom we can say that the kingdom of God is "at hand," but its fullness is "not yet." We await the *parousia,* which comes at the "end of the book" and at the end of history. If theology is to become eschatology, it must become grammatology. The study of religion as well as the pursuit of theology, as Jonathan Z. Smith reminds us, is not about "something" we call religion. It is about texts.[21] There is no sacrality without the text, or at least the text that sacralizes what heretofore had been mere mythic credulity and ritual performance. Yet the text is full of "holes," if by the "meaning of the text" we signify that meaning does not inhere in, but spins out of, the text in its precession. The gaps and holes in the text are what Derrida calls the "spacings *(espacements),*" which are its very "texture." The texture of the text is a "deconstruction" of what we thought was its unitary meaning, a meaning we did not have until we began to read it some more and acknowledged that there was much about it we did not understand. Before deconstruction, signs were not viewed as crucial to an assessment of the signification of the text as a whole. The text was subordinate to the "order of being," which it supposedly represented. "In determining Being as presence (presence in the form of the object, or self-presence under the rubric of consciousness), metaphysics could treat the sign only as a transition. Metaphysics is even indistinguishable from such a treatment of the sign. And neither has such a treatment somehow overtaken the concept of the sign; it has constituted it."[22]

DECONSTRUCTION AND FAITH

Derrida tells us, however, that metaphysics can never substitute for faith. Metaphysics is the attempt to circumscribe God by stripping him of his inter-personal character, his relational authority, which is illimitable. Metaphysics and religion are not by any extension of the mind interchangeable attributes. Metaphysics gives "reasons"; religion makes demands. "Is a religion imaginable without sacrifice and without prayer? The sign through which Heidegger believes ontotheology can be recognized is when the relation to the absolute Being or to the supreme Cause has freed itself of both, thereby losing access to sacrificial offering no less than to prayer."[23]

The history of Western thought, including the history of theology, has been the narrative of ontotheology. But ontotheology can never under any circumstances become a surrogate for faith. Though the Western theological legacy has given lip service to the role and importance of faith, it has subrogated the term to the mastery of discourse. Faith is submerged within the propositional calculus of philosophical reasoning. It is hidden amid the shifting composition of interwoven signs and significations. Faith expresses itself in memory and hope, in the recollection of God's delivery of the people of Israel from bondage in Egypt, in the sorrow of Calvary and in the jubilation at the sight of the empty tomb. Faith cannot brook concepts; it requires symbols. "Ontotheology encrypts faith and destines it to the condition of a sort of Spanish Marrano who would have lost—in truth, dispersed, multiplied—everything up to and including the memory of his unique secret. Emblem of a still life: an opened pomegranate, one Passover evening, on a tray."[24]

Faith is waiting and anticipation. It cannot under any circumstances count on the temporal exactitude of correspondence between an assertion and its verification. The very notion of a messiah, or messianic presence, insinuates that there is nothing we can gauge from present history to ascertain how God is going to manifest himself in the future. Deconstruction and messianicity are bound up closely with each other, inasmuch as the deconstitution of the sign brings about a total openness to how God can reveal himself, or does reveal himself, in a concrete setting. The Christmas story—God having been born in a stable—is a complete deconstruction of all the texts of messianicity that had preceded it.

> This messianicity stripped of everything, as it should, this faith without dogma, which makes its way through the risks of absolute night, cannot be contained in any traditional opposition, for example, that between reason and mysticism. It is announced wherever, reflecting without flinching, a purely rational analysis brings the following paradox to light: that the foundation of law—law of the law, institution of the institution, origin of the constitution—is a performative event that cannot belong to the set that it founds, inaugurates, or justifies.[25]

Faith can only be received in the desert. By "desert" Derrida means not merely the literal wilderness, but an unfortified framework of signification that is not limited by predications and inferences. Faith is the gesture that seeks to speak *to* God rather than *about* God. The theme of faith as it appears in Judeo-Christian writings is unique among the religious literature of the world, because it cannot position God anywhere specifically within the text, even though it is in and through the "holy" text that such a God speaks and makes himself known to those who would seek him. God is holier than any theology. Theology depends on the parceling out of reality in the nominative quanta of formal language and draws on the categorical schemes of Greek metaphysics. Theology ends where faith begins. "The chance of this desert in the desert (as of that which resembles to a fault, but without reducing itself to, that *via negativa* which makes its way from a Greco-Judeo-Christian tradition) is that in uprooting the tradition that hears it, in atheologizing it, this abstraction, without denying faith, liberates a universal rationality and the political democracy that cannot be dissociated from it."[26]

DERRIDA AND NEGATIVE THEOLOGY

Derrida's use of the Latin expression *via negativa* is instructive here, because it indicates where Derrida himself recognizes his deconstructive approach to language and logic is headed. In the last decade or so Derrida has taken up the issue of what in traditional Christian thought has been called negative theology. Negative theology, in vogue in the Middle Ages, is rooted in the precept "*omne negatio est determinatio* (all negation is determination)." In short, all we can say determinatively about God is what we must deny about him. The typical predicates that metaphysical theology summons to "speak of" God suggest this incapacity of human language to contain or express his nature. We cannot positively state God's scale or character. We can only assert that he is *in*finite, *im*mutable, or *un*changing. Negative theology provides us with a primitive roadmap for overcoming metaphysics and nihilism, since it self-consciously relativizes all pretensions to ontotheological certitude while at the same time permitting a peculiar language of faith that is at once specific and filled with humility.

Negative theology is technically known as "apophatic" theology, from the Greek *apophasis* (to speak differently from). Negative, or apophatic theology, *sounds* nihilistic, but it is actually the reverse. In that sense it is not theological in the usual connotation of the word at all, inasmuch as it lets *logos* bow before *theos* rather than the other way around. Negative theology accomplishes within the religious ambit what Heidegger has sought to accomplish by a more sophisticated route of reconstituting philosophical language. "Negative theology would be not only a language and a testing of language, but above all the most thinking, the most exacting, the most intractable experience of the 'essence' of language: a discourse on language, a 'monologue' . . . in which language and tongue speak for themselves and record . . . that *die Sprache spricht.*" In other words, negative theology permits God to speak indirectly through language that cannot contain him—not symbolically, not allegorically, not metaphorically, but *apophatically.*

Apophatic language is *unrealistic.* That is because God is impervious to all our grammars. He transcends everything we can possibly know. Derrida, therefore, calls for a faith language that is not accommodated to the logical precision of either ordinary or "scientific" language. Such a language must be iconoclastic to the extent that it discloses the idolatry of all philosophical and theoretical idioms, even dialectical ones. "Whence this poetic or fictional dimension, at times ironic, always allegorical, about which some say that it is only a form, an appearance, or a simulacrum. . . . It is true that, simultaneously, this arid fictionality tends to denounce images, figures, idols, rhetoric. An iconoclastic fiction must be thought."[27] Apophatic language is the only appropriate argot for making *faith claims,* as opposed to *truth claims,* because it reveals both the diversity of all possible forms of God talk and the inexhaustibility of the "object" of such expressions. "Sorry, but more than one, it is always necessary to be more than one in order to speak; several voices are necessary for that. . . . Yes, granted, and par excellence, let us say exemplarily, when it's a matter of God . . ."[28]

This "matter of God," Derrida suggests in his later writings concerning religion, matters more than philosophy or theology hitherto have taken seriously. It is interesting that Derrida, who during his earlier career was rebuked as a purveyor of "atheistic nonsense," should be decrying the faithlessness of Western thought at the turn of the millennium. At one level Derrida's detractors have been accurate. Deconstruction, like Heideggerian ontology, is *a*theistic, because its apophatic character requires that we cannot make any kind of nonstop or plenary statement about the divine presence. Theistic representations are not only inadequate, but when they pretend to be adequate, they become idolatrous. As we speak of God, we warp and raddle texts, yet the presence of God is not to be experienced in the text per se, but in the "margins," "holes," and "gaps" that surround and penetrate the text. That does not mean the texts are empty or meaningless. They are *meaning-full.* But their meaningfulness can only be appreciated when we recognize that the meaning occurs in the negativity of the text.

In a strange way Derrida is rereading Plato as a negative theologian, unlike Heidegger, who sees Plato as the metaphysician par excellence. According to Heidegger, metaphysics builds upon the insight that the presence coming to be "represented" in thought endures as an eternal "idea (*eidos* [in Greek])," or concept. The perdurance of presence foments the illusion that concepts are ultimately true and inalterable as to their "real" signification. Plato's epistemology, founded on the quest for knowledge of eternal forms, is responsible for this curious kind of intellectual optics that we know as metaphysics. But Plato, as far as Derrida is concerned, also discovered another principle—the key to the deconstruction of formalistic thought, which can be found in his dialogue *Timaeus*. That principle is what in Greek is known as *khōra*, the space of the negative. *Khōra* is what "delimits" being and therefore serves as a brake against the overconfidence of metaphysics. Being only *is* by virtue of this "absence" that constrains it.

Hence Plato—and the history of subsequent philosophy—may also be read deconstructively and therefore Hebraically.

> Should one henceforth forbid oneself to speak of the philosophy of Plato, of the ontology of Plato, or even of Platonism? Not at all, and there would undoubtedly be no error of principle in so speaking, merely an inevitable abstraction. Platonism would mean, in these conditions, the thesis or the theme which one has extracted by artifice, misprision, and abstraction from the text, torn out of the written fiction of "Plato." Once this abstraction has been supercharged and deployed, it will be extended over all the folds of the text, of its ruses, overdeterminations, and reserves, which the abstraction will come to cover up and dissimulate. This will be called Platonism or the philosophy of Plato, which is neither arbitrary nor illegitimate, since a certain force of thetic abstraction at work in the heterogeneous text of Plato can recommend one to do so. It works and presents itself precisely under the name of philosophy.[29]

THE RETURN OF RELIGION

We can, therefore, construe Plato not as a metaphysician but as a "heterogeneous" thinker. The word "heterogeneous" is used routinely and sometimes elliptically by most French postmodernists. It connotes the concern of philosophy with differentiation, plurality, and alterity as opposed to the traditional metaphysical interest in similarity, analogy, and logical identity. It is the opposite strategy of logocentrism. The heterogeneity of postmodern thinking engenders an anxiety that the cosmos is no longer solid and well fortified. But Plato himself recognized the impossibility of any foundationalist understanding of how the universe is put together. Though Plato did not have an inkling of the biblical Creator God, his own creation theory allowed for intelligent design, which he ascribed to an ambiguous figure he designated as the Demiurge. In shaping the world the Demiurge confronted "refractory" existence, negativity, *khōra*. Thus the intelligible cosmos of Platonism ends up not a little squishy as well as spongy. The modernist fantasy that everything is constructed with conceptual cement blocks and mortar is only a partial, and perhaps erroneous, account of the Platonic project. A postmodern Platonism recognizes that intelligent design involves fluidity and fungibility. Modern physics in the past century, of course, through the influence of both relativity physics and quantum theory, has carted us beyond foundationalism to a view of the cosmos that considers all things as transformers of energy and matter. In such a scenario the solidity, or "substantiality," of matter is no longer viewed as the root metaphor for nature. It is the fact that the universe is full of "holes" (the Platonic *khōrae*)—"black holes, white holes" and what the famous theoretical physicist John Wheeler called "wormholes" in the fabric of space and time—that allows for the holiness of God to shine through.

What Derrida himself labels the "return of religion" and the revival of faith in the postmodern era is only conceivable because of the breakdown of substantialist metaphysics, which was closely associated with not only modernist rationalism but also atheistic materialism. Atheistic materialism is altogether incompatible with postmodernist thought. Its last gasp was scientific socialism, which collapsed along with pure philosophical rationalism on the world historical stage about the same time. What postmodernism has done is force us to retrain our common sense to embrace a cosmos where the God of faith is more recognizable and can work in our lives more effectively. Perhaps this new common sense requires its own alternative rationality that will enter into the formation of a postmodern and *post-theological* theology. But before we map out that new common sense, we must take a brief look at the career of another French philosopher who has been gaining notoriety in the English-speaking world of late.

DELEUZE AND THE NEW NIETZSCHE

Though he has never attained the notoriety of other postmodern philosophers such as Derrida, Gilles Deleuze is the premier historical occasion for the emergence in France of the movement that was initially known as post-structuralism. It was Deleuze's reading of Nietzsche, who hitherto had been largely ignored, that sparked the movement. The interest in Nietzsche sprang from publication of Deleuze's book *Nietzsche and Philosophy* in 1962.[30] Although it would be excessive to ascribe this development exclusively to Deleuze, his study of Nietzsche was the first in France to treat him as a systematically coherent philosopher. Deleuze's reading of Nietzsche opened up questions that became central in subsequent Nietzschean studies and in French post-structuralism in general.[31]

Derrida arrived like a Lafayette figure in the United States, brandishing the sword of deconstruction to aid the simmering "war of independence" among post-1960s religious intellectuals against the logicism and linguistic formalism of Anglo-American philosophical thought. Deleuze, on the other hand, remained in France, wrote in France, and made alliances that were not in the short run productive for the international ascent of his career. When the revolutionary events of May 1968 rocked France, Deleuze took an active political role and teamed up with a renegade Marxist psychologist named Félix Guatarri to carry his academic work on Nietzsche into a more popular venue. In 1972 the two of them published *Anti-Oedipus,* which attacked the structuralist and rationalist orthodoxy of the postwar era head-on by challenging traditional psychoanalysis and the state-run mental health apparatus.[32] By assailing the psychological establishment, not just in France but in the entire Western world, Deleuze improvised with a strategy that had already proved popular in the United States. The antirationalism of the American counterculture had already turned into a crusade against psychological authoritarianism as a tool of social control, which found a shrill voice in the writings of R. D. Laing and philosopher Herbert Marcuse.[33]

During the late 1960s and early 1970s the American publishing industry churned out a sequence of dense but relatively popular books by these authors and others contending that modern society was a complex and creaky siegeworks of reason engineered against the instincts, especially sexuality. These thinkers were lumped together as so-called left-wing Freudians. Although they basically accepted Freud's tripartite psychology of the id, ego, and superego, they held that the repression of the instincts by the rational conscience and morality was unhealthy, and called for "instinctual liberation" as the precondition for social emancipation of various marginal groups and constituencies. The various ideologies of sexual freedom, including gay liberation, stem from the influence of the left-wing Freudians. Deleuze, however, was not really concerned with sexuality, or with Freud for that matter. *Anti-Oedipus* was a testament against the "scientific" orthodoxy behind Freudianism and its manifestation in modern institutions of mental health care.

Deleuze had been convinced all along that Nietzsche was onto something of sizable proportions, and he sought to combat the larger modern Western thought tableau that dominated physics, philosophy, psychology, and the social sciences. Nietzsche's aphoristic style and his descent into madness had obscured the new "image of philosophy" that he was indeed putting forth. Deleuze believed that *Anti-Oedipus* was a kind of coming-out party for Nietzsche, at least in the public arena. Its immediate success, however, actually gave him celebrity status not as a philosopher but as a social critic, which in turn obscured his growing philosophical reputation, never anticipated even in France.

The thrust of *Anti-Oedipus* was a reassessment of the conventional theory of schizophrenia. Conventional theory regarded the schizophrenic as someone for whom the structure of consciousness had been overrun by, or flooded with, impulses from the unconscious. Conventional theory was modernist in this sense. It presumed a hierarchy of cognitive functions with the "rational" ego ruling over the irrational mechanisms of the psyche. Deleuze and Guattari, on the other hand, inverted the modernist psychological model and advanced what they rather tendentiously termed a psychiatry of the "natural man *(homo natura)*." Schizophrenia does not a constitute "disease" at all. It is the pure instantiation of the natural mind, which consists in ever-shifting flows and "productions" that are synthesized as specific human "desires." The natural mind knows no hierarchy of agencies and processes. Deleuze and Guattari looked to *Anti-Oedipus* doing for psychiatry what Nietzsche had attempted to do with philosophy—expose its soft underbelly and show that what had historically been constructed as "real" and "true" could be reconstructed as a clash of opposite forces within nature itself.

ACTIVE AND REACTIVE FORCES

In his earlier studies Deleuze had refined and to a certain extent codified what Nietzsche had only made rhetorical and epigrammatic stabs toward. For Deleuze, what Nietzsche termed the "will to power" was the dynamic explanation for human history and consciousness. While modern psychology had made experience and sensation into a reactive process of the mind embedded within "nature," Nietzsche saw them as "active" forces internal to the organism itself, which at the same time was an expression of the will to power. The will to power is the genealogy of all forces—both active and reactive. It is the single "phenomenon" hovering behind the footlights of the entire phenomenal world. According to Deleuze, Nietzsche was more radical than even the phenomenologists of the late-nineteenth and twentieth centuries. Philosophy is not about making clear our concepts. It concerns giving some kind of spokenness to what has always remained mostly unspoken or cannot be spoken in and for itself. Philosophy, in Deleuze's famous term, is a "symptomatology." It signifies a surveillance of consciousness, but consciousness is not something that should be conveniently taken for granted. Consciousness—specifically rational consciousness—is not something independent of sensation and experience. Consciousness, sensation, and experience are by-products of the play of the active and reactive qualities of force.

What Freud called the "pleasure" and "reality" principles, Deleuze viewed not as elements in contention with each other, but as different directionalities of the flow of force. When the libido, or sexual instinct, takes aim at a particular enticement, there is either fulfillment or resistance, depending on the force vectors. The Freudian ego, or conscious awareness, is a particular and "reactive" vectoring. The struggle between reason and instinct, or between the conscious and the unconscious, comes down to a binary patterning of these vectors. Phenomena are signifying complexities. They are not the outward display of a concealed reality that is beyond iteration, as in Heidegger, nor are they shadows of the real, as in Plato and Greek metaphysics. They are constellations of vigorous force, of what the Greeks called *physis*. Nietzsche, Deleuze contends, was the first to comprehend this set of relationships and to have an intimation of this "new image" of philosophy. From his vantage point concepts do not "represent" some ethereal order of existence, but are indices, or signs, of the configuration of the flux. Thus, Nietzsche was not only a "symptomatologist"; he was also the first "semiotician," the diagnostician of how these natural discharges are funneled, channeled, intermingled, coordinated, and fused with each other.

Deleuze holds a distinctive place among postmodern philosophers because he set the most radical of agendas—to overcome modernism by creating a whole new pictorial grammar and vocabulary that will seed a new and unparalleled "common sense" of the world. Just as the antirepresentational initiative of so-called modern art a century ago and the counterintuitive thrust of the new physics in the last fifty years have upended the prestige of realism in culture and thought, so also Deleuze undertook to leverage Nietzsche in such a way that philosophy itself might speak differently, or at least postmodernistically. In Ronald Bogue's estimation Deleuze, in contrast with Derrida, takes us beyond post-structuralism, and we might add, perhaps beyond postmodernism per se. "The world is not a text in which signs only refer to other signs, but a network of forces in which signs are symptoms of forces—and philosophy is a semiology only in the older sense of the word—a symptomatology. The play of differences . . . is innocent because the affirmative will try to find the world guilty, not because signs are arbitrary and have no relation to reality."[34]

Modernism, Bogue suggests, has "found the world guilty." It has tried to become judge in advance of the last judgment. It has served as both judge and jury of all sensation and experience, and lashed them to its own discursive protocols. However, a courtroom is not the most appropriate metaphor for the new image of philosophy. For Deleuze, it was *drama*—the action of the stage, of theater, of cinema. The theater does not "represent." It follows the classical, and prephilosophical, Greek strategy of *mimēsis,* of exhibition and performance. The rule of theater is not simulation or replication. It is not representation, but *presentation.* In the theater, meaning is display, or enactment. Elsewhere, I have made the case that the "performance principle" is what encapsulates postmodernism.[35] But the performance principle is what turns replication into Deleuze's "active force."

> Theatre is a real movement, and it extracts real movement from all the arts it employs. . . . This movement, the essence and the interiority of movement, is not opposition, not mediation, but repetition. Hegel is denounced as the one who proposes an abstract movement of concepts instead of a movement of the Physis and the Psyche. Hegel substitutes the abstract relation of the particular to the concept in general for the true relation of the singular and the universal in the Idea. He thus remains in the reflected element of "representation," within simple generality. He represents concepts instead of dramatizing Ideas: he creates a false theatre, a false drama, a false movement.[36]

POSTMODERNISM AS A THEATRICAL PHILOSOPHY

Postmodernism is authentic theater because it does not dissimulate. A dissimulation is the same as a false appearance. But the very idea of dissimulation implies that there is the script and the performance, the text and its recital. The script, or text, is pure, eternal, and real. The enactment, or simulation, is what we offer up for critical review and analysis. The concept of "simulation" is crucial in Deleuze because it takes us away from the usual, Platonic dyad of reality and reproduction, the original and the copy. Deleuze's point is simply that nothing is "repeated" or replicated exactly. There is always a relationship of similarity, but not of correspondence. Platonic metaphysics talks about the difference between the general and the particular. But what is the general? When we put on a play, the script is always interpreted, or performed, by different directors in different ways. The countless performances of Shakespeare's *As You Like It* or Beethoven's Seventh Symphony are never exact duplications of each other. Hence, we cannot say there is the general or generic version of the play or the symphony. The sense of generality is fostered by repeated performance.

Repetition is not generality. Repetition and generality must be distinguished in several ways. Every formula which implies their confusion is regrettable. . . . Repetition and resemblance are different in kind—extremely so. Generality presents two major orders: the qualitative order of resemblances and the quantitative order of equivalences. Cycles and equalities are their respective symbols. . . . Generality expresses a point of view according to which one term may be exchanged or substituted for another. That is why the empiricists are not wrong to present general ideas as particular ideas in themselves, so long as they add the belief that each of these can be replaced by any other particular idea which resembles it in relation to a given word. By contrast, we can see that repetition is a necessary and justified conduct only in relation to that which cannot be replaced.[37]

The notion in formal logic of the general and universal, which takes precedence over the particular and singular, is founded on a kind of perceptual blunder in thought. Because something recurs, it remains the same; it is identical with itself.

The history of the long error is the history of representation, the history of the icons. For the Same, or the Identical, has an ontological sense: the repetition in the eternal return of that which differs. The Similar has an ontological sense: the eternal return of that which makes dissimilar. . . . However, the eternal return itself, in turning, gives rise to a certain illusion in which it delights and admires itself, and which it employs in order to double its affirmation of that which differs: it produces an image of identity as though this were the end of the different.[38]

Every performance, in effect, is distinctive. Nietzsche insisted that time and destiny are like a cosmic stage performance. Ever since Plato, philosophers, theologians, and metaphysicians tend to project into the play of temporal events an "eternity" of sameness perduring beyond the pageantry we envision on the stage. But what we are seeing is really an infinite diversity of singular moments, or events, appearing to be one and the same. Identity is an illusion foisted through repetition. The identity of a human being arises from cellular and genetic processes, electronic perturbations in the brain that we describe as musings and memories. All of these fleeting frames of experience are different, so shown if somehow we were to be able to take a snapshot of the entire compilation at any given moment. The state of affairs at any allotted instant has no permanence; it is a bare virtuality. Deleuze writes: "A life contains only virtuals. It is made up of virtualities, events, singularities. What we call virtual is not something that lacks reality but something that is engaged in a process of actualization following the plane that gives it its particular reality."[39]

Classical metaphysics—and by extension Western philosophy on the main—has always been like masonry architecture. It has attempted to assemble and lay stone upon stone the building blocks of thought and experience, with the aim of erecting a stone wall of truth standing atop a permanent foundation. It has sought to adduce these "hard" truths from first and indubitable principles or undergirding entities that it has called "grounds" for truth. But, Deleuze tells us, "what the ground has to ground, therefore, is only the claim of those who come after, all those who at best possess secondarily. It is always a claim or any 'image' that requires a ground or appeals to a ground: for example, the claim of me to be courageous, to be virtuous. . . . As such, we may distinguish between the ground or ideal Essence, the grounded in the form of Claimant to a claim."[40]

But "grounding," if we share Nietzsche's perspective, is really the molding and contorting of the flows in optimal paths, or circuits. From the metaphysical angle every ground is always at the base of the process, or it is at the beginning. Yet "the two senses of the ground are nevertheless united in a third. In effect to ground is always to bend, to curve and recurve—to organize the order of the seasons, the days and the years."[41] *Grounding is a kind of "rounding."* The "over and above" and the "at the outset" are a means of drawing temporary boundaries. These boundaries convey a sense of vertical structure to reality. But the flows are always part of a horizontal system of markers and coordinates. This horizontal character of reality Deleuze calls the "plane of immanence."

THE PLANE OF IMMANENCE

The "plane of immanence" is Deleuze's linchpin concept for a "revisionary" metaphysics that overcomes metaphysics as it has been conventionally construed. Whereas classical metaphysics is accustomed to visualizing order in terms of "substructures" and "superstructures," "grounds" and "substances," "beginnings" and "endings," the notion of a plane of immanence allows us to chart the realm of "becoming" without these architectural, or masonry, metaphors. In the same way that modern physics required a new geometry to account for multiple dimensions of space and time, postmodern "metaphysics" demands a different kind of metaphorical gridwork. It is necessary to transcend the familiar philosophical discrimination between reason and experience, form and matter, ideas and sensations.

The history of philosophy has more or less absorbed, more or less digested, empiricism. It has defined empiricism as the reverse of rationalism: Is there or is there not in ideas something that is not in the senses or the sensible? As in science fiction, one has the impression of a fictive, foreign world, seen by other creatures, but also the presentiment that this world is already ours, and those creatures, ourselves.[42]

The concept of the plane of immanence gets around this difficulty by ordering existence not as a hierarchy of levels, which require the usual metaphysical differentiation between immanence and transcendence. Instead, the concept entails the dynamic expansion and contraction of the flux itself. Deleuze's description compares favorably to models in contemporary astrophysics.

> From chaos the plane of immanence takes the determinations with which it makes its infinite movements or its diagrammatic features. Consequently, we can and must presuppose a multiplicity of planes, since no one plane could encompass all of chaos without collapsing back into it; and each retains only movements which can be folded together. The history of philosophy exhibits so many quite distinct planes not just as a result of illusions. . . . Every plane of immanence is a One-all: it is not partial like a scientific system, or fragmentary like concepts, but distributive. . . . The plane of immanence is interleaved.[43]

Thought itself stretches out from this plane. Rationality is part of the more encompassing process. Although Deleuze seeks to articulate a language that catches the flavor of Nietzsche's kinetic universe, he is also aiming to produce a new image of philosophy that allows for conceptuality without metaphysical dualism. "Philosophy presents three elements, each of which fits with the other two but must be considered for itself: the prephilosophical plane it must lay out (immanence), the persona or personae it must invent and bring to life (insistence), and the philosophical concepts it must create (consistency). Laying out, inventing, and creating constitute the philosophical trinity—diagrammatic, personalistic, and intensive features."[44]

Without doubt Deleuze is even more difficult to read than Derrida. The concept of the "plane of immanence" does not automatically comport with our intuitive picture of the relationship between "reality" and the operations of thought. But that is precisely Deleuze's objective. His "naturalism" or "immanentism" at first glance does not seem at all hospitable to a postmodern faith. And it may also strike us as inimicable in many ways. But Deleuze is concerned almost exclusively with philosophy. Just as Einstein's construct of "curved space" within a space-time "continuum" resisted common sense, yet worked well mathematically, so Deleuze's suggestion of "curved concepts" within a plane of immanence may function more felicitously than any paradigm of predication. Deleuze has intended all along to counter within the context of philosophical analysis the transposition of the "Christian-moral view of the world" into nihilism.

The implication of his voluminous, and often odd, prose is that the "end" of metaphysics, as was true for Nietzsche, anticipates the liberation of both language and the imagination, the passage of philosophy into art and logic into aesthetics. The upshot is a more fluid and supple image of thought that may allow for the language of faith to become more relevant, not less. When "God is dead," can faith be reborn? The notion seems paradoxical, but only if we do not understand Nietzsche's critique of the metaphysical God. In tracing the genesis of religious postmodernism, we shall learn that it was the very search for an altogether uncharted God language that brought us to the present juncture.

3

THE RELIGIOUS LEFT BANK

Origins of Religious Postmodernism

THE SAGA OF RELIGIOUS AND theological postmodernism is less complex and has a shorter time line than the biography of postmodernism as a whole. Postmodern theology, as it is now commonly but inappropriately called, materialized about the same time as the post-1960s evangelical revival in America, which came toward the end of the Carter administration and at the outset of the Reagan administration. The motive force behind theological postmodernism, however, had little to do with a resurgent evangelicalism. It was preeminently a reaction within theological liberalism against liberalism, just as the New Left radicals of the 1960s were not challenging political conservatism as much as they were protesting against what they considered to be the complacent and cowardly liberalism of their own parents.

With a few pertinent exceptions, the earliest postmodern theology was a more academically and rhetorically sophisticated version of what in the late 1960s had been known as radical theology, or death-of-God theology. Derrida's philosophical sensibility and difficult diction gave far more gravity to the message of the radical theologians, who had been more cultural critics and polemicists than sophisticated thinkers. The iconoclasm of the religious writers of the 1960s acquired a technical vocabulary that had not been available to them before. By 1982, when the first major collection of essays in this genre,

69

Deconstruction and Theology, was published, the inexorably aging radicals of the Vietnam years had become postmodernists in what was increasingly a more conservative political and religious environment.

The complete story of the early phase of theological postmodernism has not yet been told, and it has also been obscured by the fact that when the expression finally became trendy, it was appropriated by a hodgepodge of individuals and groups who all wanted to clamber on to the pomo bandwagon. Curiously, however, the story is also an extremely personal one. As the author of the little book published in 1979 and reissued recently as *The End of Theology*—which most observers agree gave the initial impetus to the careening snowball of theological postmodernism—I can only confess to have harbored a much more modest intent than what eventually ensued.[1]

I began writing the book on a cold and damp Halloween in the year 1977. Looking back, I can say that the event was not anywhere as dramatic or important as what Luther (always my hero) undertook on the same evening 460 years earlier. Both initiatives, however, had long-term, unintended consequences. Like Luther, as a young man I was troubled by what I perceived as a pervasive but false theological hermeneutic that had overtaken the theological world, both on the right and on the left. That false hermeneutic was contemporary Anglo-American philosophy in its fascination with propositional argument and empirical confirmation in matters of faith. I had begun my own academic career in the early 1960s as an aspiring physical scientist. I was entranced with the inferential method of reasoning, and throughout high school—and at least through my junior year in college—I had proudly settled on that method to silence pious churchgoers and religious enthusiasts. Although raised in the Presbyterian church, I had little concept of theological conviction, let alone living faith. As far as I was concerned (and my parents, who reinforced the view), the church was not so much a spiritual milieu as a community for moral growth and social training. My pastors and mentors were, as far as I was concerned, what the economist John Kenneth Galbraith at the time said of his detractors in the profession—some of "the greatest minds of the eighteenth century."

Residing in the San Francisco Bay area of California throughout the decade of the 1960s, of course, changed that perspective. The social turmoil and cultural anarchism of the period had a definite effect on me, as it did for most of my contemporaries. When my father suddenly died of a heart attack in the summer of 1967—the so-called summer of love in the Haight-Ashbury district of San Francisco—a personal as well as a social era came to an abrupt end.

Just about the same time my earthly father died, I unexpectedly met for the first time my heavenly Father. The second incident was not a direct consequence of the first. I had entered a Presbyterian seminary in the fall of 1966, not so much because I wanted to become a minister as to obtain my intellectual and emotional bearings after graduating from college. The Bible and church history curriculum at San Francisco Theological Seminary was as rigorous as one could possibly imagine. I found myself absorbed for at least ten hours a day in the task of committing to memory the structure, history, and terminology of the Bible, all the while steeping myself in Hebrew and Greek grammar. It would be an understatement to call it an immersion experience. At first I considered it a sort of Sisyphean labor, with little more productive outcome than the thrill of working excruciatingly hard at something I had never experienced in my past. It was similar to rock climbing. I enjoyed it because it was challenging and it was there.

But my attitude also was gradually colored by my Bible teacher, an elderly and distinguished professor of Bible named James Muilenburg, who had retired from Union Theological Seminary and devoted his last years to teaching the introductory Old Testament course in the quiet of the Marin County hills. To this day I can say that Dr. Muilenburg did not merely teach. With his flowing white hair, jut jaw, and ferocious gaze, he had the mien of a biblical prophet. He did not approach the Bible as merely a holy book or a puzzling text. He constantly spoke of it as God's "Word," a phrasing that had never made much sense to me before. What he said made sense because he did not entertain the notion of the "Word of God" as a theological abstraction or a catchpenny phrase. "When you open this book," he would say, "you must be prepared to know that God is speaking to you." And he would quip: "You know why I know God is real—because we're speaking to each other." In other words, he made me recognize that the mystery of God is contained in the mystery of the Holy Writ, and the enigma of the very language that goes into the making of the Word of God. The familiar doctrine that God has, and wants to have, a "relationship with us" suddenly had commanding implications that cannot be captured in either homiletical slogans or garden-variety theological assertions. Only God can create beings who are capable of relating to each other, who can enter into dialogue, who can open their hearts and share the depths of their inner persons. Language from the Creator's vantage point is not propositional at all. It is intersubjective. It is relational!

At the time that realization was overpowering. In April 1967 I dropped out of seminary temporarily because I was bothered and bewildered by the thought that God was truly a personal God. The thought was so overwhelming that I could no longer concentrate on my day-to-day course assignments. I took a leave and started wandering and camping with the flower children along the California coast. I was searching for something. I tried to talk with them, but most of them were too stoned to carry on an intelligent or interesting conversation. Then one evening while the sun sank behind fiery cloud banks as I lay supine on the beach near Carmel, I believe God for the first time in my life actually spoke to me. I will not elaborate on that experience, because it is too remote in my memory and now too crusted with theological and psychological deliberations that I have unfortunately amassed since that moment. But it changed me once and for all. Returning to seminary the following winter, I grew close as a student to "Jim," as he wanted me to call him. He envisioned that I would become a biblical scholar like himself. But I knew I was a theological thinker, or at least a historical theologian.

When I arrived at Harvard for doctoral studies in the fall of 1969, I knew that I had my work cut out for me. I was a little like Luther when as a young priest he spent time in Rome and found himself aghast at the pervasive splendor and venality of the "holy" Catholic Church, which he thought was far less concerned with saving souls than merchandising the means for doing so. As I saw it at the time, the same venality had overtaken the traffic in theological and philosophical ideas. At the time Harvard University was a citadel of linguistic analysis, as that philosophical school of thought has been called. Virtually all philosophy courses were designed to help us "get our heads on clear and straight," as one famous professor worded it. There was no serious interest among either professors or students in asking or dealing with what the philosophy of that era dismissed as "metaphysical" (that is, religious) questions.

Religious believers themselves of even the most gentle ilk were put down as "enthusiasts"—a word that had been used contemptuously by high-church clergy against revivalists in colonial America. The only passion that could be detected among the students was found in those political activists who avidly studied Marxism. Students and instructors at the divinity school, where I tended to hang out, were a little better, but they were often prostrating themselves like palace flunkies to agree with their philosophy instructors "over in the yard." The theology of language that Dr. Muilenburg had advanced and the "theory" of language taught at Harvard were as disparate as night and day.

Was a theory of language possible that not only had philosophical weight, but accommodated faith? In a stab at answering that sort of question, for my doctoral dissertation I wrote on the religious thought of the great eighteenth-century German philosopher Immanuel Kant. He was a rationalist, but he had also been steeped in German Pietism, which stressed priority of the affective relationship between the believer and God. Religion was essentially moral and rational, Kant held, but it also had a "transcendent" quality that stretched the limits of philosophical rationality. Kant's most famous line conveyed this paradox: "The starry heavens above me and the moral law within me." At least Kant took the starry heavens seriously. At the time I did not consider myself by any means an evangelical, and I did not even know that most evangelicals had much the same opinion about Kant as Willard Quine, the famous logician. Quine was no longer teaching in any serious capacity at Harvard, but I had a chance meeting with him at a university soiree and struck up a conversation. He was a kindly old man, but when I told him what I had selected as a dissertation topic, he wrinkled up his nose and sniffed, "Oh, Kant, you mean that mystic!" If Kant, the true watershed figure of modern philosophy, was too mushy-headed for the tastes of contemporary philosophers and theologians, I lamented, the Lord help us.

The Kantian Context

Kant, unfortunately, did not really have a theory of language to counter what I was taught at Harvard. But he did have a theory of knowledge that could be updated for the purpose I had in mind. That purpose was to come to grips with so-called ordinary-language philosophy, which had been the meaning motif in twentieth-century philosophy. Ordinary-language philosophy in a profound sense was nothing less than Reid's commonsense realism refracted through the lens of twentieth-century linguistics and mathematical logic. Significantly, Kant himself had many of the same predilections as Reid. He did not trust professional or, as they were known in that age, "speculative" philosophers. As a son of the Enlightenment, he adhered to the "republican" ideal of the virtues and intellectual prowess of the common man. Kant wanted to bring philosophy down to earth. Yet Kant was also a Prussian, both gifted and cursed with the complexity of the German language, and educated in the ornate rationalism that had captured the universities of Central Europe within a century after the start of the Reformation. To this day Kant's thought poses a formidable challenge: it is addressed to the commoner, yet it is virtually impossible to comprehend, even in its native tongue, without extensive philosophical training.

Because Kant is so difficult to read, he is easily misunderstood as well as reviled for his lack of "plain-spokenness." Though Kant took the intellectual culture of Europe by storm for the next century after his death, he was an object of suspicion and consternation in most of the English-speaking world. Kant's main innovation was what he himself referred to as the "Copernican revolution" in philosophy. The expression is slightly misleading. Copernicus stipulated that the earth, from which human beings view the celestial spaces, revolves around the sun, rather than the sun around the earth. Kant's "revolution," on the other hand, rested on the claim that human knowledge "revolves" around the self, or subject. Kant never said, nor seriously entertained the premise, that all knowledge is "subjective" or, even worse, "relative." Nor was he the author of the philosophical view that many automatically ascribe to him, what has come to be called perspectivalism.

Perspectivalism is the capacious notion that whatever we know depends on our direction of vision, or perspective. Just as we cannot perceive any object simultaneously from both the front and back, so we cannot immediately grasp truth "in itself," according to perspectivalism. Subjectivism, which can mean many things to many different people, is simply a more hard-edged—and not necessarily more coherent—variant of the perspectivalist argument. If we cannot know anything in toto, subjectivists contend, then all we know is what we know from our own personal vantage point. That is largely the sentiment producing the puerile statement, "If it's true for you, it's true." Whoever wants to blur the boundary between perspectivalism and subjectivism can use even more pungent language. One can hurl the damning epithet "relativist," which can signify just about anything. It is one of those terms like "Communist" or "fascist," which aims to damn by its usage alone, rather than identifying what is actually troubling in an opponent's discourse.

On the other hand, a certain measure of relativism (and to a minimal extent subjectivism) has been embedded in the Western philosophical heritage since Plato. Even the church fathers might be considered perspectivalists, if one chooses to employ the term loosely. From the age of the apologists onward, the fathers had sought to defend the new faith by demonstrating its rational ramifications. But to make the faith intelligible, they knew they were starting with faith, not with natural philosophy or argument. Their audience was those who could not assent at face value to the Christian witness of Jesus dying on the cross for all of humanity and rising from the dead. Kant himself was aware of this tension within his own philosophical lineage. His "apology" was that of a pious Lutheran coming foursquare against the empirical science of Isaac Newton, the skepticism of David Hume, and the inductivism of the English and Scottish thinkers. In a preface to *The Critique of Pure Reason,* Kant set forth what can be considered the rallying cry of all reformations, including the next one. He stated that the purpose of his philosophy was "to remove knowledge in order to make room for belief."[2]

Why would such a monumental and ponderous philosophical effort be conducted "to remove knowledge"? Some translations render the German as "to abolish reason," an even more hyperbolic contention. Kant's subjectivism—his appeal to the subject as the arbiter of what we can and cannot know—was in fact an effort to rescue objective knowledge by authorizing its proper boundaries. When the limits of reason were established, Kant held, faith could flourish. An instinctive rationalist and admirer of the new experimental science, Kant surely was not one to suggest that the world of the private individual *is* the world. Such an extreme philosophical position has quite a hoary pedigree. It is called solipsism, an extreme form of skepticism. When contemporary critics rail about the "subjectivism" of contemporary religious and moral values, they are picking out a popular attitude that can best be characterized as solipsistic.

Solipsism, nevertheless, has never been a tenable philosophical stance: it easily fractures from its own self-contradictions. Popular solipsists are really saying that they acknowledge neither moral nor intellectual standards of any general type—a strand of libertinism that has been fashionable since the Vietnam decade. Such popular solipsism is not philosophical, nor does it represent postmodern thinking. It is merely a cultural pathology founded on a crude species of anti-intellectualism. But Kant was not a solipsist by any gyration of the imagination. Kant's Copernican revision of philosophical epistemology, or the general theory of how knowledge is obtained and processed, rested on the insight that the "objectivity" of knowledge hinges on the necessity of a *common cognition*. And this commonality of our ideas and experience can be explained by the fact that we all have a uniform capacity as human creatures for exercising the aptitude of reason, with which God has endowed us. The utilization of reason extends beyond sense observation and reflection. It impacts the moral life as well. Kant termed this moral application our "practical reason," as contrasted with "theoretical reason." Theoretical, or scientific and logical, reasoning must be humble and understand the precincts outside of which it cannot make claims or adduce "facts." Practical, or moral and religious, reasoning nonetheless does not need to abide by such limits. Faith itself is limitless.

FAITH SEEKING UNDERSTANDING

In an exceptionally intricate manner Kantian philosophy encapsulates the inaugural principle of Christian apologetics, codified in the fifth century by

Augustine of Hippo—"*fides quaerans intellectum* (faith seeking understanding)." And it was because of Kant that thought on the European continent did not draw a line in the sand between philosophy and theology, or reason and faith, as happened in England and America. Anglo-American philosophy reversed the formula from the mid-eighteenth through the early-twentieth centuries, setting up what the philosophers of that age termed the "understanding," or the empirical intellect, as the yardstick for faith. For Kant, the understanding was incapable of cognizing God. Faith could become rational, but reason could never substitute for faith. English-speaking philosophers from Reid forward, however, took the opposite tack. When we suppose there is anything grander or less explicable than our everyday picture of how the universe holds together, they argued, instead of questioning our own posture we should rigorously analyze our concepts to make sure we have not overburdened them with beliefs that somehow warp common sense. In short, truly novel or overpowering ideas are probably just perceptual indigestion.

The Cambridge philosopher G. E. Moore, who represents the bridge between nineteenth-century empiricism and twentieth-century "analytical" philosophy, put the matter soberly. Our customary beliefs are sacrosanct, he argued in *A Defence of Common Sense* (1925). If we are troubled by their pedestrian character, we simply need to get clearer about those propositions that seduce us away from them. Moore and his brilliant student Ludwig Wittgenstein were probably the most influential British philosophers of the twentieth century, but they also spawned a mind-set that allowed little space or opportunity for the kind of passionate self-examining and God-searching that epitomizes the person of faith in struggling with an incomparable and holy Deity. Moore could never have chimed in with Augustine in his confrontation with God: "A man must implore Thee before he can know Thee."[3] The point is not to sit down and determine how straightforward the concept of God really is. God is never straightforward. Moore, who brutally repudiated the fervent Christian evangelicalism of his prepubescent years, succeeded in coming clean about where commonsense realism was gravitating. It could not really support belief. The unavoidable result is atheism, or at least what Moore proudly dubbed "complete agnosticism." Evangelical thought of the Anglo-American variety has long been engaged in a dance with the devil, a perilous and tricky two-step that employs for its apologetics the very methodology that more elegant philosophy has successfully exploited to crush Christian belief. Kant's transcendental philosophy, as it was called, never really secured a foothold in England or America.

Commonsense realism, which in the twentieth century became ordinary-language philosophy, always carried the day. But "Continental philosophy"—a byword for German and French thought—with its Kantian patrimony was able to make inroads into the Anglo-American establishment by the late 1970s because it had something to offer that the theory of ordinary language painfully lacked. Continental philosophy no longer was puffed up with the kind of metaphysical swagger that had earmarked it since Kant and Hegel. Continental thought was beginning to take the problem of language seriously. Yet it approached the problem from an altogether different angle. While Anglo-American philosophy sought to uncover the ordinary meaning of everything we say, Continental thinkers aimed to give some account of how language functions at an extraordinary level. The impulse came from Heidegger, the well-known existentialist, right after the Second World War. But most of Heidegger's postwar writings—the so-called later Heidegger—had not been translated into English until the end of the Vietnam conflict.

HEIDEGGER AND LANGUAGE

What distinguished Heidegger in his later career was the discovery that language is not simply about explanation, evidence, and the analysis of propositions; it has a profound "revelatory" function as well. Heidegger, like most German thinkers, was an avid scholar of classical Greek philosophy. He pursued the point that some linguists and anthropologists had discovered several decades earlier—that discursive rationality is not a universal trait of human language. Languages as diverse as Hebrew and Hopi yield meaning not through predication, the joining of a subject to a predicate, but through adumbration—the process of bringing slowly to light. To say something is "true" in the propositional sense that S is P, as Aristotelian logic demands, is an affectation of advanced Indo-European idioms such as Greek, Latin, Italian, or English. But "truth" can be communicated in other ways as well. Heidegger contended that he had discovered a more primitive or "originary" paradigm of both language and truth in Greek philosophy before Plato, among those obscure and nonsystematic writers we remember as the pre-Socratics. This paradigm both antedates and challenges post-Platonic tradition (and thereby most of Western philosophy). In the pre-Socratic setting truth was understood not as inference, but as "revealing" or "unconcealing." That is how Heidegger, with a certain etymological fidelity, translated the Greek word for truth, that is, *alētheia*. Everything we "know" as true is true because truth has somehow crept out of "hiding."

But for everything clear and visible, there is always a dark penumbra, an obverse and invisible side of what can be glimpsed that "withdraws" from our sight, while at times emerging back into the light. Heidegger was convinced that propositional logic constitutes a betrayal of this ancient philosophical insight into the nature of truth. The goal of philosophy is to think about things in a fashion that has not been thought before, that in Heidegger's jargon remains "unthought." "Thinking the unthought" is what philosophy is all about. Heidegger maintained that when he studied classical philosophy, he was undertaking to "think the Greeks" in a manner "the Greeks never thought." When philosophy confronts language, it does not come up against the everyday and obvious; it stands like Moses before the burning bush, face-to-face no longer with clarity but with mystery. Language is not intrinsically logical; it is poetic.

Although Heidegger regarded himself as a philosopher and not by any stretch as a theologian, it was apparent to anyone sensing the rhythm of his oracular observations about language that he had somehow recaptured the biblical sense of the infinite Deity who makes himself known to us by speaking to us. Heidegger's choice of words concerning the hide-and-seek of Being echoes Luther's paradox concerning the God who is simultaneously "*Deus absconditus* (the hidden God)" and "*Deus revelatus* (the revealed God)." Furthermore, Heidegger had dismissed the propositional view of language as an idea of "schoolmasters."

When I read the later Heidegger in translation for the first time during the summer of 1977, it was like an unexpected thunderclap from distant clouds gathering over a long-parched landscape. What Heidegger has been saying all along is that the predicative structure of philosophical argument and analysis, which reaches its essential expression in Aristotle's *Categories,* tends to obscure what is ultimately going on in the act of thought itself. Thought and reason are qualitatively distinct from each other. One analogy that catches the drift of what Heidegger is doing is the familiar saying "the map is not the territory." Maps are two-dimensional illustrations of a three-dimensional landscape. They are easily recognizable and synchronized sign systems that enable us to navigate across large-scale topographies. But they do not coincide directly with what they represent. Maps are not the same as portraits. They are what Kant termed "schemas." A schema incites the imagination to retrieve from memory an actual picture that is appropriate to the signs in play. Particular sign systems, on the other hand, can be schematized in various manners. When we see a relief map with peaks and valleys, for example, we can conjure up in our minds all sorts of vistas from the Alps to the Rockies to the mountains of the moon. The more carefully the signs are delineated, the more a concrete panorama of what is "mapped" emerges. Yet, no matter how meticulously we map an explicit terrain, we can never even come close to an image, or photograph, of the same scene. Maps and images belong to different series of signification.

For Heidegger, Western thought on the whole, and Western philosophy and theology in particular, has mistaken the map for the territory. This confusion is so ingrained in our perception that we instinctively regard the error itself as a matter of common sense. Such an error has been institutionalized in what philosophers have labeled the correspondence theory of truth. The average person—and most commonsense realists—take for granted that words correspond to things. This belief is almost as old as Western philosophy itself. The word "road" corresponds to a real and locatable entity that is somehow "identical" with it. In the classical and medieval worlds, philosophers sought to characterize these generic objects to which individual words, or "names," correspond. Philosophers known as realists asserted that these genera were physical in some sense of the term. Idealists contended that they were mental, not physical. In the late Middle Ages there emerged a school of philosophy propounding that those "things" which language signified did not have any relationship to the terms themselves. These philosophers came to be called nominalists. They adopted a position similar to cultural linguists in the twentieth century. According to the nominalists, words are random signs that have meaning not because of any clear correspondence between the act of reference and the actual referent, the thing referred to. They have meaning because everyone who uses the language can agree on what the terms mean.

The modern counterpart to nominalism is what has been dubbed "linguistic conventionalism." Linguistic conventionalism was the linchpin of Saussure's structural linguistics. Saussure taught that the relationship between the sign and the event of signification was completely arbitrary. It should be noted, of course, that linguistic conventionalism is not the same at all as conceptual relativism. This historical observation is crucial, insofar as structural linguistics constitutes the philosophical matrix for the development of post-structuralism, which became postmodernism. As innumerable intellectual historians have confirmed, it was the nominalist assault on both realism and idealism that laid the groundwork for the Reformation doctrine "by faith alone." Luther himself was schooled in nominalist philosophy and harbored a strong suspicion of Catholic dogmatics, which evoked the classical correspondence of truth to warrant (ground), what Luther considered unbiblical teaching. Luther's concern needs to be appreciated anew when one mulls the challenge of postmodernism to commonsense realism. The notorious "relativism" of postmodern philosophy is, in point of fact, the revival of nominalism under the aegis of post-structuralist linguistic philosophy. Such a nominalism is a key to understanding the relativity of finite linguistic patterns to reality itself.

According to Heidegger, the syntax of language does not duplicate the structure of reality any more than a map reflects the territory. The "is" of a predicative judgment (for example, the proposition that x is y) does not correspond to what metaphysicians term "Being" itself. It is strictly a logical operator, a nominalistic function. When we speak of Being itself—as the medieval Schoolmen talked about God as Being itself, or Being qua Being—we cannot possibly have in mind "something" that can be an object of reference. Nor can we compass it as an isolated concept. Being cannot be demonstrated by argument and inference; it can only be thought. On Heidegger's terms, for something to be "thought" is to be "glimpsed" simultaneously in both its visible and invisible facets. Again, we return to the problem of perspective. We cannot view a three-dimensional entity in its entirety. We can only scrutinize one particular side of it. But when we approach something from a singular perspective, we sense the presence of the whole, even if it is not transparent to us. That perception of presence provokes continued thinking and consideration, which yields successive insights and instants of understanding.

This analogy was driven forcefully home to me on a recent occasion when a young Christian missionary friend showed me snapshots and gave an account of his first visit to Mount Fuji in Japan, where he had been assigned. The young man had obviously been awed by the sight of Fuji, which is one of the most spectacular summits on the planet. He pulled out a sheaf of photographs for me to browse through. But while I was thumbing through the photographs, he kept apologizing for the inability of his camera to capture both the grandeur of the mountain and the fascinating features of the soil and rock he espied while hiking the trail that spirals toward the summit. "You simply had to have been there," he sighed, "and even then you're not completely sure what you're looking at." His exasperation can be compared to a devout person who hears a secular philosopher give a smug explanation of why God does not exist. In the mind of that listener, the God whom the philosopher has ponderously dismissed seems to bear little resemblance to the awesome and almighty Lord he worships. The god of that particular philosopher is not by any means comparable to the God whose majesty and unfailing love do not seem to require "proof" any more than opening the curtains in the morning to behold Mount Fuji requires reading a travel guide that attests how stupendous the landmark really is. Once we lay eyes on the mountain itself, rather than a simple photograph, we dare not pretend that the picture is somehow commensurate with the thing itself. We cannot survey at once the entire mountain with all its crags, ridges, and promontories. Yet we can climb and circumambulate the mountain in order to obtain a closer and fuller view, a vague sense of which we acquire when we gaze out the window. If we accepted our initial vision of the mountain as its totality, we would of course be quite foolish. Even if we laid out on the table a hundred different photos, as my friend did, we still could not claim we had come anywhere near to representing the mountain as it is. But ironically, that is what theological reasoning often strives to accomplish. The snapshot approach to ultimate reality is what propositional logic, even "theo-logic," undertakes.

Tourists who have come back from Mount Fuji would rarely presume that their satchels of pictures and postcards—or in this age the memory cards in their digital cameras—afford any more than a thin approximation of what they have encountered firsthand. Yet philosophers and theologians, past as well as present, usually go in the opposite direction. The confusion of propositional logic with thought in all its richness and immensity is akin to the naive supposition that a few clicks of the shutter can replicate somehow the experience of the mountain. Heidegger himself constantly emphasized this point. Western philosophy, Heidegger contends, has been ensnared for centuries in this confusion, insofar as it mistakes particular beings for Being itself. It misunderstands that words or concepts are mere sketches—not even approximations—and can never measure up to the real presence of the Most Holy One in all his grandeur and exhaustless *personae*.

The confusion of presence with representation harks back to Plato and his identification of God as the "idea" of "the good," Heidegger says, and has given most of Western thought a unique character and coloring, what he terms "ontotheological," or "metaphysical." Heidegger coined the term "ontotheology" in order to put across the notion that metaphysics treats the conceptual representation of God as God himself, or the idea of ultimacy as ultimacy per se. The metaphysical God, he wrote, is not a God we can bow down before or offer sacrifices to, yet such a God—whom the seventeenth-century religious thinker Blaise Pascal named the "god of the philosophers"—is given higher priority within the tradition than the God of Abraham, Isaac, and Jacob.

The God of the philosophers is *logical*. The God of Abraham, Isaac, and Jacob is *relational*. And because God is a Being not in himself, but a Being in relation, we know him through his Word and through the testimony of many who have borne witness to his mighty works. To talk about God as an

ultimate *fact* in the metaphysical sense is more egregious than any misapplica-
tion of logic. It is to reify the Supreme Person who seeks us for a relationship
with him. It is to finitize the One who is, and who was, and who is to come.
In other words, metaphysics is the most insidious lapse into idolatry. As the
Scriptures remind us, idolatry is never self-evident. It is usually detectable
by a haughty self-assurance. Otherwise, it would not be idolatry. Idolatrous
worship pretends to be true worship, just as idolatrous thinking pretends to
be true thinking. But true faith descries the difference.

IDENTITY AND DIFFERENCE

Heidegger's definition of conceptual idolatry is what he designates as the
"ontological difference"—the "difference between Being and beings," or
between presence and representation. Derrida's reframing of Heidegger's
"ontological difference" as *différance*—the difference between writing and
presence—has been more influential in the last two decades on the recognizable
rhetoric of postmodernism. But the theological implications of Heidegger's
insight, from which Derrida borrows, are far more stunning.

It was this sense of difference that I originally deployed to ignite the first
postmodernist skyrocket in contemporary religious thought. Because of the
careening popularity of Derrida in academic circles during the late 1970s and
1980s, the popular correlation of postmodernism with deconstruction—which
in itself came quickly to be associated with slippery oratory, like Lewis Carroll's
nonsense verse—took hold in the general culture. Much of what seemed to
make deconstruction interesting at the time is that it was utterly unlike anything in America that had called itself philosophy. In short, it was not making
a philosophical or theological statement "about" anything at all. In the 1960s
the wildly popular and upcoming young rock singer Bob Dylan had been
asked in a magazine interview what his songs were "about." Dylan's music,
which he wrote himself, had the same bardic and playfully obscure lyrics as
Derrida's writings. In response to the question, Dylan did not hesitate or bat
an eye. "Oh, some are about two minutes, some are about three minutes,
some are about five minutes," Dylan said impishly.

Dylan's reply was prompted by an intuition that the preposition "about,"
which suggests a referential relationship between the order of signs and the
givenness of the world, was altogether irrelevant. Dylan had adopted his own
name from the Welsh poet Dylan Thomas. The power of Thomas's poetry
did not derive from the loftiness of the subject matter, but from the driving
and assonant force of the poet's language. Dylan Thomas's poetry was in-

tended to be read out loud, not in silence. The same was true for Bob Dylan's couplets. The significance lay in the rhythm and the sound, not in whatever conceptual representation came to mind when one listened to the songs. The representational theory of language, so indispensable to commonsense realism, was helpless in the company of a lyrical genius.

Deconstruction was designed to eliminate the prepositional pipe fitting that, according to standard philosophy, links two planes of reality, the verbal and the essential. This two-planes prototype of meaning and significance had thrived in some guise since the Middle Ages. In addition, deconstruction undercut the presumption that language necessarily mirrors a world outside of language. Although deconstruction was not at all a theory, it had profound theoretical applications. In comparison with correspondence theory, deconstruction took cognizance of language as an endlessly unfolding immanent plane of signifiers. A text is not unlike the game of hangman. One draws a line, then another line along a different track, and so on until the outline of the hangman emerges. Like the effigy of the hangman, the meaning of the text is not in the text but in its ongoing extension. That is one of the overarching reasons Derrida has appealed in some respects more to literary theorists than philosophy. Literary theory is not beguiled by the thesis that philosophy is inherently, to use Richard Rorty's phrase, a "mirror of nature." Literary theory knows that it is dealing with a fictional subject matter, which on close analysis proves not really to be subject matter in the least. Because literary theory is not encumbered by its own metaphysical assumptions, it therefore can concentrate on how the text functions as a skein of tropes and sentences, on its texture rather than its substance, on what happens in the experience of reading and writing instead of what supposedly is buried, like pirate treasure, beneath the surface.

Deconstruction did for the representational, or correspondence, theory of meaning in philosophy what modern art in the twentieth century did for the representational quality of painting. Artists from Matisse to Mondrian undertook to "see through" the illusory representation on the canvas in order to achieve a "painterly" concentration on the elements of painting itself, such as color, geometry, brush stroke, and illumination. Similarly, deconstruction zeroed in on the theory of writing as writing, as the composition of meaning. In fact, some philosophers increasingly profile Derrida not as a philosopher at all but as a writer. This typification naturally is aimed at expelling Derrida from the exclusive club of Western philosophers, but it contains an intimation that offers a harsh judgment more on philosophy itself than on Derrida.

If philosophy is not "about" some not-so-apparent and undetectable gridwork that somehow cements together our thought and ideas, but in practice a technique of bringing the purport of philosophical—or theological—writing to light through writing, then Derrida really is a writer. Philosophers such as Pascal, Nietzsche, Kierkegaard, Wittgenstein, and in a certain measure Heidegger were more writers than philosophers in the classic sense of the term. Indeed, since the end of the Enlightenment, philosophy has become increasingly "writerly." There is no systematic plan, or topic area, for Derrida's writings. Postmodernism is less about the death of God than the demise of the expository. Even theology is becoming "grammatology."

Of course, that process was not new to Christianity. Paul and the early apostles did not write treatises, but epistles. Letters, like divine speech, are eminently relational. They are pitched to someone in a certain situation with the intent of clarifying an issue, or supplying some wisdom, that is pertinent to that individual. The theological message of Paul's epistles, for example, materializes out of the context to which each is addressed. Its sacred, or inspired, character can be inferred from the manner in which it keeps playing out in people's lives and predicaments from century to century, from generation to generation. The alleged discrepancy, or dreaded conflict, between the author's intent in writing ("What did Paul mean?") and the theological point ("What does God mean?") becomes irrelevant. Both Paul and God "wrote" the text, and it is not contradictory to make such a statement. The meaning is in the application, in the meaning as extension.

Like the hangman, the outline emerges as one continues to read and to write.

The old Jewish rabbinic attitude that the "word" of Scripture subsists in the mind of God, but has to be teased out through laborious interpretation and commentary—including commentary on commentaries—is thoroughly ingrained in Derrida's work. Derrida, of course, is Jewish. If Christian thought from the era of the apologists had not for the most part "gone Greek," it probably would have been unnecessary for modern theologians to fight bitterly about the "literal" versus the "historical" meaning of the biblical text, or over whether the Scriptures were divinely "inerrant" or humanly flawed. The Reformation doctrine that the Holy Spirit mediates between the errant reader and God's infallible Word amounts to an early form of what we might term a postmodern process of hermeneutics—the faith that God will show us what he means to show us, and continue to show us even more, as we become "mature in Christ."

When I wrote *The End of Theology*, I drew heavily upon Heidegger's most important discovery, namely, that the history of Western philosophy is the history of metaphysics, and that this nearly two-and-a-half-millennia epoch has exhausted itself and come to closure; it has reached its "end."

> Metaphysics and theology share the same territory for investigation, insofar as they constitute a hunt for some kind of *archē* for human experience. The theologian calls this *archē* "God." The metaphysician may choose a term with less anthropological connotations, such as what the Greeks denoted the *ontos on* [the being of being], the "highest being," . . . or the Sufficient Reason. In endeavoring to determine the *archē*, both metaphysics and theology are in pursuit of a semiotic quarry. The quest for God is fundamentally a search for the ultimate *significandum*, for the re-presentation of re-presentations.[4]

When Heidegger spoke of "the end of philosophy," he was arguing essentially that ontotheological reasoning had come to an impasse, specifically with Hegel's discovery that the subject and object of thought are inseparable from each other. Modern philosophy was inherently "subjectistic," Heidegger maintained, deliberately turning a phrase to distinguish what he had in mind from the attitude we now call subjectivism. Subjectivism is the reduction of ontology to the consciousness of the subject. It is the wider claim that we can only know what the individual subject knows. Subjectivism is the uncomfortable family secret of empiricism and commonsense realism, inasmuch as it confines the truth of the experience of the things of this world to what we can tangibly hear, see, taste, and feel. Paradoxically, commonsense realism has both begotten and made possible the very subjectivistic orientation that is now accepted as a matter of course in contemporary Western culture. Subjectivism and nihilism, as Nietzsche himself proclaimed, portend the implosion and collapse of the ontotheological tradition itself, like a dying star. The exit from this collapse is a "way of thinking" that emboldens us to "overcome" metaphysics overall. The end of theology is the conclusion of the Western metaphysical project, which has nowhere else to go. But it is also the beginning of a new path of thinking; it is thinking about the identity of Being as the difference between Being and beings, or between thought and representation.

DERRIDA AND EARLY POSTMODERN THEOLOGY

By the mid-1980s Heidegger's revolutionary insights about thinking were for the most part ignored, and the glamour of Derrida's work was now ascendant. Furthermore, the textualism of Derrida had quite a number of uncharted consequences when it was deployed in the area of theology. These consequences could have been avoided if the spell of Derrida himself had not been so embracing and absolute. The preoccupation of theologians with Derrida, and the neglect of Heidegger, can largely be ascribed to the impact of the writings of Mark C. Taylor, who burst onto the intellectual scene in the early and mid-1980s. Taylor was, and is today, one of the most prolific authors in the academy. The sheer mass of his published writing has been sufficient to turn theological attention to the topics and figures he has shepherded.

Taylor first took serious account of Derrida in an essay he wrote during the summer of 1980 entitled "Gnicart Tracing." The article was first published in a volume I edited,[5] then subsequently in the book *Deconstructing Theology.*[6] The strangeness of the anagram in the title was intended by Taylor to introduce some of the basic yet rarefied dimensions of Derrida's "grammatology." The title implies, as Derrida says, that writing lays bare all forms of signification as a "trace" of what has been inscribed and deposited, not as the alleged referential edifice of the text. "Writing is tracing, interweaving which is fabrication. The fabrication of the text, however, always has loose ends. Ever unfinished, the text is a 'permanent metamorphosis' which transforms reader into author and author into reader."[7]

When we hold a tracing up to a mirror, as in the act of representation, we view it "backward." This inversion of the trace is what theological "reflection" amounts to. At the same time, it remains a trace, a reverse writing. There can be no representation in the purely intellectual sense of the word. There are only the different directions writing and rewriting might take. Writing takes place on a single horizontal plane, as contrasted with the phantom "second order" of correspondence theory. Meaning is not a mystical foil to the text. It is text superadded to text. All meaning requires further textuality. Text and meaning are what Derrida dubs "the double sentence."

Is theology, therefore, simply writing? And is theological meaning merely the commentary, or midrash, on theological writing? Taylor, who originally became prominent as a commentator on Hegel and Kierkegaard, was torn. Half of him was drawn to the lifework of Kierkegaard, who attacked the systematic (i.e., "metaphysical") rationality of Hegelian philosophy, demanding all along that he be treated not as a "speculative" thinker but as an author. The other half was swayed by Hegel, who argued in the preface to his *Philosophy of Right* that the "real is rational and the rational is real."[8] If writing is the only "reality," so to speak, then it has an intrinsic rationality to it that defies the simple comparison with Kierkegaard the "existentialist," who teased us constantly with pseudonymous treatises and essays as well as personalized journals, all of which underscore the acutely idiosyncratic and antimetaphysical slant of the written word itself.

When it came to proffering a personalized writing style and theological signature, Taylor opted not for Kierkegaard the writer, but for Hegel the philosopher. Hegelian idealism had asserted the rationality of the real through its version of dialectics—the sublation or "taking up" through thought of opposites in the synthesis of a new identity, what Hegel referred to as "identity in difference." Identity in difference is the product of dialectical consciousness, the progressive negation of what has been affirmed until one achieves the unity of all differences, including the difference between subject and object, or self and other, in the pure "concept *(Begriff)*." But where consciousness of identity in difference is attained through the historical self-reflection of philosophy, in Taylor it comes to pass in the surface of the text. The text by its very nature is "superficial." It has neither height nor depth. It is only a striation of marks and jottings that continually unfolds its "meaning" through a movement of displacement of one sign by the next. It is a play of white and dark spaces, of a "hide-and-seek," in Taylor's language, between absence and presence.

In Hegel's system being and nonbeing "contradict" each other only to engender a conflictual energy that creates a synthesis of opposites over time. For Heidegger, absence and presence are necessary for the self-revealing of Being. For Taylor, they are simply plus and minus, what in Gestalt psychology are known as the white figure and black ground that can be read like an equation both ways. Taylor stresses this point in an aphorism that is both textual and visual: "The negative is positive and the positive is negative."[9]

Or as he puts it unabashedly: "Identity is difference and difference is identity."[10] There is no resolution of the two. The resolution is simply in the writing.

Although virtually all of Taylor's midcareer works are sportive and experimental, they are at the same time serious academic monographs with unyielding academic gravity. In a critical respect Taylor adapted Derrida's theme of meaning as writing, and writing as meaning, to the genre of the history of religious and philosophical ideas. Portions of Taylor's most well-known books read a little like a documentary for the Public Broadcasting System. Every original insight is carefully coded and explored in terms of the history of contemporary thought and scholarship. Taylor has always been a sufficiently polished and adept scholar to make light of scholarship. But he has consistently maintained a deference to the standards and protocols of scholarly argument to prevent him from taking the daring and truly innovative flights of style as well as presentation on which Derrida has repeatedly embarked. The result was a distinctively academic theology that was sober enough to be highly respectable and appropriately outrageous to garner literary attention.

By the early 1990s Taylor had for the most part repudiated his own reputation as a theologian, however, and began to ply the role of an art theorist and philosopher of culture.[11] He moved from the department of religion at Williams College to an endowed chair and a humanities institute. He invited Derrida to the inauguration of the institute. During this period he began to publish books that were visually compelling and, at least from a scholarly point of view, not a little scandalous. Like late-modernist painters, Taylor progressively sought to call attention to the "surface" of the work itself, including even the paper and the ink. On that score Taylor was infusing the spirit of modernism into a perennially tradition-bound and metaphysically minded academy. Postmodernism in the broader sweep of the term was not at stake.

But there was a decidedly postmodern motif in what he was doing that antedated his cultural and aesthetic writings. In his first major essay on theology as deconstruction, or deconstruction as theology ("Text as Victim"), Taylor construed Derridean textualism as a kind of incarnation of the Word. The language and metaphors were taken directly from the writings of radical theology and "the new Dionysianism," a popularization of both Nietzsche and the countercultural ethos of the late 1960s.

> Sacrificial appropriation is, of course, a transgression which turns against itself by reincarnating the Word it victimizes. . . . The dissemination of the Word establishes the identity of sacrificer and sacrifice, victimizer and victim. In the act of transgression, the communicant discovers not only parricide, but also fratricide, to be suicide. If sacrifice and sacrificers are one, then victimizer is also victim. A death of God (a)theology, which is really a radical Christology, finds its completion in the crucifixion of the individual self and the resurrection of universal humanity. The end (or beginning) is realized through the dissemination of the Word.[12]

The metaphor of writing as "flesh" and reading as communion was not as bizarre as it appears on first inspection. At this stage of his career Taylor was strongly influenced by the work of Thomas J. J. Altizer, who had summoned forth Nietzsche's notorious slogan to declare once again in the last half of the twentieth century that God was "dead." There was nothing that was either startling or complex in Altizer's theology, even though Altizer face-to-face was a highly colorful character. About the time President Lyndon Johnson escalated the Vietnam War in the mid-1960s, Altizer, an obscure professor of religion and literature at Emory University, gained abrupt, global notoriety for his book *The Gospel of Christian Atheism*.[13] While the title itself was oxymoronic, it had adequate shock value, in a decade of raging social libertinism, to be taken quite seriously and of course to be roundly condemned by conservative theologians and clergy.

The message of the book, however, was not nearly as outré as the title. Altizer, who had been trained in Barthian neoorthodoxy, found postwar mainline Protestantism dishonest in many ways. Barth's emphasis on the utter transcendence of God found its cultural instantiation in churches that only had to take the passionately human character of a crucified Christ with a grain of salt, Altizer sensed. Altizer resonated with the cry of Nietzsche's madman that the churches of the Western world were nothing more than "the tombs and sepulchers of God." But while Nietzsche's announcement of God's death had an air of foreboding, Altizer was prepared to appeal to the same statement as cause for celebration. It was not that Altizer was deliberately "a-theistic." His argument was ingeniously unchallenging, even if it was baldly heterodox. Altizer's theological point was that God was dead because he had "died on the cross," a premise Nietzsche never elaborated.

Actually, the position had originally been established by Hegel, who used the phrase "God is dead" long before Nietzsche. Hegel, in turn, had borrowed the adage from Luther, who meant something different by it. Hegel said that the Incarnation is the fulcrum of world history. The Incarnation is simultaneously God becoming humanity, and humanity on its way to becoming God. The apotheosis of the human in the "progress" of the West is the fruition of God's "death."

When he wrote *The Gospel of Christian Atheism*, Altizer was caught up in the heady humanism of the Kennedy and Johnson years in America just before the tragedy of Vietnam. Altizer considered himself something of a prophet of a triumphant and well-nigh sacred secularism. It was a secularism that could not brook the otherworldliness of classical Christianity. It was the time of sexual, political, and intellectual revolution. Modern Christianity was its own kind of revolution. It was the revolutionary realization that everything about modern life could be affirmed and honored. For the transcendent God had died; he now lived in the immanent joy of what Harvard theologian Harvey Cox called "the secular city."

As the Vietnam conflict wound down, Altizer discarded this theme of joyous secularism—it was no longer the mood of the day—and began focusing on the theme of divine immanence. This theme captivated Taylor. What could be more immanent than the *immanence of writing?* In the article "Text as Victim" Taylor compared the text to the host of the Eucharist: "*Hoc est corpus meum* (this is my body)." The "this" signifies the corpus, the "body" of writing.

The Jesus we have is the Jesus of the Gospel writings. Our faith rests upon these writings. The significance of the text arises from what we say about the text, how we remark upon it, how we apply it homiletically, how we "deconstruct" it in each successive moment of reading and rereading. To deconstruct the text is to disassemble it, to rend it into pieces as Christ was torn apart on the cross. But it is also to partake of it. If, as Derrida has intimated, there is nothing "outside" the text, then the sacred text is the same as sacred presence. As respondents to the text, we are its "disciples." As believers and interpreters, our condition is a kind of "nomadism" that cannot settle down into any permanent theological point of view. Deconstruction, Taylor insinuated, was the liturgy of the scholar. "Salvation" was to be found in "dying" to our representations and being born anew as readers.

There was a curious but irrefutable logic to Taylor's approach, even if it came across as bizarre and incongruous with the perspective that one would normally consider theological. In his book *Erring,* Taylor produced a name for this commission, inspired by Altizer. Taylor named it "deconstructive a/theology," or simply "a/theology." In a/theology "the death of God can be understood in terms of a radical Christology that prepares the way for reinterpreting the notion of the divine. From an a/theological perspective, Jesus is manifested as word, and word is read as writing. Writing . . . is not to be understood in the ordinary sense of the term." It is "the interplay of presence/absence and identity/difference that overturns the polar opposites of classical theology," since "everything is always already inscribed within the generative/destructive play of (the) word(s)."[14]

Writing, including the writing that is Scripture, is what Nietzsche named "eternal recurrence." As eternal recurrence Scripture "both manifests the infinitude of finitude and the finitude of infinitude and reveals the eternity of time and the time of eternity."[15] Scripture is "the eternally errant medium in which all differentiation is produced and destroyed," while at the same time it "cannot be re-presented in distinct categories and clear concepts."[16] At times Taylor has been faulted for taking Derrida much too seriously, and perhaps even too literally. It has been Taylor's key accomplishment to take the ludic and makeshift discourse of deconstruction and turn it into a systematic theology of sorts—an intensely serious a/theology that parodies traditional Christian exposition while it erects a seemingly post-Christian formalism of the very parody of philosophy that comprises Derrida's own extensive writings. Derrida's well-known, and regularly misapprehended, statement that "there is nothing outside the text" was applied to Scripture. Scripture is text, or textuality *en bloc*. The text is "eternal milieu," the recurrence of the "divine" differentiation of signs from each other and their ongoing dissemination. Scripture is the "incarnate Word."

The death of God, therefore, becomes the infinity of writing. Altizer's "total presence" now becomes uninterrupted textuality, trace upon trace vanishing without a trace. "Eternity" is the featureless and unrelieved desert of signs, interconnected and disconnected from each other, in which the new literary bedouins of the postmodern epoch ceaselessly wander. Reference, truth, and meaning no longer can be understood as orders or processes that have to be inscribed within fixed borders. Like deconstructed textuality, they constitute flows that are both global and borderless all at once. "Meaning is a function of signifiers and patterns of signification that are temporally dispersed." The "metonymic chain" of signifiers "does not properly begin or end."[17] The milieu is always incomplete and "unfinished." The semantic context remains indeterminate.

> The absence of an identifiable *archē* and a definable *telos* transforms "the meaning of meaning" into the "infinite implication, the indefinite referral of signifier to signifier." The radical temporality of signification renders meaning both transitional and transitory. Floating signifiers yield only migratory meaning. Within the nomadic economy, meaning . . . can neither settle nor be settled. . . . As a result of the endless drift of meaning, erring can never be overcome.[18]

In his subsequent book Taylor referred to it as "altarity," a pun on the technical philosophical word "alterity"—or otherness—that was coming into persistent use within the postmodernist vocabulary. Taylor made his points by clever wordplay. The objective was to underscore the instability and roguishness of postmodernist discourse. Interestingly, however, Taylor's work to date has not inspired any emerging school of "a/theology." The reasons are somewhat murky and complex. The central reason is most likely that Taylor's eccentric, though not unclear, style does not transfer well into other intellectual settings. The same holds for Derrida. At the same time, Derrida himself has moved in a direction few of his admirers would have guessed two decades ago. Taylor has taken the opposite course. While Derrida in recent years has moved beyond the iconoclasm of his language philosophy into explorations of faith and religion that could best be described as "neo-Kierkegaardian," Taylor has immersed himself more routinely in cultural theory, including media studies and the academic theory of religion.

EVANGELICALS AND POSTMODERNISM

At the same time evangelical thought has developed its own fascination with the postmodern and since the early 1990s at least has been plunged into its own kind of paradigm shift. The shift underway in evangelicalism notably has had little to do with theological, philosophical, or epistemological concerns, although postmodernist philosophers have grown ever more au courant because of their general prestige and relevance to issues of contemporary cultural change. Because evangelicalism as both a theological community and a movement is thrust forward by church growth and the practice of evangelism, it has been forced to confront the dynamic peculiarities of contemporary postmodern culture. Evangelicalism has been far more attuned to what is going on in the new hip global consumer society than the old liberal churches, which since the late 1960s have tended to side with the now-muted Marxist critics of market civilization. The old liberals have tended to make the mistake of Marxist philosopher Frederic Jameson, who saw postmodernism itself as a politically grounded ideology, the distinctive "logic of late capitalism."

As even the French theoreticians of contemporary culture have pointed out, on the other hand, postmodernism is less an ideological system masking economic interests than a transformation of both thought and communication arising from the absorption of knowledge and ideas by media images. Postmodernity is what the French philosopher Jean Baudrillard characterizes as "the death pangs of the real and of the rational that open into an age of simulation."[19] By "simulation" Baudrillard means the circulation of signs and images that do not refer to anything at all, but keep generating and reproducing themselves as part of the psychological landscape of the consumer society. He has in mind such things as product brand logos, celebrity posters, cartoons and political icons, film and television scenarios. Popular movies such as *The Matrix* and *The Truman Show* have dramatized Baudrillard's philosophical ideas, which in their original format are even more difficult to read than Derrida's. In the Baudrillardian universe we take the creations of media not only as a level of reality, but as reality itself. These creations Baudrillard defines as "simulacra," entities that are constantly simulated from nothing in order to provide a substitute for organic perception. A simulation is not a copy or representation of something else. Like a video game, it becomes a proxy for actual experience. Simulacra are not just real; they are "more real than real," according to Baudrillard. He generates the neologism "hyperreality" to convey what is going on in our media-saturated environment.

Evangelicals are quite familiar with media-saturated reality. A generation ago the expression "evangelical" was strongly associated with the word "televangelist," which became a veritable cultural stereotype. The word "televangelist" came into existence as a consequence of leading evangelists using the airwaves to propagate the gospel message. When the new Christian music exploded in the 1990s, evangelicals were far more "wired" and responsive to electronic sound as a means of both witnessing and worship than others. The same was true of the Internet. Inasmuch as today's American market-culture media is so inextricably intertwined with message, that larger segment of the Christian church which depends on communications technology is more apt to "get" what postmodernism, at least from a sociological standpoint, is all about. Historians have stressed how the Reformation of the sixteenth century would have been inconceivable without the invention of the printing press several decades earlier. It would have been silly for Reformation preachers to exhort Christians to read their Bibles if there were not Bibles in abundance to be read. By the same token, the Next Reformation—the reformation of the twenty-first century—would be unthinkable without the sublimation of everyday language into media signs and simulacra, as Baudrillard has chronicled.

What is generically known these days in evangelical circles as modernism—that is, the Enlightenment view that all authority resides in reason and must be tested by experimental evidence—has faltered in the midst of what the sociologist Pitirim Sorokin identified as the "sensate culture" of consumer desire and satisfaction, inexorably mediated by advertising and strategies of product promotion and visual enticement. Modernism was always what one twentieth-century philosopher has called the "fortress of deductive reasoning." Since at least the seventeenth century, evangelical theology has been as deductive as the Catholic Church in the High Middle Ages. While Catholicism and Scholasticism in the thirteenth and fourteenth centuries deduced religious truths primarily from the correctness of tradition, Protestantism only exchanged the Bible for the church as the source of authority. It did not alter the method of drawing implications from that authority. Thus, by the early-nineteenth century evangelical Protestantism found itself in an unusual place. It often reasoned from the precise texts of Scripture as if they were premises of Aristotelian syllogisms. Classical Protestantism was far more Catholic and hence medieval than it admitted. The focus on proof-texting betrayed those leanings.

But Aristotelianism was never compatible with the biblical faith perspective, as Luther discerned, and neither was deductive reasoning. The inductive methodology of modern science, starting with the data of everyday observation rather than biblical revelation, brought a formidable test to theology on the whole. In the modern epoch the struggle between theology and science had far less to do with competing worldviews or divergent systems of suppositions than it did with inductivism versus deductivism. Inductive theology, of course, was nothing new. The seventeenth-century German Pietists and the eighteenth-century Methodists focused on religious self-awareness as much as Scriptural exegesis and dogma. John Wesley even added the category of experience to the venerable Christian theological canons of reason, tradition, and Scripture, to round out the famous Methodist quaternary. So-called empirical theology flourished among Protestant liberals from the First World War through the Vietnam era. We can even search all the way back to such church fathers as Origen and Augustine and recognize them as inductivists. Augustine's *Confessions* may be regarded as the first great tome of inductive theology.

On the same score the deeply rooted heritage of revivalism in American evangelical life has inherently skewed sensibilities toward religious experience. The strength of conservative Christianity in America has not in any significant fashion emanated from what evangelical theologians over and over again tout as a habit of reasoning from "solid, biblical principles." The accent in evangelicalism has always been on preaching and conversion. That has been the situation even with such towering theological figures as Jonathan Edwards. It is always the state of the soul that ultimately matters in evangelicalism, not a cogent framework for answering questions and settling disputes. Evangelical theological analysis and evangelical ministry were always—at least with respect to modus operandi—at cross-purposes with each other. And it was evangelical ministry that carried the day.

Popular culture, especially musical culture, was consistently on the same wavelength as evangelical ministry. It is no happenstance of history that contemporary pop music—from blues to bluegrass, from rock 'n' roll to soul—had subterranean roots in African-American gospel singing and Southern Anglo revivalism. The wild and cavorting stage performances of popular artists since Elvis have been adapted from circuit riders and traveling evangelists. The sensuosity and visual theater of revivalism has enhanced the propensity of evangelical thought for the postmodern turn. Deductive rationalism was always a luxury for high-church ecclesiastics. Postmodernism as a philosophy better expresses the vibrant populistic pulse of American society, including its strains of irrationalism and anti-intellectualism. Postmodern American evangelicalism is exceptionally American.

RADICAL ORTHODOXY

Fascinatingly, the same postmodern propensities toward experiential theology have more recently surfaced in the United Kingdom, but with a different sort of vector. The movement acquired a name that suggests a double entendre—"radical orthodoxy." Various critics of the movement have scoffed that radical orthodoxy is neither radical nor orthodox, but they largely miss the point. Radical orthodoxy was conceived as an alternative to the kind of secular postmodernism embodied in thinkers such as Altizer and Taylor as well as Charles Winquist, who combined psychoanalytical theory and symbolical analysis with Derridean textual scrutiny.[20] Radical orthodoxy had its beginnings at Cambridge University, which unlike Oxford had been historically friendly to the "softer disciplines" of the humanities. It was at Cambridge early in the twentieth century that the school of "ritual theory" sprang up among anthropologists. The Cambridge school of anthropology exerted serious leverage in the subsequent transition within the academy from theological to religious studies.

Following the same cue, radical orthodoxy centered on ritual itself as the experiential correlate to faith. The intellectual streams that feed into radical orthodoxy are diverse and on many counts somewhat odd in their confluence. They include linguistic analysis, social theory, Scholasticism, liturgical theory, and patristics—all of which are somehow fitted together with the issues brought forward by postmodern philosophers and theologians. Radical orthodox thinkers have a reputation for trundling out some antiquated or forgotten figure in the Western tradition in order to provide a more historical perspective on a topic in which postmodernists revel. On the other hand, postmodernism has a reputation for slighting the historical. If in its staging radical orthodoxy comes across as a maddening sort of intellectual pastiche—like postmodernity itself—it has a common sphere of attention and interest. That commonality is Christian liturgy. The leading personalities in the movement all tend to be high-church Anglicans, or Anglo-Catholics. The radically orthodox find themselves troubled with the disregard for the importance of tradition and sacrament in the theology of the Church of

England. Radical orthodoxy conceives itself as somehow reviving the deep feelings for pageantry and ceremony that were the mainstay of the Catholic faith for over a millennium. According to the movement, Christian faith is defensible because of the fundamental Christian "experience" of participating in the Eucharist, the sum and substance of corporate church life. In Holy Communion the Word truly becomes flesh, and all Christian dogma and theological demonstration proceed from this experience of partaking in the fact of Incarnation. Sacramentalism, while of course familiar to contemporary evangelicals, is quite intelligible, but it can never suffice for the power of individual conversion and the life of sanctification. Radical orthodoxy, therefore, can be considered a unique European take on the new freedom of religious expression and aestheticism conveniently labeled postmodernism. The type of postmodernism that old-time evangelicals want to despise is really a latter-day version of frontier-style religious enthusiasm, which has been a burr in the saddle of denominational polity since 1801. The regular clergy were aghast at the howling and barking of those who were saved during the Cane Ridge camp meetings (Aug. 7–12, 1801, Bourbon Co., Ky.).

The most prominent spokesperson for radical orthodoxy is University of Virginia religion professor John Milbank. In his most comprehensive book, *The Word Made Strange,* Milbank argues that all the would-be efforts of postmodernism to "overcome" metaphysics and theology are actually "theological" gestures in their own right. "Only theology overcomes metaphysics" is Milbank's slogan. Rejecting Heidegger's and Derrida's historicizing, Milbank regards theology not as a Hellenistic innovation but as a unique sort of "pre-alphabetic," or pre-grammatological, orchestration of signs in a postmodernist fashion. Milbank calls this sign-symphony a "metasemiosis," which is not the same as metaphysics. There is no

> liberal enclave in which one can shelter from "mystical nihilism." The real cultural issue lies between this nihilism and theology. Christian theology has been able, like skeptical postmodernism, to think unlimited semiosis. It is therefore not a mere dialectics concerning the mutual presence of reason, but a "trialectics" which articulates the deferral of the sign. The contrast with postmodernism lies at the level of metasemiotics, where the nihilists seem only able to think of signified absence in terms of a necessary suppression, betrayal or subversion.[21]

Milbank has insisted—not always convincingly—that the postmodern project is in a lot of ways old hat. The emphasis of classical Christian liturgy on the "real presence" of Christ in the bread and wine, which Calvinists and later Reformers repudiated, is antimetaphysical and therefore "postmodern."

Even Aquinas was not really a metaphysician, because of his doctrine of the "analogy of being *(analogia entis)*," which is closer to Heidegger than we realize.[22]

American theologian Paul Lakeland, however, has professed that radical orthodoxy is not really postmodern, but "countermodern." According to Lakeland, its sacramentalism harbors a high ecclesiology that is actually pre-Reformation. He notes that Milbank pulls no punches about the revival of what he calls "Christian social theory," which can be construed as medieval and authoritarian. "Hidden away within all Milbank's erudition there is . . . a kind of ecclesial absolutism."[23] Milbank talks about postmodernity as a "strange kind of return" of the premodern. Indeed, at times Milbank sounds a little like an esoteric. His concluding essay in *The Word Made Strange* commends "gothic" or "complex space." Gothic space involves the mysterious and "sacred" unity that holds together the wild plethora of heterogeneous signs and experiences. It is the solution to the enervation of the secular, to Nietzschean nihilism. Milbank cites Gothic architecture—the antithesis of the classical aesthetic of harmony and proportion—as an example. The Gothic solution entails finding mystic "order out of an irreducible diversity," a "measure between diverse things that are, as Aristotle said, inherently incommensurable." Such an order "tends to be imbued with a 'sacred' character because it cannot be defined, and is always being repeated with a same yet different character . . . according to the *social Christology*."[24] Milbank goes on to say that "the gothic vision therefore acknowledges sublime indeterminacy and the inescapability of aesthetic judgment." For

> without this binding by pre-given rules, or by what is 'manifestly' observable, the Kantian sway of a self-sufficient immanence is undone; in complex space every judgment 'exceeds' . . . [and] must seek again the harbor of transcendence, . . . the possible truthfulness of the human imagination. To envisage the possibility of judging objectively, without rules, is to envisage the reality of the God, and the inevitable religious character of the just society.[25]

A "sacred" totality of the social order—a "social Christology" that is integrally aesthetic or "Gothic" and can be based on the human imagination sufficing as "God"—is, however, a perilous prospect. It comes close to what the political theorist Peter Viereck a generation or more ago called "metapolitics," the fusion of an indeterminable sense of the mysterious with a reverence for social solidarity. As Viereck notes, metapolitics is the main historical ingredient in fascism and other historical experiments in totalitarianism.[26] Milbank and other representatives of radical orthodoxy stretch the bounds of what may be termed postmodern. Postmodernism has always been antitotalizing, not just antirational. The appeal to mystery is not sufficient in itself to transcend the ontotheological constitution of Western thought. Mystery is its own brand of ontology.

There is no intersubjective constituency, no relationality for Milbank. Evangelicalism, as opposed to radical orthodoxy, is rooted in the appeal to mystery rather than faith. If radical orthodoxy seeks covertly to reestablish some form of clerical triumphalism and medieval hyperauthoritarianism under the pretext of "overcoming metaphysics," it is doomed to failure. The "freedom of a Christian" can only necessitate submission to one's God and one's friends and neighbors in love, as our own Master commanded, not some mythopoetic politics.

This will not be about the return to magic and mystery. That was the Aquarian gospel of the 1960s, which is incommensurable with the gospel of Jesus Christ. The Next Reformation will be about faith, and *faith alone*. Here we stand. We can do nothing else.

4

SOLA FIDE

Beyond Worldviews

PRESUPPOSITIONALISM

Before postmodernism became a household word, evangelical Christianity perceived itself as locked in battle with something called "secular humanism." As a sizable proportion of the theological literature from the 1950s through the 1980s makes evident, secular humanism was perceived as the paramount threat to Christian values and belief. In many respects the dangers attributed to secular humanism echoed much of what is asserted about postmodernism at present. Secular humanism was a blatant contradiction to Christian views and principles. It had infected the general culture and undermined Christian faith and morality. Most of the literature was never precise about what secular humanism entailed. But in large part it amounted to everything in the intellectual climate in the late-twentieth century that could not be immediately reconciled with the "Christian worldview," especially its touchstone of doctrine and morality.

In the United States secular humanism was frequently equated with the ideology behind the strict separationism that influenced the Supreme Court from the late 1940s onward, supporting the ban on prayer in public schools and the gradual extrusion of biblical symbols and concepts from the public square. But, curiously, the huge potpourri of intellectual fashions and so-called isms that gained visibility during this period had one common feature—they all denied the transcendence of God and the defense of Christian morality on the grounds of biblical revelation alone. In short, secular humanism was a covering word for intellectual modernism, which—ever since Descartes and Locke—had always touted the secular over the supernatural.

The peril of intellectual modernism, according to the writers of this era, was its rejection of a personal God as the source of order in the universe, and its avowal of mechanistic and "naturalistic" explanations for life and consciousness. Christian evangelicalism had been fighting a hundred-years' war—or perhaps a two-hundred-years' war—with the Enlightenment. It was not jousting with the Enlightenment as a philosophical methodology. It only quarreled with the Enlightenment's conclusions. The choice was between a rational biblical metaphysics and a rational scientism, which denied the authority of the Bible. Subjective human reason remained supreme.

Enter Francis Schaeffer. A pastor and missionary by training and profession, Schaeffer rose to prominence in the 1970s as the leading light of the new apologetics movement in evangelical circles, which sought to confront secular humanism straight on. The new apologetics movement arose out of the Christian Reformed tradition and in many ways mirrored classical Calvinism before the latter became entangled with the various controversies over predestination in the seventeenth century. Unlike Anglo-American fundamentalism, the new apologetics took seriously the need for philosophical literacy and a certain measure of sophistication in defending evangelical Christianity against secular humanism. It regarded biblical truth not as something indefeasible and self-evident, but as a "worldview" that made eminent sense if one pursued the "argument" for Christianity carefully and decisively. At the same time, the new apologetics was not dependent at all on the tradition of commonsense realism. In fact, the opposite was the case. While commonsense realism emphasized the transparency of the biblical text, which could be grasped immediately by the average person without any erudite exposition, the new apologetics dwelt on the need to provide "reasons" for accepting Christianity.

This approach was already familiar in the writings of C. S. Lewis, whose fame preceded Schaeffer by nearly a generation. But it acquired philosophical cogency in the work of Reformed theologian Cornelius Van Til, who was one of Schaeffer's teachers. Van Til is usually considered the father of the Reformed school of thought known as presuppositionalism. Presuppositionalism is the scion of Dutch neo-Calvinism, which gained momentum at the end of the nineteenth century and furnished a stratum of theological thought among evangelicals distinctly alternative to commonsense realism and the

Princeton school. The watershed for neo-Calvinism is the writings of Abraham Kuyper (1837–1920). Kuyper is generally credited with introducing the notion of "worldviews *(Weltanschauungen)*" into evangelical apologetics. He also propounded the idea, later refined by Schaeffer, that the modern age is a battleground for two irreconcilable *Weltanschauungen*—secularism (or "modernism") and Christianity. One has been "developed by those who have remained under the influence of sin, the other developed by those who have been partially restored," or regenerated.[1]

In light of this peculiarly Calvinist dualism, Kuyper took exception with Reid's commonsense realism, which he associated with the Enlightenment and by extension with Pelagianism. According to Kuyper, faith is not the handmaiden of knowledge. Instead, knowledge is impossible without faith. In contradistinction to the Princeton theologians, Kuyper refused to identify faith with "wisdom." Faith does not require "evidence." Indeed, if it does demand evidence, it is not faith. Faith acquires the clarity of the regenerate mind. "Common sense," on the other hand, is tainted by sin and therefore cannot be the sole foundation of theological argument. For Van Til as well, faith can never be accommodated to facts. Indeed, the "facts" of the believer are of an indelibly different color than the "facts" of the unbeliever. One person's "fact" is another's "interpretation," which is dependent on the presuppositional framework within which they maneuver. That, of course, was the point made by Nietzsche. Ironically, presuppositionalism bears some discernible analogy with postmodernism, or at least with the kind of comic-book postmodernism that many present-day evangelicals hold up to ridicule. Although presuppositionalism was never considered "heresy" by fundamentalists in the way that postmodernism frequently is, it can be seen as a transitional theology to postmodern evangelicalism.

In the philosophical sphere presuppositionalism is of the same genealogical stock in twentieth-century philosophy as logical positivism and what has come to be termed "moderate foundationalism," although it also represents a peculiar adaptation of the work of Kant. Although people like Van Til saw themselves as countermanding Kant's "critical philosophy," the template for their theology bears an unmistakable Kantian stamp. Presuppositionalism derives from the late-modern standpoint that we have no direct knowledge of the world, but that we start in our search for understanding with certain beliefs, or "presuppositions," which we do not question at all. These beliefs are taken for granted, and they may vary from person to person, from language to language, from culture to culture. From our presuppositional parapets we spin intricate webs of cognition, which congeal in just-as-familiar and higher-order structures of belief and interpretation that we call worldviews.

Presuppositionalism—the theology of worldviews—was part and parcel of a sea change in the general intellectual climate that began with Albert Einstein and the physics of relativity. Until the twentieth century, philosophers had tended to agree that knowledge itself was made up of basic "building blocks," and that these blocks were laid atop a number of key principles, which served as the foundation for truth and understanding. Such a view was foundationalist, and it could be traced all the way back to Descartes. The high-water mark of foundationalism was the efforts at the turn of the century by Bertrand Russell and Alfred North Whitehead to assimilate these principles to pure mathematics, which engendered the discipline of symbolic logic. This led to a search by subsequent thinkers for the scientific holy grail of a purely formal language to which all so-called natural languages, including the academic language of philosophy itself, could be reduced.

That quest faltered rapidly in the 1920s, not only because of the general disillusionment that engulfed Europe after the Treaty of Versailles, but also because of the discovery by anthropologists and linguists that there really was no completely intelligible and uniform set of rules for all the different human languages. After the First World War that generation of Western intellectuals for the first time proposed the notion of "cultural relativism," which of course implied both moral relativity and the impossibility of any unified theological position that was not historically contingent. In Anglo-American philosophy this new attitude favored the spread of linguistic analysis, which held that language is multidimensional and that different "grammars" make it possible for us to characterize the same "thing" in entirely different ways. The philosopher Ludwig Wittgenstein, whose writings propelled the movement of linguistic analysis, made the now-celebrated distinction between "seeing something" and seeing it "as something." He cited a well-known drawing adapted from Gestalt psychology, the so-called duck-rabbit. If one looks at the figure from a certain angle, one sees a duck. If someone else looks closely at it, they may behold a rabbit. In an "ontological" sense the picture, or "depiction," is neither a duck nor a rabbit. It can be either one, or it can be both.

On the face of it this argument is similar to perspectivalism. However, perspectivalism assumes there is indeed one monolithic and self-consistent entity that nevertheless cannot be viewed from a single angle of vision. If we somehow add up all the different possible "perspectives," we can apprehend the thing, just as if we carefully cut and paste together a series of photographs of a sweeping mountain scene, we will generate a full-scale panorama. Presuppositionalism, on the other hand, is more self-consciously "relativistic" than perspectival. The presuppositionalist contends that the picture we ultimately "see" depends on what we intended, or thought we were going, to see in the first place. In other words, if for biographical or psychological reasons we are disposed to see a duck, we will see a duck. If we are inclined to see a rabbit, the converse will occur. It is very difficult, if not well-nigh impossible, to convince a "duck" person that he or she is actually seeing a rabbit, and vice versa. It is never the case that the duck person is seeing wrongly, or rightly. The duck person merely sees what he or she sees as a duck. There is no "meta-object" that is in any logical sense both a duck and a rabbit.

As a philosophical tack presuppositionalism would have seemed to be the archenemy of foundationalism. And even more so it would appear to have been inimical to the certainty of belief that evangelicalism prizes. Presuppositionalism and foundationalism strike us as incompatible options. Nonetheless, the incompatibility may only be perspectival. In certain respects perspectivalism and foundationalism *are* comparable to the duck and the rabbit. Foundationalists since Descartes have maintained that the certainty of our conclusions proceeds from the indubitability of our premises. Presuppositionalists agree that it is the other way around. We start off with nothing more than what we "postulate," or presume. But as in a geometric proof, these postulates serve as the grit and gravel for a clear and unshakable demonstration of certain truths. If the argument does not pan out, it shows that our presuppositions were off base to begin with. An argument or worldview that in the long run makes eminent sense proves the validity of our presuppositions. Van Til, Schaeffer, and other Christian presuppositionalists have repeatedly made the claim that the Christian worldview pans out far better than all other ones.

The details of how this "apology" works in practice have never been consistently elaborated; but much of the line of reasoning was patterned after Kant in his *Critique of Practical Reason*. Kant argued, for example, that it is more "reasonable" to assume that God exists than that he does not exist. For if God did not exist, our efforts to live rational and moral lives would turn out to be absurd. Kant was adamant that it is impossible, in the way foundationalists might attempt, to prove—by ascending in an order of inference from one cogent step to the next—the existence of God. But God must exist in a "practical" sense, according to Kant. The existence of God has to be "assumed" if the universe as we experience it is to make any sense at all. The presuppositionalists spoke in largely the same fashion, although they "assumed" the unsurpassed rationality of not only a generic Christian God but also most of historic Christian doctrine. At the same time, Christian presuppositionalism takes us far beyond theology. One needs to assume most of what Christianity teaches if the other epistemological, aesthetic, moral, and cultural perplexities of our age are ever to be sorted out.

SCHAEFFER'S APOLOGETICS

For Schaeffer, who considered himself neither a philosopher nor a theologian but an "evangelist," presuppositionalism is the only course to take in this "post-Christian" era when people no longer think thoughts that are automatically anchored in the Christian outlook. Humanism has to be put to the presuppositional test by Christianity, as Elijah did with Baal on Mount Carmel. Schaeffer constantly criticized evangelical Christians for defaulting on the intellectual challenges posed by secular humanism. "True education means thinking by associating across the various disciplines," Schaeffer wrote, "and not just being highly qualified in one field, as a technician might be. I suppose no discipline has tended to think more in fragmented fashion than the orthodox or evangelical theology of today. Those standing in the stream of historic Christianity have been especially slow to understand the relationships between various areas of thought." When the apostle Paul warned Christians to keep themselves unsullied by the world, "he was not talking of some abstraction. If the Christian is to apply this injunction to himself, he must understand what confronts him antagonistically in his own moment of history. Otherwise he simply becomes a useless museum piece and not a living warrior for Jesus Christ."[2]

Schaeffer termed the tendency of biblical Christianity to refuse serious engagement with contemporary intellectual culture "the great evangelical disaster." Faith must be aggressively intellectual, not anti-intellectual: "The orthodox Christian" has been remiss in "defense" of the gospel for failing "to think and act as an educated person." Modernity poses a critical choice between two worldviews. In the one worldview human existence is simply the random output of the processes of matter and energy. In such a worldview the universe is "ultimately silent, with no meaning and purpose," and human life is without moorings. In the other view life is shaped by an intelligent designer and by the sustaining love of the Creator. We either submit to God's purposeful design or we willy-nilly aim to "fill the void by hedonism or materialism."

Nevertheless, one cannot make a case for the Christian worldview by either inductive or deductive reasoning alone. Even the most airtight case for Christianity will not necessarily be accepted by nonbelievers, inasmuch as they most likely have a prior commitment to a different worldview. "People have presuppositions, and they will live more consistently on the basis of these presuppositions than even they themselves may realize. By presuppositions we mean the basic way an individual looks at life, his basic worldview, the grid through which he sees the world. Presuppositions rest upon that which a person considers to be the truth of what exists. People's presuppositions lay a grid for all they bring forth into the external world. Their presuppositions also provide the basis for their values and therefore the basis for their decisions."[3] When two "grids" such as Christianity and secular humanism confront each other, the only means for arriving at an appropriate conclusion are to draw out the logical thread of each one and take account of where they respectively end up. At certain points the two threads may become intertangled, and it is the task of the apologist to show how the Christian strand takes the discussion in the direction both parties assume it is going.

In an important respect Schaeffer was sketching out an apologetic method that might be labeled "Christian Socratism," though that probably is not terminology he would have found most congenial. The Socratic method has always been to start with the assumptions of the interlocutor and let them play out to a climax where they self-destruct and become absurd, or they crystallize into some disclosure of the truth. Schaeffer never really followed this method himself in any significant measure, but he saw it as a strategy for combating the dictates of humanism. In stark contrast with Tertullian's version of Christianity, where Athens and Jerusalem have no commerce with each other, Schaeffer was confident that Jerusalem itself could out-Athens the Athenians. There was no precedent for this confidence in the history of Christian theology. But Schaeffer, like his "foundationalist" predecessors, was persuaded that Christianity could best modernism on its own turf. Christianity, in essence, would always prove itself to be the superior "worldview." "When all is said and done, when all the alternatives have been explored, 'not many men are in the room'—that is, although worldviews have many variations, there are not many basic worldviews or basic presuppositions."[4]

The most basic presuppositions can be found in Christian theism, including the formulations of the Nicene Creed. These presuppositions are the mightiest of them all. The presupposition of God triumphs over all others. The rationale is evident. All of Western culture itself is based on Luther's paradox of Christian liberty: the Christian is totally free in his personal faith and subject to no one except the infinite God. On the other hand, the Christian is at the same time subject to the regulations of civil society, which express absolute human equality as ordained by a sovereign God who has no equal. "Democracy, freedom without chaos, as we know it in northern Europe, was built on the Reformation, and it has not existed anywhere else, and this includes the small city-states in Greece long ago. . . .When one removes the Bible, in which God has spoken propositionally, and the resulting Christian consensus, freedom without chaos will not long remain. It can't. Something will take its place, and it will be one of the elites."[5]

Schaeffer's compelling mission seems to have been to restore Protestant Christianity as the preferred or "elite" worldview in the West. If the Reformation worldview had indeed spawned modernism, it was time for Christians to reclaim their intellectual inheritance, out of which secular humanism had somehow skillfully and persistently defrauded them. In reading Schaeffer one catches a whiff of historical nostalgia as well as regret. If only we could do the sixteenth century all over again! On the other hand,

> the Reformation was certainly not a golden age. It was far from perfect, and in many ways it did not act consistently with the Bible's teaching, although the Reformers were trying to make the Bible their standard not only in religion but in all of life. No, it was not a golden age. For example, such overwhelming mistakes were made as Luther's unbalanced position in regard to the peasant wars, and the Reformers showed little zeal for reaching people in other parts of the world with the Christian message. Yet though they indeed had many and serious weaknesses, in regard to religious and secular humanism, they did return to the Bible's instruction and the example of the early church.[6]

Modernism was like a virus that had somehow infiltrated into the Reformation's conceptual genetic code and sired a Frankenstein-like image of things. The Christian intellectual needs to unwire this Frankenstein by following through on the intellectual promise of the Reformation, which was unintentionally aborted centuries earlier.

Unfortunately, Schaeffer's neo-Reformed gospel of Christian cultural magisterialism did not outlast him. Schaeffer died of cancer in 1984 after a little less than two decades of influence among Christian evangelicals. There were several factors in the failure of Schaeffer's message to have a long-term impact, particularly in America. The first was Schaeffer's partisanship toward the European Reformed tradition over Anglo-American evangelicalism. Schaeffer's establishment of the L'Abri Fellowship in Switzerland in 1951 as his hub of operations fostered a cosmopolitan identity for his new brand of evangelicalism, but it failed to counteract the "spirit of the age" that Schaeffer consistently exhorted Christians to resist. Schaeffer was never a sufficiently potent thinker in his own right to make a difference on the Continent, which was becoming totally secular and apathetic about any effort to revive some sense of Christendom.

Nor did Schaeffer enjoy the kind of cachet that would have made him a leading light in American evangelicalism, which was always suspicious of the kind of Swiss Calvinist "Renaissance man" that Schaeffer aspired to be. In the long haul presuppositionalism was a far too heady brew for American evangelicalism, which gravitated toward either popular revivalism or the biblical systematics of the old Princeton theology. Many of the intellectual adversaries that Schaeffer named in his writings were only dimly understood or appreciated by the average American evangelical. Since American evangelicalism, until at least the 1980s, had exhibited a cultural secessionist mentality, the need to engage the popular isms of the twentieth century, as Schaeffer referred to them, was barely intelligible, let alone compelling.

Second, Schaeffer's presuppositionalism grated against the hard-core objectivism that the old Princeton theology had imbued in the American evangelical mind, or perhaps the American mentality on the main. There was always a lingering suspicion that presuppositionalism and the assimilation of Christianity to one worldview among many—even if it was the supreme worldview—was disguised liberalism. Although with their insistence on biblical faith as the absolute ground of any enduring worldview, Van Til and Schaeffer upheld a rigorous monotheism, such an unimpeachable "presupposition" remained a mere presupposition. Evangelicalism wanted to be hard, not soft. The truth of Christianity did not have to be argued. It was surmised to be self-evident. In particular, it did not have to be confirmed in some kind of agonistic contest with its atheistic adversary.

Moreover, the dependence of presuppositionalism on the rhetoric, if not the content, of logical positivism was too much for any sworn "evidentialist" to bear. Along with the logical positivists, Schaeffer admitted the possibility that any worldview, including the Christian one, could in principle be falsified by data. Schaeffer therefore came to be considered a "verificationist"[7] of sorts, which means that the Christian worldview was putatively forced to compete with other modernist *Weltanschauungen,* including Darwinism, historical materialism, and existentialism. Rationalistic evangelicalism did not share Schaeffer's optimism that in the intellectual arena—the Roman circus of twentieth-century isms—the play would ever be entirely fair, or that there could in principle be a level playing field.

Third, Schaeffer's cultural triumphalism was easily trumped by a less irenic and highly controversial form of evangelical Calvinism—Christian reconstructionism or dominion theology—whose star began to ascend at approximately the moment when Schaeffer's was setting. Reconstructionism can be mostly defined as the effort to put Van Til's theology into political action. Unlike the remainder of evangelicalism, reconstructionism moved away from epistemological issues and began to focus upon a political theory that served to concretize triumphalist doctrine. Reconstructionism, or "dominionism," began as an attempt to replicate on the American scene the merger of church and state that was the original program of European Calvinism and was instantiated in the city of Geneva. Reconstructionists look forward to a truly godly society controlled by Christians and recognizing the ultimate authority of both church and family.

Like Calvin, reconstructionists sought to apply Old Testament law to society. Christians have a "moral obligation" to subjugate all aspects of society to the reign of Christ, or to create a "heaven on earth," or what some reconstructionists dub "theonomy"—the imposition of God's law within this world, the *saeculum*. Jesus' new covenant of grace does not replace the old covenant, as much of post-Reformation theology has presumed. Christian reconstructionism has been closely connected to the work of Rousas John Rushdoony, Greg Bahsen, and Gary North. Schaeffer and Van Til, through most of his career, were positive that a new cultural and moral reformation could happen in the Western world if Christianity could just acquire the right intellectual troops and armaments. However, the social anarchism and anti-Christian radicalism of the 1960s, in particular the death-of-God movement, pushed the presuppositionalists toward legal and political coercion rather than philosophical persuasion. Although historians cannot agree on what was the main impetus in the early 1980s toward political activism among evangelicals, it was the spirit, if not the actual thinking, of the reconstructionist movement that performed a major role.

Like Calvinism itself in the sixteenth and seventeenth centuries, presuppositionalism waned as a theological innovation and became increasingly an ideology of social and political change.[8] The politicization of evangelical Christianity in America was probably inevitable, given the religious history of the nation itself. But periods in which politics take precedence over the "habits of the heart," if we may use Alexis de Tocqueville's phrase, generally are harbingers of historical conflict and upheaval, in which the spiritual potency of evangelicalism is sapped. That was certainly the case in the late-eighteenth century, when American evangelicalism, repeating the 1640s in England, sparked rebellion against the Crown. The conclusion of the War of Independence, however, ushered in an epoch when the strength of religious faith and conviction reached a nadir in American history. The same happened in the mid-nineteenth century as the fires of the Second Great Awakening ignited the militancy of abolitionism, resulting in civil war and subsequently the apathy and cynicism of the Gilded Age. The evangelical resurgence in the 1970s and 1980s spilled over into the new politics of Christian conservatism during the 1980s and 1990s, culminating in the election of 2000.

FROM NEO-CALVINISM TO THE NEXT REFORMATION

One can only conjecture what the next decade or two will bring. Will the relative political successes of evangelicalism lead to the final establishment of a "Christian America" leading the world in the paths of righteousness, as the reconstructionists hope? Or will it yield a mounting political fractiousness, a left-wing backlash, and a recrudescence under some guise of the "culture wars"? The culture wars themselves were the outgrowth of the presuppositionalist rendering of the Reformation. Will the Next Reformation be a victory for this particular approach? Will it be the vanquishment of one worldview by the other through worldly stratagems, the final defeat of "secular humanism" by a uniquely Christian politics that, unable to win in the amphitheater of ideas, succeeds in reversing the trend toward separation of church and state? Will it represent the trouncing of modernist secularism by a relentless modernist "theonomy"?

Or will the Next Reformation represent a turning away from the culture wars approach entirely? As shown by the collapse of the Soviet Union in 1991, along with the abrupt and unanticipated end of the Cold War between capitalism and communism, the weakness of the enemy is often more surprising than the threat he initially appeared to pose. Modernism is not unlike communism. Just about the time Christian politics was gathering a head of steam for a direct clash with secular humanism (or secular modernism) in the electoral arena, secular modernism itself was beginning to crack under the pressure of its own internal contradictions, as the Marxists might have said. The contradictions were roundly philosophical and epistemological, as we have seen. They boiled down to what Heidegger regarded as "fundamental ontology." They had to do with the Western and Greco-Christian conception of reality, which may have been confused with, but was not necessarily tantamount to, biblical truth and God's majesty.

Luther was the first to acknowledge such a contradiction in the Heidelberg Disputation of 1518, where he set forth the critical Reformation distinction between the "*theologia crucis* (theology of the cross)" and the "*theologia gloriae* (theology of glory)." The theology of glory is "philosophical" theology. Luther had harsh words for the Aristotelianism of his day, and his declarations concern any attempt to explicate the truth of God purely discursively and by appeal to propositional calculations. "That person does not deserve to be called a theologian who looks upon the invisible things of God as though they were clearly perceptible," Luther asserted. "He deserves to be called a theologian, however, who comprehends the visible and manifest things of God seen through suffering and the cross."[9] It is impossible for fallen humanity not to misuse rationality and to misrepresent the knowledge of God. "Now it is not sufficient for anyone, and it does him no good to recognize God in his glory and majesty, unless he recognizes him in the humility and shame of the cross. Thus God destroys the wisdom of the wise."[10]

Theologies of glory—whether they be Scholastic, Calvinist, commonsense realist, Hegelian, positivist, foundationalist, or presuppositionalist—all share the common trait of making the claim that a particular reformulation of our understanding of truth and language is sufficient for understanding God. Theologies of glory, on the other hand, given their hubris and sense of self-sufficiency, have a tendency to misname what they name. "A theology of glory calls evil good and good evil. A theology of the cross calls the thing what it actually is," insofar as "he who does not know Christ does not know God hidden in suffering."[11] Theologies of glory always necessitate "political" solutions, because they require "good works." Reconstructionism is as hoary, and as misplaced, as Constantinian Christianity. Christian foundationalism goes at least as far back as Aquinas. Both are spirits contrary to the Reformation. The spirit of the Reformation is that of radical grace. "The love of God does not find, but creates, that which is pleasing to it. The love of man comes into being through that which is pleasing to it." That is because "the love of God, which lives in man, loves sinners, evil persons, fools, and weaklings in order to make them righteous, good, wise, and strong. Rather than seeking its own good, the love of God flows forth and bestows good. Therefore, sinners are attractive because they are loved; they are not loved because they are attractive."[12]

Religious postmodernism, as we are slowly coming to comprehend, is the *spirit of the Reformation*. Luther touched off the Reformation of the sixteenth century by discovering that authentic theological thinking is about cross, gospel, and grace rather than self-glorification, metaphysical disputation, and law. If this is truly so, then the Next Reformation will be all about radical humility and the lack of pride not just in our lives, but in our thought. On both the left and right, Protestantism—with its denominational, ministerial, and ecumenical councils, its political action committees, its preoccupation with palaces proffered as church buildings, its elaborate financial schemes and fund-raising—has swallowed the theology of glory with one gargantuan gulp. It has buttressed these totally worldly ambitions with a regal rationalism that aggrandizes the institution of the church and its claims at the expense of broken souls crying out for grace and forgiveness.

Even more significantly, the Reformation itself was a reaction against modernism in its late medieval manifestation. The word "modern" derives from the Latin *moderna,* meaning "recently" or "just now." Modernism thus implies an affiliation with conceptual developments that are the latest trends. "Modern" intellectual history begins with a movement in the late-fourteenth, fifteenth, and early-sixteenth centuries that called itself the *via moderna*. The moderns, adherents of the *via moderna*, included such theologians as William of Ockham, Gabriel Biel, and Pierre d'Ailly, who tended to be "nominalists" and thus skeptical of most authority. They numbered among those Renaissance thinkers who were not satisfied with the return to pure classicism and the authority of ancient texts, including the Bible. They wanted to be more up-to-date. They were not interested in studying Greek or Hebrew and figuring out the "original" meaning of, for example, the Letter to the Romans. They regarded themselves primarily as innovators and only secondarily as custodians of the past. Like the Pharisees of Jesus' time, they were looking for a ready-made, pragmatic application of the texts. They were "liberals" masquerading as "conservatives."

It was the theological novelties of the *via moderna* in treating the doctrine of grace that especially stuck in Luther's craw. Luther was an Augustinian. He found the arguments of the *via moderna* specious when it came to the scriptural understanding of salvation and looked upon them as sheer recycling of the Pelagian heresy of the fifth century, which Augustine had routed. Pelagius himself had claimed to have the "orthodox" reading of Scripture, which required human will and effort to reach heaven. Augustine took the contrary position. The human will is utterly corrupt, he stressed. There is not a thing anyone can do to save oneself or to contribute to one's own salvation. Modernism of all stripes and Pelagianism have always been close cousins.

As theological historian Alister McGrath has stressed, these "modernists" purported to be biblical, but they did not fully comprehend what Scripture indeed was saying. They took a somewhat recent theological construct and attributed it to the whole of "biblical" theology. The *via moderna* professed what nowadays we would consider a "covenantal" interpretation of faith and Scripture. "God had ordained that he will justify an individual, on condition that the individual first fulfills certain demands. These demands were summarized using the Latin tag *facere quod in se est*, literally 'doing what lies within you,' or 'doing your best.' When the individual met this precondition, God was obliged, by the terms of the covenant, to justify him."[13] This interpretation appealed very much to the "common sense" of the age, insofar as social and economic transactions in late feudal society were based on this rule of reciprocal responsibility. But such a "modernist" reading of Scripture was fatally flawed, especially if one really consumed the Pauline texts, and *in context*. Although Luther knew he had the right, discerning reading of Scripture, his Catholic critics were quick to pounce on him. The charges against Luther were quite similar to what many evangelicals say about postmodernists. According to these critics, Luther "seemed to suggest that God despised morality, having no time for good works."[14] Luther was tarred as an "antinomian (antimoralist)," or what today we would call an anarchist or relativist. Many of the early Reformers were indeed "postmodernists" on this score.

DECONSTRUCTION AND FAITH

John D. Caputo, one of the foremost contemporary postmodern thinkers and exegetes of Derrida's writings, equates the spirit of the Reformation itself with the spirit of deconstruction. "Deconstruction is not out to undo God or deny faith, or to mock science and make nonsense out of literature, or to break the law." On the contrary, it is the thought "of an absolute heterogeneity that unsettles all assurances of the same within which we comfortably ensconce ourselves." Caputo, an Augustinian by background like Luther, has deeply appreciated the impossibility of stuffing God in the box of legalism, or the gray tweed jacket of analytical philosophy, and sees deconstruction and postmodernism essentially as the task of "dehellenizing Christianity," or more specifically, of "dehellenizing biblical faith." The idea of deconstruction as dehellenization, according to Caputo, "is as old as Luther, and older still, tracing its origins back to the first chapter of First Corinthians, and older than that, given that the prophets never heard of the science that investigates [Being as Being]."[15] By "inscribing" theology inside the Derridean trace and ensuring that it is always "marked" by difference and "undecidability," deconstruction demonstrates that "faith is always faith," not something else.[16] *Sola fide!*

Deconstruction is not faith per se, Caputo insists, but it leaves a wide berth for faith. It is the trek into the desert so that faith can come into its own, so that there are no accessories to faith, so that faith can experience the pure presence of the One who is not present as an object at all. One cannot be saved by philosophy or even by theology. Every destiny is God's, and God's alone. The undecidability of radical faith for both Derrida and Caputo has nothing to do with some conscious violation of the parameters of predication and judgment, with some irrational, unphilosophical gesture. Deconstruction assists faith because it is "a pact with the *tout autre* (wholly other)." God can only be "known" through faith—through stripped down, bare-bones, noncontentious, unassuming faith. At the same time it is an "alliance" with what is coming, with advent, what Derrida refers to as *l'avenir*—not "the future" in the literal sense of the French word, but with the meaning that can never be iterated within the bounds of any given syntax, with the signification that God is continuing to supply as we seek his face, with the plenitude of unthought thoughts and unsaid sayings with which the Holy Spirit continues to provision us. We respond to God in faith because we allow our systems of thought to be crucified and rejected, so that God may raise us up. There can be no faith without the preparation that the deconstructive power of postmodernist discourse offers us. "God," remarks Caputo, "is clearly on the side of the deconstructor."[17]

In his seminal essay "Faith and Knowledge," Derrida talks about faith as a different kind of "errancy" than Taylor's, as a sojourn in the "desert."[18] The question is "whether the desert can be thought and left to announce itself 'before' the Desert that we know (that of the revelations and retreats, of the lives and deaths of God)."[19] The desert does not distract. It is not a site, as would be a lovely Greek isle, to contemplate the contours of the world we envision, to meditate upon its patterns and symmetries, peer at its harmonies and essential connections. The desert is where we *cannot* philosophize. It is where the sand bites at our beard and the wind howls in our ears. In the desert we imagine the vastness of a vacuous terrain that approximates God's time, a "time" wholly other than our own. The desert deconstructs our Greek eye for geometry and detail. It is where we are tempted, as was Jesus by the devil, to translate our infinite spiritual longings into material satisfactions and dominance. In the desert there is nowhere to look back, but only to anticipate what is on its way, what has in no manner yet arrived, what is *l'avenir.* In other words, the desert of faith turns our hearts and minds toward everything that is wholly not our own and what is wholly God's.

Postmodernism is not nihilistic in the usual sense of the term, Caputo contends. But it is in the same breath "messianic." Postmodernism as a philosophical style is most capable of uttering the phrase *Maranatha.* Like the Spirit and the Bride, it says "come." Postmodernism awaits the coming of the full presence of the God who has tabernacled with us on earth, who has become flesh but is yet to be revealed in the kingdom of his presence. Postmodernism replaces ontology with eschatology. Faith and ontology have nothing in common with each other. For ontology prefers a kind of backward-reading in place of the sure preface for the stories we have narrated in the past, the mooring of our history, the securing of our identity, the once-and-for-all *ipse dixit* (he himself says) for our theology. The philosophical quest for unfailing presuppositions is not Christian; it is *outright paganism.* It is theoretical hearth and home, where the pagan "household gods" of our epistemological conceits and ethical parochialisms, like the Asheroth in the Judean high places, subtly supplant the living God, who is Alpha and Omega, who is and who was and who is to come, the Almighty.

The loss of "foundations" in postmodernism is a welcome development, because faith itself—not some discursive banner of certitude—is the only sure "foundation." Faith is not in itself a superior presupposition that warrants somehow an equally superior worldview. Faith is not a presupposition at all. Faith is prior to all presuppositions, or presuppositionalisms. Faith is *presupposition-less*. Faith shatters the idols of the age. Faith is open to radical thought, even a radical thought that seems to question the very precept of "foundationalism," because it is secure in itself. It is secure in itself because it is secure in the illimitable Lord of all time and history, who offers no ultimate security—theological, scientific, ontological, or otherwise—besides the security of faith. There is no security whatsoever in the desert.

In his essay "Des Tours de Babel," Derrida—whom Caputo facetiously refers to as Saint Jacques the "desert father"—compares the history of theology, which is both Jewish and Greek in its patrimony, to the tower of Babel. Theology is "naming" God, singularly identifying God as the "father" of all names. Like the poet Shelley's description of the ruins of the empire of Ozymandias, which he encounters in the waste spaces, Derrida looks at the history of giving a name to the One who has the name of names from the standpoint of the desert. "The name of God the father would be the name of that origin of tongues." Such a name would be an undiminished, translucent, and "foundationally" secure name. It would be, in Derrida's idiom, "pure presence." It would be the metaphysically prior and correct "name." It would be knowable to all as part of the *consensus gentium*, the common sense of humanity. Yet the tower upon which the history of metaphysics and theology has sought to place the capstone with the name of names engraved upon its shining, alabaster surface—that tower has been sent hurling down by the One whom they sought to glorify and honor. God "sows confusion among his sons."[20] The confusion of language is at once the confusion of grammars. And the confusion of grammars is a divine sign that the One whose name is above all names must be honored not with sound and consistent theology, but with a contrite and humble heart. If postmodernism is vilified by philosophers and theologians today as "sowing confusion," then from a biblical perspective it is on the side of the angels. The specter of the tower accentuates the Reformation dictum of *sola fide*. There is nothing that can please God except faith. The ruined tower is the only acceptable worldview in the eyes of faith. Within that worldview we behold an endlessly expansive horizon. That is the view from the desert. Faith, however, has no compulsion without content. *Sola fide* is an empty cry apart from another Reformation dictum: *sola scriptura* (by Scripture alone). What would a postmodern reading of this dictum look like? What would be its consequences?

5

SOLA SCRIPTURA

Beyond Inerrancy

FROM REFORMATION THEOLOGY TO ENLIGHTENMENT RATIONALITY

The Reformers replaced the authority of the church with the authority of Scripture. John Gerhard, one of the leading lights in later Lutheran orthodoxy, insisted that the authority of Scripture was not a matter of faith per se; it was "the *principium* (the foundation)" on which other statements of faith might weigh. Thus, by the sixteenth century faith was no longer the *crucifixio intellectus* Luther had apostrophized in the Heidelberg Disputation. It was a conceptual bedrock for the erection of a new cathedral of Protestant systematic theology. Faith and reason were no longer in tension with each other. Faith was the Protestant version of the Cartesian *cogito*—in this case the first principle of a rational theology.

The Enlightenment took this process one step further. If faith were merely a first principle of reason, then reason alone might be adequate. And if faith cannot know God except through reason, then reason does not require God. Thus the Enlightenment exchanged the authority of Scripture for the sovereignty of reason. And the new empire of reason was no longer ruled by a supernatural monarch. The new sovereign was the human subject, which

115

wielded the scepter of reason. "*Cogito ergo [ego] sum* (I think, therefore I am)." The ego became grand vizier, and theology bowed down. That transition could be called a "reformation in its own right," mainly because it had nothing to do with the church and the attitude of the faithful.

The Enlightenment was spawned out of what the twentieth-century philosopher Paul Ricoeur has termed the "conflict of interpretations"—in this case the interpretation of the import of Scripture. The Enlightenment of the eighteenth century would have been impossible without the wars of religion of the seventeenth century. In many ways it was not about reason at all in the philosophical sense. The philosophers of the Enlightenment never explored what the expression "reason" really meant. It was well-nigh intuitive. The method of philosophical reason of the eighteenth century was aimed at discerning a middle ground between the seemingly incompatible dogmas of Protestant and Catholic, Lutheran and Calvinist, orthodox and pietist, Puritan and monarchist. This mediating principle could not be located in any particular religious perspective, since the previous century had confirmed the toxicity of all authoritarian attitudes. The rule of sovereign reason was the irrepressible outcome of the Reformation exaltation of personal conscience.

If the individual believer was the only true "priest," he or she was also the only certified "philosopher." The sanctification of commonsense rationality in the Scottish and British Enlightenment derived from the eighteenth-century inversion of the hierarchical metaphysics of the Middle Ages. In the medieval era the universe was conceived as a "great chain of being," with God at the summit and the theologian, ordained and consecrated by the church universal, as supreme arbiter in matters of both reason and faith. That was why theology was considered "queen of the sciences." The queen was second only to the king—in this context the self-revealed God. Theological reason took precedence over all other demonstrations of rationality because it was moored in the *mysterium* of faith. Ironically, the same relationship held true in the career of the Enlightenment. Private, or commonsense, rationality became the touchstone of philosophy, because it was the natural expression of "Christian liberty," the self-certification of faith alone.

What today we call the hermeneutics of Scripture—the invocation of a precise theoretical method to decode the biblical text—was never really on the table during the Reformation. The Reformation—both the so-called Radical and Magisterial Reformations—adhered to the conviction that the Holy Spirit could guide each believer (or the church community as a whole, in Calvin's view) to a patent understanding of the meaning of Scripture. From a theological vantage point, that really signified that there can be no "hermeneutical," or even "theological," skewing of Scripture in the late-modern sense. The power of God to reveal himself through his Word was taken as a given, not as a conundrum. The Word had authority because it could speak directly to the heart of the justified sinner. The Word of God was intimate and divine communication, not an impersonal ontological benchmark reinforced by a secondary calculus that correlated between text and the order of existence. The latter "methodology" was elaborated by post-Enlightenment philosophers who happened to be enamored with experimental science. For the most part, it was an "inductive" version of Scholasticism, which the Reformers had repudiated. It was a stance totally foreign to those who staked their lives and careers on the authority of Scripture. In their own way the Reformers maintained what we now term a "dialogical" reading of biblical authority. God does not simply speak through the Bible; God speaks to us. Just as Christ, as Luther put it, is always "*pro me* (for me)," so also is God's Word.

That was not "subjectivism" even by any metaphor or analogy. It is basic biblical theology. The Magisterial Reformers upheld the dialogical, or personalistic, reading of Scripture as paramount in the face of claims by their radical counterparts, such as some Anabaptists and the Socinians, or anti-Trinitarians. The most radical of the radicals truly advanced a "subjectivistic" agenda. They insisted that individual experience, as well as private interpretation of that experience, could be taken as authoritative, even at the expense of Scripture. They were therefore closer to the commonsense philosophers of the Enlightenment than their magisterial antagonists. They were the bona fide "subjectivists." In arguing that Scripture takes precedence over human self-revelation, the Reformers were planting the seeds for a genuinely postmodern (and hence postsubjectivistic) hermeneutic that was far more biblical than the so-called biblical approach that old-school evangelicals routinely prize. For the Reformers, Scripture is authoritative because it mediates God's magnificent reality to each one of us as persons on our own terms. Calvin described this process as the work of the Holy Spirit. Scriptural authority ensures that each one of us hears God as God, not through the filter of our own wants and expectations. This experience of God is neither objective nor subjective in the strict sense—it is "intersubjective," or interpersonal. The concept of intersubjectivity, frequently misconstrued as subjectivity, is the key to postmodern theology and to its attendant hermeneutics.

LÉVINAS AND POSTMODERN BIBLICAL HERMENEUTICS

In order to size up postmodern biblical hermeneutics, we must turn to the thought of the Jewish philosopher Emmanuel Lévinas, who is rapidly eclipsing Derrida in importance as the torchbearer of postmodern religious thought. Like most major postmodernist writers, who are invariably French, Lévinas also has an opaque style, informed less by freewheeling idiosyncrasies (as with Derrida) than his location within the earlier school of French phenomenology. The tradition of French phenomenology includes such figures as Jean-Paul Sartre and Maurice Merleau-Ponty. Phenomenology in its French version is even more daunting than in German. But as soon as one works through Lévinas's complex verbal constructions, one comes to appreciate the revolutionary impact of his biblical hermeneutics. In a critical fashion Lévinas's thought represents a surpassing of the old dichotomy between Athens and Jerusalem, or biblical faith and Greek philosophy. Lévinas's writings signify the biblical perspective—or at least the Old Testament perspective—transformed into "philosophy."

In his early and most important book *Totality and Infinity*, Lévinas writes that "the interlocutor alone is the term of pure experience." In the following sentence Lévinas qualifies this saying: "What presents itself as independent of every subjective movement is the interlocutor, whose way consists in starting from himself, foreign and yet presenting himself to me."[1] Language, at least in the biblical milieu, cannot possibly be construed as "propositional." Biblical language necessarily involves the "interlocution" of address and response. Interlocution implies that there always are two inseparable poles for every experience—self and other. But in contrast to nineteenth-century existentialists such as Kierkegaard and speculative idealists like Hegel, neither of these poles can ever be collapsed into one or the other. Subject and object, self and other, are always in extreme tension with each other. Neither can stand for the sphere of "truth." The "word" of God, according to Lévinas, is not "logical." It is what he terms "vocative," that is, dialogical. In grammar the vocative indicates the second person, which can never be either the subject or predicate of a sentence. When we "invoke" something, it is not really a "thing" at all we are calling upon; it is a "person." We invoke someone who is capable of answering back, of giving a response.

The alleged divide between "subjective" and "objective" experience, therefore, is a false dichotomy. We know only because we are in relation to what we know, and "what" we know somehow "knows" us. The *what* is really a *Who*. That is exactly the sense of the Hebrew word *yada'*, normally translated as "to know," as in "to know the Lord." There is no "thing in itself." When it comes to God, the very notion of a "thing," which suggests an independent and unresponsive entity, becomes untenable. The idea of God as an entity knowable by propositional analysis is metaphysical, a survival of heathen philosophy. The sense of God as a person, as personal presence, is uniquely biblical, and thereby *Christian*. The same goes for our reading of the Bible. Scripture is not a transcendental billboard for which we need the proper hermeneutical "glasses" in order to view. It is the "voice" of him who meets us and engages us, as he did Abraham and the prophets, in our distinctive personal situation and in accordance with our own capacities to give a reciprocal response.

According to Lévinas, personal reality has to be apprehended quite differently from ontological reality. The God of Abraham, Isaac, and Jacob is not the God of ontotheology. Ontological reality is "read off" by matching up our language with our sense of what is exterior to language. Personal reality cannot be read at all. Personal reality confronts us whether we want that confrontation or not. *Personal reality is relational.* Ontological reality is disclosed through our experience of entities, or "phenomena." Personal reality is manifested, for Lévinas, in the "face." The "epiphany" of the face, he says, constitutes "a relationship different from that which characterizes all our sensible experience."[2] Common sense is literally "speechless" before the "face" of either God or another human being made in the image of God. Lévinas's use of the term "face" is a literal transposition of the Hebrew term *panim*, closely associated in the Bible with flashes and fulgurations of God revealing himself. But Lévinas's term also suggests *the priority of personal over propositional reality.* When we encounter the "face," whether of God or those created in the image of God, we are not dealing with an inert object to be judged and appraised as linear syntax, as if we might analyze the proposition "All cats are four-legged." Any predicative statement we might make about a person cannot possibly exhaust the reality of who he or she is from God's point of view. That is why the Bible warns against us becoming "judgmental." The warning does not imply that we should avoid utilizing critical standards, either in assessing our own behavior or that of another. It emphasizes that there is always more to people's history, motives, character, or destiny than any statement we might make about them can encompass. Only God knows for sure. God's passionate love for them trumps every critical posture, even if they ultimately reject God's initiative.

As far as Lévinas is concerned, God's "infinity" overwhelms all finite determinations of who someone is, because who God is can only be adduced through the "interlocutory" relationship between the I and the other. The subtitle of Lévinas's *Totality and Infinity* is *An Essay on Exteriority*. In the ontotheological tradition of the West, "exteriority" is either privileged over mere "subjectivity," or it is downgraded in favor of the actual experience of the subject. In the latter case "interiority" itself is privileged. For Lévinas, this dichotomy arises from the metaphysical mentality. Only when metaphysics is set aside, and the "vocative" prioritized over the predicative, can the "real" truly be known. The real, for Lévinas, is sequestered in God's summons and address to us. If indeed Scripture is the pure vocative text, then no "scientific" reading of the text is possible. Indeed, hermeneutics itself—the theory of the teleportation of the text from one order of meaning into a cognate order—is impossible. The Bible is not science. But that does not mean it is "historically conditioned" and contains "errors." The Bible is the "authoritative" and "infallible" Word of God insofar as it flows directly from God's infinite personality and from his call upon us. But does that mean it is "inerrant," as twentieth-century biblical evangelicalism has maintained? In order to answer this question, we have to consider what the doctrine of inerrancy genuinely entails.

THE DOCTRINE OF INERRANCY

In the autumn of 1978 approximately three hundred evangelical leaders met at the Hyatt Regency O'Hare Hotel in Chicago at a congress called by the International Council on Biblical Inerrancy to draft and approve what has come to be known as "the Chicago Statement."[3] Signers of the statement included J. I. Packer, Francis A. Schaeffer, R. C. Sproul, Carl F. H. Henry, Norman L. Geisler, James M. Boice, and John H. Gerstner. The statement begins: "The authority of Scripture is a key issue for the Christian church in this and every age. Those who profess faith in Jesus Christ as Lord and Savior are called to show the reality of their discipleship by humbly and faithfully obeying God's written Word."[4] So far we have a simple recapitulation of standard Reformation doctrine. But the statement puts the alternative almost in the "anathema" form of the classical church councils. "We are persuaded that to deny it [the authority of Scripture] is to set aside the witness of Jesus Christ and of the Holy Spirit and to refuse that submission to the claims of God's own Word which marks true Christian faith. We see it as our timely duty to make this affirmation in the face of current lapses from the truth of inerrancy among our fellow Christians and misunderstandings of this doctrine in the world at large."

These opening considerations are followed by what the committee that drafted the propositions (articles) on inerrancy calls "a short statement":

1. God, who is Himself Truth and speaks truth only, has inspired Holy Scripture in order thereby to reveal Himself to lost mankind through Jesus Christ as Creator and Lord, Redeemer and Judge. Holy Scripture is God's witness to Himself.

2. Holy Scripture, being God's own Word, written by men prepared and superintended by His Spirit, is of infallible divine authority in all matters upon which it touches: it is to be believed, as God's instruction, in all that it affirms; obeyed, as God's command, in all that it requires; embraced, as God's pledge, in all that it promises.

3. The Holy Spirit, Scripture's divine Author, both authenticates it to us by His inward witness and opens our minds to understand its meaning.

4. Being wholly and verbally God-given, Scripture is without error or fault in all its teaching, no less in what it states about God's acts in creation, about the events of world history, and about its own literary origins under God, than in its witness to God's saving grace in individual lives.

5. The authority of Scripture is inescapably impaired if this total divine inerrancy is in any way limited or disregarded, or made relative to a view of truth contrary to the Bible's own; and such lapses bring serious loss to both the individual and the Church.[5]

Again, the first three statements, and for the most part the fourth one, comport in an unqualified sense with standard Reformation teaching. The Reformers, like the church fathers who preceded them and whom they regarded as reliable biblical interpreters, generally took the absolute truthfulness of Scripture for granted. They did not have to defend the Bible against charges that certain passages were "erroneous," because that was never raised as a serious issue.[6] The Reformers were more exercised about the Roman Catholic claim that church tradition can count along with Scripture as God's "special revelation," a position that became the official Counter-Reformation stance after the Council of Trent. Calvin and Luther did note that certain transcriptions might have resulted from "copying errors," but they reckoned that the original manuscripts themselves had to be flawless. Proponents of biblical inerrancy have parried charges from critics that the claim is nowhere to be found in the history of theology; they correctly point out that most Christian doctrine has arisen in response to episodic challenges to what the early believers called the "rule of faith." All doctrine, therefore, is mainly apologetic rather than expository.

On the other hand, it is clear that the doctrine of inerrancy has been shaped by the commonsense realism of Reid's philosophy. Before the nineteenth century the different theological models all derived from a triadic structure of scriptural authority based on three crucial terms—*dictation, inspiration,* and *infallibility*. The degree of tension between the first two terms determined the meaning of the third. The Jewish rabbis believed that God's revelation had been "complete" in the Torah, or five books of Moses. Even today Judaism refers to what Christians call the Old Testament as the Law and the Prophets. While the Torah, or Law, was "dictated" to Moses, according to rabbinic exegesis, the prophetic writings were "inspired" by God's Holy Spirit, mainly to summon the refractory people of Israel back to obedience to the revelation given to the generation that fled Egypt. Even the very letters and their vocalization of the Torah came "from heaven," according to the rabbis. That was not necessarily true of the prophets.

The Christian church, however, has taken the contrary view of the place of the prophets. Focusing particularly on the messianic passages, Christianity has seen the prophetic books as "shadows," prefigurements of the ultimate promise of human redemption in Jesus Christ. Inasmuch as in the original Christian hermeneutic, all Scripture points backward and forward to Christ, believers have always been more disposed to a "literalistic" reading of the text, which has its final and unequivocal meaning in one positive fact—Jesus' death on the cross and his resurrection, opening the gates wide for the salvation of all humanity. Thus, evangelical Christianity—particularly under duress throughout the modern period from historicist and contextualist challenges to the factual authenticity of certain scriptural passages—has gravitated toward the principle of infallibility. If the Scriptures are not infallible, then the centrality of God's redemptive act in Christ may appear shaky. Augustine himself put the matter bluntly: If any tiny portion of the Scriptures is questionable as to its veracity, then the whole of Scripture comes under the umbrella of doubt, which is impermissible. The word "mistake" cannot apply to even the most miniscule segment of the Bible. So-called inerrantists frequently cite Augustine's position to underscore that their hermeneutic is of ancient, rather than modern, provenance. But it is dubious that Augustine's contention that Scripture does not contain any "errors" was intended to be as strong, or as exacting, as present-day inerrantist theory.

The original Christian concept of scriptural infallibility was never intended to guarantee a precise, literal, "factual" truth of every single biblical sentence. That innovation really belongs to the old Princeton theologians, in particular Archibald Alexander and Charles Hodge. Hodge is the patriarch of the inerrantist movement and the progenitor of what has come to be termed "fundamentalism." Hodge regarded the theologian as simply a higher-order "scientist," whose business was to collect and assemble biblical "facts." Theology and science are equivalent because "the external world," like God himself, is revealed as exactly what it is. Divine revelation is at the same time commensurate with common sense. Although Hodge, a Calvinist by background, held that sin had darkened the human intellect, he was convinced that the regenerate mind would invariably see things clearly—both natural phenomena and the supernatural realm laid bare through the proper reading of the biblical text. Hodge first enunciated what we now call the inerrantist claim in 1866 in a sermon.

Later, in his *Systematic Theology,* he honed the idea into a careful refurbishing of the classic view of scriptural infallibility. "The Scriptures of the Old and New Testaments are the Word of God, written under the inspiration of the Holy Spirit," he insisted. "They are therefore infallible, and of divine authority in all things pertaining to faith and practice, and consequently free from all error whether of doctrine, fact, or precept."[7] So far so good. There was nothing in such an assertion that would not have sounded familiar to Calvin, Augustine, or even Clement of Alexandria, for that matter. The precept of what church tradition dubbed "plenary inspiration"—the supposition that the entirety of the Bible, not just portions, are God's pure and immediate communication—necessitated such a viewpoint. But Hodge was prepared to transform what throughout Christian history had been primarily a soteriological perspective into a straightforward *epistemological* claim. "Inspiration," he wrote, "extends to all the contents of these several [canonical] books. It is not confined to moral and religious truths, but extends to the statements of facts, whether scientific, historical, or geographical. It is not confined to those facts the importance of which is obvious, or which are involved in matters of doctrine. It extends to everything which any sacred writer asserts to be true."[8]

Hodge's "extension" of the principle of inspiration to what Derrida might call the "grammatology" of the Bible—the formality of the inscription regardless of context or genre—brought about an almost impalpable transformation of classical Christian hermeneutics. It was not the rabbinic, or medieval, view of scriptural inspiration as divine dictation. Nor was it the rudimentary Augustinian and Reformed presumption that if the Word of God is to be understood as the "saving" and providential word, then there can be no logical discrepancies within the broader fabric of Scripture in toto. Hodge essentially made the unprecedented claim that the saga of the parting of the

Red Sea, Elijah's miracle on Mount Carmel, or Jesus' ascension all had the same ontological status as the rain in Spain or the annual flowering of the cherry blossoms in the nation's capital. In other words, God's extraordinary acts in history were really quite ordinary. There was no room for the Reformers' faith response to Scripture. Faith was really rather incidental. The Spirit and the letter no longer remained in contention. Everything was the letter. As Kevin Vanhoozer asks about the old Princeton theology:

> Is every word in Scripture literally true? The problem with this question is its incorrect (and typically unstated) assumption that "literal truth" is always literalistic—a matter of referring to history or to the "facts" of nature. It is just such a faulty assumption—that the Bible always states facts—that leads certain well-meaning defenders of inerrancy desperately to harmonize what appear to be factual or chronological discrepancies in the Gospels. In the final analysis what was new about the Princetonians' view of Scripture was not their understanding of the Bible's truthfulness but rather their particular view of language and interpretation, in which the meaning of the biblical text was the fact—historical or doctrinal—to which it referred. Their proof-texting was more a product of their view of language and interpretation than of their doctrine of Scripture.[9]

But the consequences of the Princeton innovation were even more invidious. The doctrine of language inevitably displaced the doctrine of Scripture that they had inherited from the great theologians of the past. The truth of Christianity now became a truth of "plain evidence." It had less and less to do with the truth of salvation, although the traditional "evangelical" rhetoric was not at all diminished. In his *Commentary on the Epistle to the Galatians* Luther phrased the issue quite starkly:

> On the question of justification we must remain adamant, or else we shall lose the truth of the Gospel. It is a matter of life and death. It involves the death of the Son of God, who died for the sins of the world. If we surrender faith in Christ, as the only thing that can justify us, the death and resurrection of Jesus are without meaning; that Christ is the Savior of the world would be a myth. God would be a liar, because He would not have fulfilled His promises.[10]

In other words, the infallibility and "truth" of Scripture is founded on its power to fulfill God's plan for each of us in our lives. Yet under the Princeton strictures that outlook becomes largely irrelevant. Even biblical eschatology loses its soteriological significance. Eschatology is nothing more than pulp fiction or tabloid-style sensationalism, as the incredible popularity of such works as the Left Behind series attests.

A similar literalistic means of construing inerrancy can be found in Paul Feinberg's work. According to Feinberg, "Inerrancy means that when all facts are known, the Scriptures in their original autographs and properly interpreted will be shown to be wholly true in everything that they affirm, whether that has to do with doctrine or morality or with the social, physical, or life sciences."[11] The preoccupation of inerrantists with the Bible as a true picture of the facts in all spheres of knowledge, secular as well as religious, stems from the work of nineteenth-century American theologians B. B. Warfield and James Orr. Orr modified Warfield's work by arguing for what he termed "limited inerrancy." The notion of limited inerrancy was a conceptual gambit for updating and refining the Reformation viewpoint. Limited inerrancy means that the Bible is categorically without error in issues of salvation, but can be more loosely interpreted in other settings. Orr's successor referred to Warfield's stance as "total inerrancy," which was fundamentally the position of the signers of the Chicago Statement (1978).

The Chicago gathering was prompted by what advocates of total inerrancy perceived as a gradual slide among evangelicals in the direction of limited inerrancy. In two books published in the late 1970s Harold Lindsell, former editor of the magazine *Christianity Today,* maintained that all of Christian history largely constituted a "battle for the Bible," a struggle between orthodoxy and heresy. The orthodox perspective, of course, was the same as inerrancy. Anything deviating from that orthodoxy, which included not just liberalism but also "limited inerrancy," had to be confronted as heretical.[12] Lindsell attacked what he termed the new "postcritical methodologies" undermining the "orthodox" conviction that the Bible is inerrant in every detail. Lindsell defended the old Princeton theology as the flag bearer for orthodoxy in the modern era. He also made public waves with a *j'accuse* style of confrontation, naming institutions as well as individuals who in his opinion had strayed from the fold on the inerrancy matter. Lindsell denounced them as "false evangelicals."

REFORMERS AND INERRANTISTS

Over the years Lindsell's critics have charged that the battle has been less over the Bible than the political issue of who might win the hearts and minds of evangelicals. On the other hand, to spin the question of orthodoxy versus heresy simply in terms of biblical hermeneutics represents a serious truncation of the Christian legacy. Even during the Reformation there was far more at stake in the slogan of *sola scriptura* than how to render and interpret texts. The intercalating of ecclesiastical and biblical authority was always a pressing issue. The disdain of inerrantists for neoorthodoxy, which hoisted the ensign of the Reformed tradition, is instructive here. Inerrantists scorned neoorthodoxy specifically because the latter was not disposed to buy into Hodge's "extension" of soteriology into the arena of epistemology. Neoorthodoxy also made a clear distinction between the infinite God and finite human language, or in Karl Barth's phraseology the difference between "the Word of God" and the "word of man," the bone of contention for the Reformers. The Catholics did not deny the infallibility of the Bible. They merely delegated the interpretation of infallible Scripture to the curia. The Reformation dispute over religious authority really came down to a controversy over the degree to which a fallible priest could "represent" the infallible divine Word.

For Luther, the issue was not so much a view of appropriate "spiritual" qualifications to serve as a custodian of the Word. Nor did it come down to what might be regarded as a true theory of language that would somehow safeguard the biblical text from "errors" and misconstructions. Such a linguistic paradigm would not be seriously pressed forward, nor would it be deployed to settle questions of what we now call biblical hermeneutics until several centuries thereafter. But it was already implicit in Luther's arguments with the "papists" over translation of the Bible into the vernacular, and in his assault on the latter for demanding that he must attend to every single linguistic jot and tittle, if somehow the *sacra verba* were not to be compromised. In a letter composed in 1530 Luther wrote that "there has been much discussion about the translating of the Old and New Testaments. It has been charged by the despisers of truth that the text has been modified and even falsified in many places, which has shocked and startled many simple Christians, even among the educated who do not know any Hebrew or Greek."

The flash point for contention was Luther's insertion of the adverb "alone *(allein)*" to convey the Reformation motto "by faith alone" into his translation of Paul's text in Romans 3:28. His detractors howled that he was falsifying the "truth" of the Bible. Wrangles over translation have always been harbingers of more significant hermeneutical quarrels. Luther's defense, however, was quite ingenuous. The grammatical precision of the translation, he asserted, is far less consequential than the sincerity of "faith" in both comprehending and translating Scripture. No amount of "literal" correlation between parallel versions of the text can suffice for the work of the Spirit in the attitude of the believer. "Ah, translating is not every one's skill, as some mad saints think," Luther wrote in his usual, colorful, cocky, and combative style. "A right, devout, honest, sincere, God-fearing Christian, trained, educated, and experienced heart is required. So I hold that no false Christian or divisive spirit can be a good translator."[13]

The "*sola*" of *sola scriptura*, therefore, is by a curious twist comparable to Derrida's *différance*. The difference in inscription is a fundamental difference. It differentiates, or throws into solemn relief the distinction, between the appearance and the intention of what is said. It was not without reason that Luther made the repeated argument that only the Holy Spirit can unveil the import of a text. Without the Spirit the mind is blinkered. Reformation theology, therefore, refutes the "correspondence theory" of truth as it has been transmitted in Anglo-American philosophy since the eighteenth century onward. There can be no "correspondence" at the scriptural level between word and thing unless the "thing" is transparently glimpsed from the perspective of one who has received grace through faith. The "revealed" word can in no way be put into the same epistemological box as our consensual, or commonsense, experience of the everyday world.

Hodge's "extension" amounts to the most subtle metaphysics. Nevertheless, salvation and "knowledge" are not coextensive with each other. To conflate the former with the latter is a heresy in itself. It is *Gnosticism.* Ancient Gnosticism was bound up with the supposition that there is a distinctive kind of religious knowledge that remains superior to faith and can only be accessed by a small group of privileged "intellectuals" segregated from the masses of humanity. The gnostics believed that faith was not what Paul said it was—tantamount to ignorance. Gnosticism, particularly in the second and third centuries of the Christian era, made powerful inroads into the church, almost to the point where it had become so acceptable that it threatened in some dioceses to become the normative form of Christianity. Gnosticism, of course, was finally condemned as a heresy. The church father Irenaeus spilled considerable ink both profiling the heretical teachings of the gnostics and refuting them. While it would be both discourteous and impertinent to suggest that the doctrine of inerrancy is equivalent to a modern gnostic heresy, there are unsettling similarities between the two sensitivities. Although the inerrantists depart from the gnostics in their rejection of scriptural truth as elite insight, their contention that the Bible is a supreme type of knowledge compares with the standpoint of the gnostics.

A hint of these similarities can be found in the writings of Hodge himself. In chapter 6 of volume 1 of his *Systematic Theology* on "The Protestant

Rule of Faith," Hodge shows the intricate connection between "revelation" and "inspiration":

> The object of revelation is the communication of knowledge. The object or design of inspiration is to secure infallibility in teaching. Consequently they differ, secondly, in their effects. The effect of revelation was to render its recipient wiser. The effect of inspiration was to preserve him from error in teaching. These two gifts were often enjoyed by the same person at the same time. That is, the Spirit often imparted knowledge, and controlled in its communication orally or in writing to others. This was no doubt the case with the Psalmists, and often with the Prophets and Apostles. Often, however, the revelations were made at one time, and were subsequently, under the guidance of the Spirit, committed to writing. Thus the Apostle Paul tells us that he received his knowledge of the gospel not from man, but by revelation from Jesus Christ; and this knowledge he communicated from time to time in his discourses and epistles.[14]

With Hodge, Scripture does not perform a soteriological function as much as it does for the Reformers. Scripture is revelation, and revelation is prima facie the "communication of knowledge," or the impartation of "wisdom." The "heart," which Luther and Wesley regarded as the seat of spiritual discernment, is of little bearing. It is the mind that counts. For Luther, "knowledge" of what Scripture signifies starts with repentance, the shedding of all previous, false understanding motivated by sinfulness and pride. In Scripture the Christian mind achieves an elevated order of illumination—in other words, gnosis as contrasted with simple, everyday "knowledge." Hodge speaks of this knowledge as a special mode of "wisdom." Although Hodge, following Reid, characterizes the Bible as a "plain text" that every human intellect is capable of grasping, the disposition of the Christian to prefer the Bible over other literary media of communication attests to its extraordinary contents. The Bible is only "plain" when the text is approached by someone who through baptism and belief qualifies as a definite "insider." An odd sort of intellectual predestinarianism—not totally unexpected for a Calvinist such as Hodge—lurks on the sidelines, a tendency that also suggests analogies with classic Gnosticism.

The gnostic character of American fundamentalism has been elaborated, although rather idiosyncratically and not a little tendentiously, by postmodernist literary critic Harold Bloom in his book *The American Religion.* "I surmise that a sense of cultural, historical, and religious belatedness," Bloom writes, "inevitable in . . . America, increases the appetite to know, rather than to believe or to trust. The urgency of our national drive to know renders

European Protestantism inauthentic in our professedly Protestant culture, and has turned us to Gnosis these last two centuries."[15] But we will not go so far as to imply that the doctrine of inerrancy has all the earmarks of ancient Gnosticism, which had a profound streak of antinomianism not shared with fundamentalism. Beyond the preoccupation with faith as epistemology, most similarities end.

If one meticulously reads the Chicago Statement, nonetheless, it is apparent that the principle of "inerrancy" has served to sustain the soteriological aim of Scripture under the banner of defending modern epistemology and its reliance on scientific and empirical knowledge. "In our affirmation of the authority of Scripture as involving its total truth, we are consciously standing with Christ and His apostles, indeed with the whole Bible and with the main stream of Church history from the first days until very recently. We are concerned at the casual, inadvertent, and seemingly thoughtless way in which a belief of such far-reaching importance has been given up by so many in our day." Inerrantists, or at least the "total inerrantists" who cobbled together the Chicago Statement, have on the whole discounted the classical confidence that the truths of God's promise and redemption do not require certification by any means or tests other than *sola fide*.

For Paul, Augustine, and Luther, what God said was true because God said it, and God meant what he said. He was a God of his word. The Bible is God's "promissory note." God's Word is true because it has been spoken ineluctably and decisively as his "troth," as his commitment to us as justified sinners. The "infallibility" of God's Word signifies his absolute trustworthiness. It has hardly anything to do with ontology, with the reliability of reference or the coherence of grammar, as Luther thundered over and over. The term "inerrancy" betrays a certain skittishness about whether we can trust God, or profess to trust God, without some sort of "cognitive" as well as confessional insurance. In recognition of this dilemma, Tertullian made another famous remark, which always discomfits inerrantists: "*Credo quia absurdum* (I believe because it is absurd)." Centuries later Kierkegaard picked up the sentiment and stressed that it is the "paradox" of God becoming incarnate, summoning the "passion" of faith. There is no way the "truth" of Christianity can be reconciled with the sheer "facts" of the world or with the equanimity of reason.

Nevertheless, inerrantism seeks to do exactly that. "We affirm that a confession of the full authority, infallibility, and inerrancy of Scripture is vital to a sound understanding of the whole of the Christian faith. We further affirm that such confession should lead to increasing conformity to the image of

Christ. We deny that such confession is necessary for salvation. However, we further deny that inerrancy can be rejected without grave consequences, both to the individual and to the Church." Although the signatories to the Chicago Statement balked from going so far as to elevate the doctrine of inerrancy to the level of the Nicene formulation, they were trenching on such an innovation. What could be the "grave consequences" of not accepting the doctrine?

Ironically, in the very context of making such a sweeping, canonical statement, the signatories offer a sop to modern cultural contextualism. "We affirm that canonical Scripture should always be interpreted on the basis that it is infallible and inerrant," the statement continues. "However, in determining what the God-taught writer is asserting in each passage, we must pay the most careful attention to its claims and character as a human production. In inspiration, God utilized the culture and conventions of His penman's milieu, a milieu that God controls in His sovereign providence; it is misinterpretation to imagine otherwise." Genre considerations and what was once known as form criticism does indeed have some bearing.

> So history must be treated as history, poetry as poetry, hyperbole and meta-phor as hyperbole and metaphor, generalization and approximation as what they are, and so forth. Differences between literary conventions in Bible times and in ours must also be observed: since, for instance, nonchronological nar-ration and imprecise citation were conventional and acceptable and violated no expectations in those days, we must not regard these things as faults when we find them in Bible writers. When total precision of a particular kind was not expected nor aimed at, it is no error not to have achieved it. Scripture is inerrant, not in the sense of being absolutely precise by modern standards, but in the sense of making good its claims and achieving that measure of focused truth at which its authors aimed.

This "focused truth," of course, is the truth of our redemption through Christ, which takes us back to the Reformation trajectory. "As the prophesied Messiah, Jesus Christ is the central theme of Scripture. No hermeneutic, therefore, of which the historical Christ is not the focal point is acceptable. Holy Scripture must be treated as what it essentially is—the witness of the Father to the Incarnate Son." Inerrantism seems to want to have it both ways. But, just as Jesus said no one can serve two masters, evangelicalism is going to have to make a choice, which it hitherto has avoided doing. Early Christianity passed along an apocryphal story about Peter: fleeing the grue-some persecutions of Christians by Nero in Rome, he met Jesus on the road just outside the city. Jesus was heading the other way. "*Quo vadis, Domine?*" Peter asked. "Where are you going, Lord?" "To Rome to be crucified again," Jesus is supposed to have said. Peter then turned around and followed his master to martyrdom. *Quo vadis, Domine?* Does evangelical thought flee the cross, like Peter at first? The "heresy" of inerrantism is exactly what Luther understood to be the stone of stumbling for Roman Catholicism. In the name of ecclesiastical rigor it denied the true "foundation" of the faith, which is no foundation at all. It denied the cross! Like Peter, we must decide whether we are going to flee to the safety of our "Hellenic" certainties, or whether we return with the Master on the *via dolorosa*. We must ask ourselves whether we will take the leap of faith in a movement the early church called the *sacrificium intellectus,* the surrendering of our deductive and discursive apologetics. The "focused truth" of the Chicago Statement cannot be smoothed out into some simple and elegant proposition to which a revived "Christendom" somehow accedes.

DEHELLENIZING EVANGELICAL FAITH

Inerrantism amounts to the rehellenizing of the faith and a retreat from the Reformation, to the reestablishment of a mighty Christian *Romanitas* that denies all intellectual and semantic heterogeneity for the sake of universal rigor. The soul of the Reformation itself is up for grabs. The Reformers themselves displayed this kind of heterogeneity. Luther and Zwingli, for instance, disagreed over whether Jesus' statement "*Hoc est corpus meum* (this is my body)" concerning the Eucharist in Matthew 26:26 meant that the bread was "identical" with his body or "symbolized" it. No doctrine of inerrancy could have settled the issue, which became the dividing line between historical Lutheranism and the Reformed tradition. The gradual accommodation of the Reformation to intellectual modernism was in many respects the direct consequence of the growing influence of the radicals, particularly the Anabaptists in Germany and in England. American evangelicalism owes far more to the Radical Reformation than to its European counterparts, even though the word "evangelical" was originally applied only to the Magisterial Reformers such as Luther and Calvin. These radicals Luther called "fanatics," because they would not allow for any historical or modulating rules of scriptural interpretation other than their own private inspiration.[16] The doctrine of the "plain sense of the text" has devolved from the extreme subjectivism of the Radical Reformation. The Radical Reformers despised learning and tradition and held that anyone could hear the "voice of God" in accordance with his or her own inner conviction. To that end they had no need for scriptural checks and balances concerning what God was putatively saying. This extreme view of inspiration resulted in a hollowing out of the full doctrine of *sola scriptura* and incrementally supplanting it with a kind of biblical pedantry that the Reformers, many of whom were richly schooled in humanistic exegesis, would never have countenanced. After all, if there is no flexible criterion for hermeneutical judgments, the only common ground for biblical interpretation is the literal text. The overriding result was the doctrine of inerrancy.

The chief reason the Magisterial Reformers could assert *sola scriptura* in tandem with *sola fide* was because they maintained a general and "authoritative" outlook toward Scripture that at the same time took account of individual responses to the same divine voice. Modernism, however, because of its similarities with fundamentalism as well as its innate bias toward the purely subjective, has managed to resolve the dilemma of what Luther called the "liberty" of personal conscience versus general authority. It keeps oscillating back and forth between a mindless radical subjectivity and an equally trifling and jejune "objectivism." Does *sola fide* mean what it means, or is it some kind of historic artifact that has changed its connotations to accommodate the modernist mind-set? Gerstner, one of the principal exponents of inerrancy, contends that Luther did not really mean what he said about the "theology of the cross." To say the least, Gerstner has an extremely curious reading of Luther and the Reformers. "While we grant—in fact, insist—that Luther and the Reformation were launched with a nonrational, fideistic push, they soon sailed under the traditional reason-faith synthesis. In this respect, the German Reformation (having a bad beginning followed by a good course) is not unlike the English Reformation, which began with Henry VIII's lust but soon went on under its true colors."[17] Gerstner refers to "Luther's own profound rationality," as if there were no equally profound crisis of heart and soul in Luther's discovery of the primacy of faith.

What Gerstner disparages as the "fideism" of the Reformation indicates what inerrantism is really all about. It is not about the Reformation at all. The doctrine of *sola fide* is not an invitation to irrationalism, or even "nonrationalism." It does not secretly signify *sola ratione*. *Sola fide* signifies that all the God-given rational aptitudes and faculties of human beings are collapsed into, and contained within, the face-to-face relationship with God. One cannot reason one's way out of that relationship, or substitute third-person theological statements and sentences for the direct encounter. Faith is the mark of the unencumbered quality of the first-person–second-person relationship. Faith seeks "understanding," but not because it is truncated or inadequate, without a rational reckoning. Faith is always founded on the intimate, personal relationship with God that cries out "*Abba*, Father."

Yet this personal intimacy seeks communication at a wider level. The disciples who experienced firsthand the personal presence of the risen Lord were commanded to make disciples of all nations. To that end they became, as Paul did, all things to all people. They embraced the Hellenic technique of disputation as one modality—but not the only modality—of witnessing and evangelism. They paraphrased and cited Torah and engaged in careful proof-texting of the Scriptures in order to capture the allegiance of Jews like themselves. But their foremost task was to make disciples. Discipling has little, if anything, to do with apologetics. Apologetics is a defense of the faith against what is skeptical or hostile toward it. Discipling is a transformation of the life and the life-orientation of the person in relationship to the One on whom all relationships converge. Discipling is creating a relationship with someone else that is Christlike, because it emulates the Christ-relationship.

Whereas "proof" is the imprimatur of reason, discipleship is the signature of faith. Reason is inherently finite. Faith is innately infinite, because it is the relationship of the finite to the infinite, thereby establishing what Kierkegaard characterized as the "incommensurable" relationship. The faith relationship is insuperably paradoxical. In Lévinas's language, the "face" that establishes the faith-relationship is the infinite peering through the veil of the finite. It cannot be totalized. But it can be concretized. It is concretized in our relationship to Jesus Christ, because Christ is the synthesis of *logos* and *sarx*, word and flesh. In Christ, cosmic "reason" encounters us on the Emmaus road. "It" dines with us. "It" addresses us. In response we can only exclaim "My Lord!"

Sola scriptura, therefore, emanates from the imperative of *sola fide*, not the other way around. Luther affirmed the ultimacy of scriptural authority because the Bible is the "literacy" of the text that captures our understanding and leads us to the "truth" of salvation, which is no proposition at all. The truth of salvation—the one and only truth—is the Savior who saves us and does so through a relationship with us and for the sake of us. Nietzsche cryptically once remarked that "truth is a woman." But what he implied was that the Bible in general and the New Testament in particular mean something distinctive when they employ the Greek term *alētheia*, or truth. Truth lies in the sanctity of the relationship, in the "marriage" of the believer to the One in whom he believes. The English word "truth" and the word for marriage ("troth" or "betrothal") have the same etymological links. The Koine Greek has a similar force. *Alētheia* is an "unveiling," as a bride before her husband. *Truth is the intimacy of the interpersonal.* As in all intimate relationships, if one is "true" to the other, one is also "faithful." The faithfulness of the relationship—the openness and commitment to pursue the "troth" involving two persons to the end—defines the sphere of truth. Marriage relationships are covenantal relationships, or at least they are designed to be that. Broken covenants have severe and often doleful consequences. When Jesus says in the Gospel of John that he is "the truth," he is not making a logical claim about himself, as the passage is so often misunderstood. Nor is he making a representation about "what" he is in an ontological sense. He is revealing who he is. He is the redeemer. No one knows God except in relationship to him. He is saying, "Follow me, walk with me." For he is "always with us," even until the end of the age.

The "infallible" authority of Scripture, therefore, is not founded on the fact that it contains no "errors." The doctrine of inerrancy is thoroughly misplaced. It is what twentieth-century philosophers have described as a "category mistake." A category mistake occurs when one set of terms is misapplied to another discourse, ensuing not in "error" but confusion. The British philosopher Gilbert Ryle gave an example of a category mistake, supposedly adapted from Wittgenstein: A visitor to the university asked to be shown around. After a tour of all the different buildings and facilities and learning their names, the visitor asked indignantly, "But where is the university?" His host was thoroughly befuddled. He thought he had shown him the university. The problem was that the visitor thought a university was a building, not the ensemble of all the buildings and their relationship to each other. Inerrancy is founded on a kindred category mistake. The truth of Scripture is "certified" by the fact that it is God's self-revelation to us, not all at once, but progressively. God's appearance to Abraham at the oaks of Mamre is filled out four hundred years later on Mount Sinai. The revelation on Sinai, however, awaits the coming of Christ, who in turn will come again in the fullness of his glory. The troth begins with Abraham and continues from generation to generation. Scripture is the story of this troth. The inerrantist demands that the whole story be "true" as a tableau of impersonal facts, when in fact the facts themselves are signs of God's all-encompassing and awesome presence. Nothing about God is "impersonal." The inerrantist, like the visitor to the university, demands to be shown Scripture, when indeed the fullness of Scripture is the whole person of God in Christ. If that were not the case, then Jesus would not have gone to the cross. He would have simply written a better book.

THE BIBLE AS PROMISSORY SPEECH

In the postmodernist argot we can say that Scripture is not a system of "facts," but "traces" of the divine fullness. Claims about biblical "facts" are idolatrous claims to ultimacy. Traces are the medium through which the ultimate and infinite exhibits itself in a penultimate and finite manner as ultimate and infinite. The trace is a finite signal that the infinite One has been there. And if the infinite One has been there, the "fact" becomes far less of an issue. Inerrancy is an idolatry of the text. It is bibliolatry plain and simple, inasmuch as it cannot see beyond the logical lattice of the text to encounter the Other who is ever calling us into his kingdom and before his throne. As Marion notes, modern idolatry is due entirely to the Hellenic strain in our thinking. The Greeks vaunted an aesthetics of proportionality (Latin: *ratio,* whence "rationality"). The ordered, measured, and symmetrical they regarded as "divine," as is evident in their statuary. But the logic of the sculpted form—the gods "made of stone" that the prophets of Israel ridicule—is carried over as well into the temple of logic. Postmodern discourse, on the other hand, serves to "bring to light the idolatrous presupposition of every conceptual discourse on God."[18] For every conceptual discourse on God draws a perimeter around what can be "seen" about God and denies that there is more to be seen or more that is even invisible. Modern theology is a spectacle, a Roman circus, in which we cheer at intellectual gladiators but fail to see the Christlike divinity in those "martyred" representations of God, in what is torn apart by wild beasts.

The dyspepsia the inerrantist senses at the figurative or "tropic" language that suffuses postmodernist discourse arises because he cannot see God working in the breakdown of a stultified language. But this dissolution is the occasion of biblical revelation. God promises Abraham a son, a seed or *sēma* of the great nation yet to come into being. Yet he demands the sacrifice of the son on Moriah. And he tells Abraham that before what he says is fulfilled, his descendants must become slaves in Egypt for four hundred years. As Luther understood, the truth of Scripture is not propositional. It is "fideistic" in the best sense of the word, because God is faithful in what he says and faithful to those to whom the words of Scripture are addressed. "These words," as Christ says to John the Revelator at the close of the books of Scripture, "are trustworthy and true."[19] They are trustworthy and true because they are the progressive revelation of the fulfillment of God's original promise. They are true words because they are *promissory* words.

Promissory diction was for a long while a puzzle to twentieth-century phi-losophers. When one says "I promise," one is not predicating something. One is not making a statement of fact. One is not making an empirical inference or a formal deduction. As the logical positivists themselves understood, one cannot "verify" a promise. One can only carry it out, or one who receives the promise can acknowledge that the promiser has made good on the prom-ise—in other words, the promise has been carried out. Promissory truth is only possible when two persons have a relationship of trust with each other. That is the essence of a covenant. The "new covenant" that Christ makes with us is both the fulfillment of a former promise and the making of a new one—that he will come back and that we will know him as we have never known him before. We cannot "validate" God's promise to us by appealing to the "facticity" or "inerrancy" of every marking in the text. The mark-ings do not point to some higher ontology. For that reason inerrancy is not errant—it is simply meaningless. The letters of the text are traces, semiotic indices, of what the everyday mind can hardly bear and from which it seeks in its idolatrous self-satisfaction to avert its gaze. Scripture is not the ultimate fact of God. It contains the distinctive features of his "face."

The Enlightenment project, to which so much of evangelical theology has sworn unswerving allegiance, never caught on to this understanding of Scrip-ture. Locked in mortal combat with both Protestant and Catholic orthodoxy, it sought to pacify a host of warring theological positions spawned by the Reformation and establish a jackbooted empire of reason that kept even God under its heel. What today we call modernism is merely the ideology of the Enlightenment in its diffusion. Modernism and atheism are not accidental bedfellows. They are fraternal twins. The hyperrationalism and foundational-ism of Descartes that launched the Enlightenment could never abide with the awesome relationship-seeking, covenant-making, promise-keeping Deity of the Bible. It could not sacrifice the sovereignty of reason to the One who, as in the tale of Job, gives no reasons until he reveals himself in the whirlwind and puts to shame all theodicies and "moral theologies."

As most trenchant interpreters of Nietzsche have observed, the phrase "God is dead" does not mean there no longer are any rational grounds to believe in God. Nietzsche's "madman" proclaims that God has "died" because "we have killed him." The "we" here, of course, is the modernist first-person plural. We have killed him with our sophisticated apologetics and rationalizations. It is modern philosophy and theology that have "murdered God." Atheism and nihilism, according to Heidegger's reading of Nietzsche, are not the dire consequence of unbelief. They are the hidden agenda of religious "belief" itself that has shored itself with all the appropriate arguments and defenses. Atheism and nihilism are the secret core of modernist religion. Modernist religion is indeed a vast cemetery, as Nietzsche's man shows, that is strewn with the tombs and sepulchers of a dead God.

The metaphor of "tombs and sepulchers" has an uncanny ring. In the Gospel of Matthew Jesus condemns the Pharisees as "whited sepulchers" that glisten on the outside but inside contain "dead men's bones." Nietzsche's madman is a foil for the Enlightenment. He seems mad, uncontrolled, wholly "irrational." But like the vatic personalities of the Bible, he is calling a spade a spade. It is the so-called believers who are really the unbelievers, because their God is totally in the brain, not in the heart, from which all genuine faith would spring. The madman declares that he comes "too soon." Like all prophetic figures, he is mocked and despised, because those to whom he delivers the message are far too comfortable and self-assured in their "common sense," which is actually self-delusion, to lend him any credence. It may be hyperbole to compare modernism straightaway with Pharisaism, but the connection is not incidental either. As most scholars today recognize, the Pharisees were not generally seen by their contemporaries as the "bad guys" the New Testament makes them out to be. They were generally regarded as upstanding religious leaders because of their piety as well as their disciplined and principled devotion to the Law.

Nevertheless, their devotion was misaligned. What they, and most likely the majority of their contemporaries, construed as authentic Judaism, Jesus condemned as mere tradition impersonating divine truth. Modernism has always seen itself as positioned in a goal-line defense against unreason. Likewise, Pharisaism viewed itself as embroiled in a holding action against the intrusions of pagan culture. But ferociously self-protective strategies are usually self-defeating. God's judgment on Judaism came with the uprising against Rome and the destruction of the temple at Jerusalem in 70. The judgment on modernism and inerrantism is in the making. The triumph of modernism in European culture during the nineteenth century led to the almost total eclipse of Christianity, even in such "religious" countries as Germany.

A VOCATIVE READING OF SCRIPTURE

The essential difference between modernism and postmodernism at the theological level consists in what might be termed a "propositional" as opposed to a "vocative" understanding of Scripture. Propositional language is always flattened, confined to the third person. It is always "about" something else. Propositional language adjudges and describes. It relates one set of impersonal terms to another. Vocative language, however, requires the second person and expresses what is technically termed the "I-Thou" relation. The I-Thou relationship is not necessarily a mystical idea, as its detractors often contend. Although the terminology was initially imported into modern thought by the Jewish Hasidic philosopher Martin Buber in a poetic and nonexpository style, the concept itself gives hint of a fundamental "logical" dilemma in the language of second-person address. We can predicate of the second person, but we cannot make the second person a predicate. According to Lévinas, this distinction reflects the fundamental "ontological" distinction between logic and *Logos*. *Logos* is that from which all "saying" proceeds. *Logos* cannot be "said." It is neither an "essence" nor an "entity." It is the voice of the Other that addresses us.

Hellenic philosophy, Lévinas insists, reduced *Logos* to logic, saying to predication. Heidegger reiterates the same point. Whereas Hellenic philosophy always speaks of God in the third person, the Bible—as attested in the writings of Philo of Alexandria, who retained the sense of *Logos* as God's spoken "Word"—gives preference to second-person address. The Bible is not simply "about" God. It is God's Word spoken "to us." While the Bible of course contains numerous "descriptive" statements about the nature of God, the defining moments in which he "reveals" himself involve interpersonal encounter and second-person address. Among many illustrations in the Old Testament, we can cite God's epiphanies to Abraham, Moses, Isaiah, and Jeremiah. It is scant happenstance that the Ten Commandments are spoken as "Thou shalt . . ." rather than "It is the case . . . ." When we experience the fullness of God in Jesus Christ, it is by a person-to-person encounter with him, or at least the biblical account of that engagement. If the Bible were a philosophical demonstration of Jesus' divinity, the angels that confronted the surprised women at the empty tomb on Easter morning would have presented an argument, like a lawyer in the courtroom, using the circumstances of that particular scene as evidence. But that is not what occurs. Jesus shortly comes to his disciples and appears before them. In the Gospel of John he says over and over that in order to "know" the Father, one must know him in a personal manner. For he and the Father are one.

The vocative, as Lévinas tells us, is summed up in a single word—*responsibility*. When one says "you," one is acknowledging something that cannot be acknowledged when one says "he," "she," or "it." One is acknowledging the subjectivity and freedom of the other, which cannot be reduced to "my" subjectivity, or my freedom. "The responsibility for the other can not have begun in my commitment, in my decision. The unlimited responsibility in which I find myself comes from the hither side of my freedom."[20] The "hitherness" of otherness that one encounters in the intersubjective relationship makes what Lévinas terms an "ethical demand" on the person. The face-to-face relationship is always an ethical one. "The access to the face is lived in the ethical mode. The face, all by itself, has a meaning."[21] Judeo-Christianity, in effect, is an ethical tradition because it prioritizes language and revelation as the significance of the face-to-face. When Lévinas says the face has a meaning "all by itself," he is declaring that there is no inferential operation that one can perform upon it. Facial recognition in physics and psychology requires an intuitive mode of cognition that cannot be formulated in any propositional calculus.

But this irreducibility of the "face" is more than a cerebral perplexity. The irreducibility of the face—and the priority of the face-to-face relationship in the biblical context—betray a vision of language that a hellenized philosophy and theology have not been able to incorporate to date. Lévinas dubs this vision an "ontological reversal": it calls into question the very possibility of ontology itself. The Bible is the supreme text for the "overcoming" of metaphysics and of ontotheology. Lévinas makes the thought-provoking observation that the commandment to love God and one's neighbor—which Jesus himself reiterated as the "whole" of Scripture—summarizes everything about the centrality of the category of "responsibility." This commandment of commandments also underscores the significance of what we have named the "vocative." The category can also be summed up as "non-in-difference toward the other." Alterity, or otherness, is inescapably "proximity." The transcendence of God in a "theistic" sense is inseparable from the needful intimacy of our neighbor. "The face of the other, in its defenseless nakedness—is it not already . . . an asking?" Jesus' well-known saying that feeding the hungry and visiting the sick is the "same" as loving him emphasizes such an instruction.

"A beggar's asking, miserable mortal. But at the same time it is an authority summoning me to 'appear,' summoning me to respond."[22] *Non-in-difference* is what Scripture ultimately signifies.

"Thou shalt not kill" or "Thou shalt love thy neighbor" not only forbids the violence of murder: it also concerns all the slow and invisible killing committed in our desires and vices, in all the innocent cruelties of natural life, in our difference of "good conscience" to what is far and what is near, even in the haughty obstinacy of our objectifying and our thematizing. . . . The entire Torah, in its minute descriptions, is concentrated in the "Thou shalt not kill" that the face of the other signifies, and awaits its proclamation therein.[23]

In its passion to espouse the "inerrancy" of the Bible, evangelical theology has also sustained the thoroughly unbiblical perception that the Bible is "indifferent" in the sense of the term employed by Lévinas. An "indifferent" Bible is one that is "about" God, not one that draws us into an irreducible encounter with the One who speaks to us, addresses us, and holds us accountable through his Word, which is at the same time his irrevocable promissory note.

BEYOND LIBERALISM AND FUNDAMENTALISM

The doctrine of inerrancy, of course, was brought forward to counter the claims of liberal theology, which were the first hammer blows of Enlightenment skepticism. Liberal theology found its own companion propositional language to evangelical orthodoxy. Instead of being plain and self-evident, scriptural statements could be recoded as historical, moral, psychological, or general philosophical statements. Liberal theology was naturally reductionistic, transporting the general Enlightenment critique of religion into the field of biblical scholarship. Liberal theology sought to "translate" God-language into a "godless" surrogate idiom. But it was merely exchanging ontotheology for an *onto-atheology*. Over the last two hundred years liberalism has trotted out on the runway innumerable "ontological" fashions. But it has failed to dispel the specter of ontology and, therefore, an overly hellenized theology. Both standard evangelical theology and liberalism, therefore, have incarcerated themselves within the Hellenic framework. Ironically, they are not as different from each other as they may think.

Both liberals and modernist evangelicals are like inmates who fight over who is the biggest, the meanest, the toughest. Yet they do little more than define themselves as having some unique and privileged stance inside the prison house of propositions, not to mention resorting to name-calling. One calls its opponents "relativists." The other utters the slur "fundamentalists." But both are casting their imprecations from behind the same set of bars. According to Gordon R. Lewis, evangelicals have "at least three absolutes": a totally transcendent God; the "once-for-all, supernatural incarnation of Jesus Christ"; and "the once-for-all supernatural inscripturation of sound information in the biblical canon that differs from all other sacred writings not merely in degree, but also in kind."[24] Liberals have their own corresponding "absolutes": a humanly "constructed" representation that we call Deity; an eighteenth-century view of Jesus, not as supernatural persona but as a "moral" or "political" exemplar; and the historically contingent and unprivileged character of the Bible. Yet the presuppositional architecture of both theological liberals and conservatives is virtually identical. It is the modernist architecture of premises and conclusions, fundamental principles and extrapolations. One side merely chooses its own nonnegotiable presuppositional system, or frame of reference.

The Reformation debate over the Bible emerged from the medieval theological context. But the argument over the "authority" of Scripture had little to do with the linguistic theory behind it or with its ramifications. The Reformers, as some scholars have demonstrated, were animated by a more fluid perspective on the event of signification than current conservative readings of Scripture would permit. They wanted biblical hermeneutics to conform to earlier but more flexible standards as opposed to the legalistic, scholastic, pragmatic, and "politicized" methods of interpretation that epitomized the *via moderna*. Scholasticism and legalism, based on the Aristotelian syllogism, did not allow for what earlier commentators, influenced by Augustinian and Neoplatonic theology, had identified as "*aequivocatio* (equivocation)." The term *aequivocatio* means having at least two, but not necessarily contradictory, senses or readings. In no manner did it connote errancy. Only the disjunctive logic of modernism would force biblical hermeneutics into having to dispose of what today we would call the semiotic rendering of a text, the recognition that multiple explications are possible, that the tablet of words has multiple meanings, or is polysemous.

As G. R. Evans notes of the period leading up to the Reformation, "Problems posed by words with two or more significations lie at the root of the majority of difficulties of interpretation which medieval scholars identified in the text of the Bible."

> [The] hypothesis that Scripture has a multiplicity of senses rests on the assumption that it is a property of words to be capable of more than one signification. . . . Scripture has its own modes of equivocation, and the critic should familiarize himself with them, and learn how to avoid equivocation himself, before he launches attacks on the truth of the Sacred Page. Scripture's own equivocations are entirely good and helpful; it is simply a matter of studying them, to see, for example, in the case of Jesus' statement that John the Baptist was Elijah and John's own statement that he was not, how in this equivocation Christ and John the Baptist differed without contradiction.[25]

It was only because of the standard Catholic doctrine of *aequivocatio* that Luther was able to assert confidently Paul's sense of the text of Romans and achieve his breakthrough that salvation is through faith, a move that seemed to "contradict" the canonical reading. Whereas equivocations may be anathema to Aristotelian logic, they were vital, as the medieval exegetes grasped, to making human commentary adequate to the very speech of God.

The theologians of the Middle Ages, unlike present-day inerrantists, did not attempt to make God's speech "adequate" to human grammar and logic. They recognized that where human language may be "univocal"—having one strand of meaning—God's voice is often equivocal. The reason is God himself. If God made it so clear, we would not recognize him as God or depend on him in faith. Postmodernist philosophy, with its emphasis on the polymorphous nature of the text and meaning as sign-play, is closer to the medieval and Reformation approach to hermeneutics than are fundamentalism and inerrantism. It is more open to letting God's word of salvation speak for itself on its own terms. It is open to the "good news," *the eu-angelion*. It allows equivocation because God speaks "equivocally"—*in the vocative!*

Because the Bible is God speaking *to* us, and to all of us, whether we hear God or not, the term "inerrancy" becomes peculiarly irrelevant. On one level the inerrantists are correct. If there is any "error" at all, then the whole authority of the Bible hangs in doubt. But that is not because of any discursive domino effect. It is because of a simple philosophical truth. If an infinite God "speaks" in error, then that God is *not* infinite! And in the Western tradition God by definition is infinite. So the Bible either is the "Word of God," or it is not. There cannot be any such thing as "limited inerrancy" any more than there can be "limited infinity." By the same token, the liberal or "moderate conservative" argument that the Bible is "more or less" true collapses on the same grounds. The inerrantists would have a better "argument" if they ceased using the language of "error" and "lack of error" and focused on the issue that Scripture itself raises: Do we "obey" God's demands on us through his Word, or do we not? Obedience is a personal response to a vocative. If we do not believe that the Bible is what believers say it is, we do not obey. But if we do believe and obey, we really have no argument against the "authority" of the Bible. "Therefore, as the Holy Spirit says—'Today if you hear his voice, do not grow stubborn as in those days of rebellion, at that time of testing in the desert.'"[26]

The point is made forcefully by Moisés Silva in his book *Has the Church Misread the Bible?* Silva points out that the Augustinian and Calvinistic emphasis on the finitude of human self-knowledge confirms that there are "obstacles to our understanding of our God and his message—our finitude, our corruption, and, yes, our relativity. But God himself is not circumscribed by any such limitation. He who created us knows how to speak to us. He who formed our minds knows how to reach them. The task of biblical interpretation is not an autonomous human endeavor but a response to God's command."[27] We can quibble over such terms as "inerrant," "inspired," and "authoritative," but that is splitting hairs. The authority of the Bible does not rest on whether it is logically and seamlessly consistent and free of "errors," as the medieval theologians with their appreciation for the rule of *aequivocatio* understood. We can dispute endlessly over whether certain injunctions, such as we have in Leviticus or in the Pastoral Epistles, were intended as absolute "moral" requirements or as "concessions" to the mores of the time. Or perhaps as having a meaning we can neither accept simply at face value nor dismiss. We must treat Scripture not as facticity but as address, and as address that sometimes sears our conscience and provokes the trauma of self-searching in our finite shell of self-consciousness. When the infinite God speaks to finite beings, only faith can wrestle with the meaning or the application in that particular time and place. The metaphysico-logical paradigm of scriptural authority has itself reached its own "limits." It may continue to be serviceable for "science," but not for the true biblical *knowledge* of God. We can say that the Bible is absolutely and unconditionally true because it is our infinite troth. When we commit to the authority of Scripture, it is like saying "I do" in our marriage vows—in this case our vows to God. We do have the freedom as finite creatures to break our vows to the infinite Creator and Redeemer. The question is not whether we are correct in pledging our troth. The only issue is whether we mean what we say. That is the true postmodern point of view.

6

THE PRIESTHOOD
OF ALL WORSHIPPERS

From Hierarchy to Relationality

THE WORD "POSTMODERNISM" FIRST AROSE as a descriptor for new trends in philosophy and literary theory. But it has increasingly been applied to theories of culture and social organization as well. The spectrum of late-twentieth- and early-twenty-first-century writers on postmodern culture theory is sprawling and complex. It runs the gamut from neo-Marxists such as Louis Althusser to post-Marxists such as Alain Badiou, from psychoanalysts such as Jacques Lacan to feminist critics of psychoanalysis such as Luce Irigay, from cultural historians such as Michel de Certeau to cultural anthropologists such as Pierre Bourdieu, from semioticians such as Umberto Eco to theorists of media such as Jean Baudrillard.

What seems to unite these disparate theorists is a realization that the end of modernism entails a shift in conventional paradigms that were operative for both characterizing and criticizing the contemporary sociocultural world until quite recently. The fall of (U.S.S.R.) communism brought in its wake a devastating crisis of credibility for academic Marxism, which was riding high in most European universities. Marxist discourse, which had penetrated much of cultural and political analysis by the 1980s, was comprised of three

145

central threads: (1) an emphasis on struggle between different social and economic classes; (2) a focus on material forces and factors as the propellant of these conflicts; and (3) a preoccupation with "capitalism," which it viewed as verging on an ultimate and apocalyptic crisis due to its inherent "contradictions."

When revolutionary socialism suddenly crashed and crumpled as the close of the millennium drew near, postmodernism became a chic alternative to the old, now discredited, dialectical vision of history that Marx and Engels and their followers had long espoused. The postmodernist paradigm, though it can hardly be made explicit or concise, can be boiled down to the following broader traits: (1) the flattening of hierarchies at all levels of organization; (2) the development of webs of interconnecting nodes and modules, none of which have any priority over the other and which do not represent in any important sense a "chain of command"; and (3) constant and dynamic change with ephemeral and superficial phenomena taking precedence over deep and abiding structures.

Baudrillard, of course, has been the doyen of postmodern cultural theory, although his take often strikes the reader more as a surrealistic word canvas than as a viable and recognizable philosophical assessment of the current scene. What makes Baudrillard both important and poignant, nonetheless, is his insight into how electronic media and global commerce and communications have not only transformed the social order, but also our very language and values. What this new media milieu has wrought is a strange dissolution of the familiar boundaries between daily experience and culture. *Culture is everywhere and nowhere at once.* Culture is nothing more, nor less, than a gigantic sensory orgy; it is "a general aestheticization of everyday life."

This aestheticization amounts to a general anesthetization, because we no longer make distinctions between pure pleasure and pure pain, between what we affirm and what we deny. We are caught up in "a pure circulation of images, a transaesthetics of banality." Whereas Marxists "enshrined the living utopian hope that the State would wither away, and that the political sphere would negate itself as such, in the apotheosis of a finally transparent social realm," in reality

none of this has come to pass. The political sphere has disappeared, sure enough—but so far from doing so by means of a self-transcendence into the strictly social realm, it has carried that realm into oblivion with it. We are now in the transpolitical sphere; in other words, we have reached the zero point of politics, a stage which also implies the reproduction of politics, its endless simulation. For everything that has not successfully transcended itself can only fall prey to revivals without end.[1]

The much larger outcome is a "dizzying eclecticism of form, a dizzying eclecticism of pleasure," as in the baroque of the seventeenth century. "Like the practitioners of the baroque, we too are irrepressible creators of images, but secretly we are iconoclasts—not in the sense that we destroy images, but in the sense that we manufacture a profusion of images in which there is nothing to see." These images "leave no trace, cast no shadow, and have no consequences. The only feeling one gets from such images is that behind each one there is something that has disappeared." For they are "images that conceal nothing, that reveal nothing—they have a kind of negative intensity."[2] Baudrillard cites the case of the pop art of the 1960s, which proffered for the first time in the history of art commercial images that could be indefinitely reproduced. The most celebrated example, of course, is Andy Warhol's Campbell's soup can. The image in itself is trivial and quotidian. It has no unique status. It is not a typical "subject matter" for art. Instead, it is the antithesis of art. According to Baudrillard, it is an "aesthetic" object that has no aesthetic value. It "releases us from the need to decide between beautiful and ugly."[3] Postmodern culture, for Baudrillard, is one in which we lose all inkling of ontological hierarchy, of any palpable discrimination between the real and the unreal. All we have are rarefied "signs" of the real, which Baudrillard terms the "hyperreal."

The pervasiveness of media—from cable television to the Internet to billboard advertising to tabloid magazines—is the occasion for this "sublimation" of the real. But it is not the cause per se. It is part of an ongoing historical process in which mass production and consumption have touched not only our commodities, but also our symbols and ideas. Nothing has value in itself any longer. Everything is but a sign of something else, which is not a "thing" but one more correlative sign. The signs swarm and commingle. They enter into a play of simulated materiality that suffices for what is genuinely material. The hyperreal is neither unreal nor surreal—it is "more real than real," inasmuch as it is so pervasive, and thus the dichotomy of what is real and not real no longer becomes an issue. Baudrillard compares the immateriality of the "real" and material to the weightlessness of outer space. Everything floats and moves into orbit. It is not grounded. The advent of hyperreality, however, has an unintended effect. It dissolves and neutralizes the lineaments of what in the past has been identified as "society," or the social order. The proliferation of media and information "pursues an irresistible destruction of the social." Hence, "the media are producers not of socialization, but of exactly the opposite, of the implosion of the social in the masses." For "all the contents of meaning are absorbed in the only dominant form of the medium. Only the medium can make an event—whatever the contents, whether they are conformist or subversive."[4]

Baudrillard's vision of society is so-called post-structural theory writ large. Post-structuralism as a philosophical and epistemological prototype, we have seen, is built upon the principle that there can be no second-order stratum to which words refer. This perspective is labeled in postmodernist parlance as the "ruse of reference." Referentiality is like an Escher drawing. If one stares at the drawing, it seems to inhabit a three-dimensional space, when in fact everything is confined to a flat plane. The solidity of the image is an optical illusion. When one says, "The word 'house' stands for a house," the mind tricks itself into assuming that there is something apart from the skein of language—a "real" house—on which language somehow converges. The problem is akin to the prospective answer to the absurd question, "Are fantasies real?"

At one level the question contains an oxymoron, a logically self-contradictory phrase. But one is tempted to surmise by the query that perhaps any given fantasy under the proper conditions might just be real, particularly if we could adduce sufficient evidence to show that it was not a fantasy after all. The term "reality" is one of the oddest expressions in our vocabulary, and as Heidegger observes, it only makes sense because we speak a language, an Indo-European language, that allots it a privileged place. Western philosophy is an artifact of Indo-European grammar, whether we are speaking Greek, Latin, French, Spanish, English, or German. Ontological thinking itself, as the anthropologist and linguist Benjamin Whorf deduced some time back, is the peculiar harvest of Indo-European grammar. It is what Derrida has ironically nicknamed our "white mythology"—a kind of conceptual folklore indigenous to the Aryan peoples of the European and North American continents. Western thought is not the vast planetary emporium of infinite cognitive possibilities we frequently make it out to be. It is really just a little curiosity shop with a sign in the window that reads: "Metaphysics spoken here."

If reality is not as real as it appears to be, according to Baudrillard and certain other post-structuralists, then the "social order" is less an order than a simulation of order. The suspicion that social authority has no "reality" behind it, but is merely the manipulation of signs and images, has been the stuff of contemporary fiction from the musical *The Wizard of Oz* to the book and film *1984* to *The Matrix* and its sequels. Baudrillard's philosophy is not by any stretch of the imagination a cross section of postmodernist social thought. But it does concretize a motif that abounds within the writings of the postmodernists—what might be technically defined as *asymmetrical horizontal sovereignty.*

The notion of "sovereignty" is a modern political construct. It originally referred to the power and authority of a king, but during the age of democratic revolution from the seventeenth century onward, it came to connote the locus of governance. Thus, "sovereignty" in the political theory of the period was interpreted as residing in the people rather than the monarch. In twentieth-century theory the concept has been expanded to signify linkages of influence and control and has acquired a more precise sociological meaning. But it is still an exceptionally useful phrase.

FOUCAULT AND THE HORIZONTALITY OF THE SOCIAL

Up through the modern era "sovereignty" implied certain vertical relationships. Either the sovereign ruled "over" parliaments and peoples, or parliaments and peoples were the sovereign themselves. However, in the postmodern context sovereignty can be conceived horizontally. The leading postmodern theorist of horizontal sovereignty was Michel Foucault. Foucault interprets social relationships as networks of power. Power is "everywhere" and "comes from everywhere." Modernism, or the "modernist project," tends to view power as "top-down" configurations of command and control. It understands power as the exercise of constraint and repression by certain individuals, collectivities of individuals, and institutions over each other. Power may also be wielded by cognitive and psychological processes, or even somatic pressures. Thus, modernism erects its suppositions concerning human behavior upon Greek philosophy and psychology, which highlights the dominance of rationality over ecstatic religiosity, and morality as the restraint of the passions and the appetites.

Psychoanalysis, of course, turns this particular architecture on its head and places the accent on the fatality of the unconscious. But it still sustains a vertical perspective. The postmodern account of power relationships, so far as Foucault is concerned, embeds them within the "social nexus." What modernism refers to as "freedom" and "domination" become transformed into the categories of "transitivity" and "intransitivity." Just as a verb in any given syntax may be transitive or intransitive, so power performs in much the same way. The philosopher Hegel analyzed how the relationship between master and slave in traditional society calls into question the conventional paradigm of dominance. The master is not independent of the slave. His identity both requires and feeds upon him. The slave, by the same token, through the value of his labor commands the livelihood of the master. When the slave becomes conscious of this tacit mastery, he is able to achieve freedom, as happens in every revolutionary situation. All power relationships are reciprocal. They continually cross-reference each other. The vectors are bidirectional.

The genius of modern power relationships, according to Foucault, is that they do not depend on anyone having to be "over and above" anyone else. Power is "coextensive with the social body; there are no spaces of primal liberty between the meshes of its network." In addition, the interconnections of power relations are dispersed. "Heteromorphous" and "localized procedures of power are adapted, reinforced, and transformed by these global strategies."[5] The effects of power are internally exercised and monitored. Foucault views "conscience" as a modern invention. The modern individual does not need to fear the punishment of a sovereign in order to be compliant with the moral and legal system. He or she has internalized, or inscribed in one's own mind and body, the demands of the system. Foucault argues that internalized law and morality are based on the modern metaphor of surveillance. The "Big Brother" myth is paradigmatic of this surveillance organization. One is routinely aware that some invisible central authority is always aware of one's moves and predilections. By way of illustration Foucault supplies the nineteenth-century philosopher Jeremy Bentham's design of a universal surveillance system he called a "panopticon (all-seeing thing)." The panopticon would be an inconspicuous surveillance tower with the capacity to watch over everything that happened within a wide perimeter. In this utopian setting one would theoretically no longer require prisons, or other coercive methods of detention and incarceration, because one would have to assume that, no matter what one did, someone else was registering and taking note of it. The mechanisms of constraint would be purely interior. Guilt and anxiety become the premier instruments in the modernist ambit of discipline and punishment.

Like Deleuze, Foucault has been heavily influenced by Nietzsche and his critique of modernism. The problem with modernism, according to this Nietzschean rendering of history, is that it has replaced the "sign" with the "representation," the polysemous character of language with Cartesian formalism. The age of signs was the age of faith. For faith thrives on signs, not certitudes. But fateful developments set in at the opening of the modern era, according to Foucault.

From the seventeenth century onward, the whole domain of the sign is divided between the certain and the probable: that is to say, there can no longer be an unknown sign, a mute mark. This is not because men are in possession of all the possible signs, but because there can be no sign until there exists a *known* possibility of substitution between two *known* elements. The sign does not wait in silence for the coming of a man capable of recognizing it: it can be constituted only by an act of knowing.[6]

The dependence of the sign on the knowing subject, and the subject's capacity for reflection and representation, inaugurate the modern perspective. But modernism at the same time subjugates the social order of relations to knowledge. The vertical connection between God—or his appointed regent whose scepter is by "divine right"—is flipped upside down and constituted as the sovereignty of reason over society. The ideology of social engineering is the result. Foucault criticizes modern social theory because of its demand for the homogeneity of "humanistic" rationality, which necessitates the bureaucratic state. A postmodern social theory, however, demands the dissolution of the state as a construct of social life and brings to the fore the multiplicity and heterogeneity of relationships in and through society as the "immanence" of culture. A postmodern social ethics would move in much the same direction.

RELATIONAL ONTOLOGY

In one of his early essays on religious postmodernism, Mark C. Taylor lays the groundwork for a postmodern social theory in an essay entitled "Toward an Ontology of Relativism." Because of the negative connotation the word "relativism" has acquired in evangelical theology, the essay might be more properly entitled "Toward an Ontology of Relationality." "Relationality" and "relativity" have the same etymology. In the essay Taylor is not arguing for "pure relativism"—the notion that there is no underlying pattern of meaning and implication outside of surface relationships. Taylor captions this view of things "perspectival relativism," which he contends expresses the "relationality of being." Perspectival relativism overcomes both the foundationalist dogma that the reality of the real is independent of the context of relationships, and the bald relativist claim that the relationships are all that matter—in other words, that there is no unifying premise.

Both foundationalism and relativism are lopsided descriptions of reality. In metaphysics the former is cognate with the position known as "monism." The latter is associated with metaphysical pluralism. Perspectival relativism involves what Taylor terms the "socialization of being," that is, a "relational

ontology." "Monism tends to hypostatize purely abstract, self-identical substance . . . as the ontologically prior foundation of all reality in such a way
that difference or plurality is reduced to accidental insubstantial status."
Both "monism and pluralism rest on the common assumption of the irreconcilable opposition between unity and plurality, identity and difference."
Finally, "neither perspective recognizes the interconnection of oneness and
manyness through which each is constituted by relation to the other."[7] This
rather turgid presentation, at the same time, prefigures the adaptation of
Derrida's rhetoric of the trace to postmodern religious thought. According
to Taylor, "presence is present as absence," while "absence makes possible
the presenting of presence."[8] At this point in his career Taylor was aiming
to draw theological implications from the dialectical philosophy of Hegel,
although he found a more compatible voice in Derrida. And although Taylor
himself never articulated any kind of postmodern social theory, or even a
social ethics for that matter, the notion of a relational ontology is crucial to
the nascent paradigm of asymmetric horizontal sovereignty.

Stanley Grenz, one of the pacesetters in an emergent postmodernist evangelical theology, has sought to take the idea of a relational ontology one step
further and couple it directly with the Christian doctrine of the Trinity. In a
book coauthored with John Franke, Grenz explores the historical intertwin-
ing of Trinitarian theology, the biblical motif of humanity as the *imago Dei,*
and contemporary social and cultural theory. Grenz and Franke remark that
"perhaps the most significant development in the contemporary renaissance of
Trinitarian theology has been the emphasis on relationality." Such an emphasis
offers "an alternative to the metaphysics of substance that has dominated
theological reflection on the Trinity throughout much of church history."[9]
The metaphysics of substance naturally echoes the classical background of
so much early Christian thought. When Tertullian first declared that God is
one *substantia* and three *personae,* he was rendering Greek into Latin and
using an Aristotelian distinction between one *ousia* ("being" or "reality")
and three *prosōpa* ("masks" or "manifestations").

The notion of "substance" as it came to be entertained within the tradition, however, conveys more the sense of God as an independent, stand-alone
being than the sense of the One who is genuinely triune. The penchant of
Western theologians to describe God as eternal, omnipotent, and immutable
contributed to this intellectual drift. Western Trinitarian doctrine, while giving
lip service to the orthodox portrait of God as truly and paradoxically three-
in-one, tended to give subtle preference to the "aseity" or "in-himselfness" of
God, leaving critics of early Christianity to wonder whether the church really

meant what it said. For instance, in the sixth century the prophet Muhammad, founder of Islam, dismissed the Trinitarian teaching of the Christians as a covert polytheism and reasserted the Old Testament claim that God is one, and one alone. But the Greek term *ousia,* as opposed to the Latin *substantia,* does not connote as starkly this sense of God's aseity. Heidegger observes that *ousia* in its pre-Platonic setting carries more the meaning of "presence" than substance. The concept of presence, as Heidegger and subsequent postmodernists tend to interpret the tradition, has more a "dialectical" than an ontological force behind it. Presence and absence, sameness and otherness, are interstitial terms in the unfolding of what the Greeks meant by *ousia.* In other words, being "is" not in itself, but in relation to what is not itself.

The new Trinitarian emphasis on an "ontology of relation" pulls us directly, according to Grenz, toward a "reconceptualization of the nature of personhood and the self that has emerged recently in reaction to the radical individualism spawned by the Enlightenment, with its elevation of the individual viewed in isolation and as fundamentally detached from the world."[10] The modern liberal portrait of the human person as an "atomic" self that feels, thinks, and acts wholly on its own and of its own volition and in accordance with its own unique desires—that is a secular and political analogue of Aristotle's God, the "unmoved mover." This portrait is Hellenic, not Hebraic. Modernism confuses it with the biblical perspective on God, who is relational. According to Grenz, the same confusion over the nature of the Trinity shows up in theological renderings of the *imago Dei.* The "most long-standing interpretation of the *imago*" tends to accentuate "the capacity for rationality coupled with our moral nature. This view is widespread in the writings of the church fathers and the medieval scholastic theologians."[11]

The Reformers, on the other hand, focused on relationality. Human beings exist in a dependent relationship to their Maker. In themselves they are degenerate and lost. It is only in relationship to Christ, the restored image of God, that they can be restored to what they were created to be. This relationship to Christ reestablishes the *imago* not as the character, but as the destiny, of the human species. Because the "image of God" in Genesis implies the relation of male to female, it is, as the neoorthodox theologian Karl Barth put it, not based on the ontological comparison that Thomas Aquinas termed the "*analogia entis* (analogy of being)" but on an "*analogia relationis* (analogy of relationship)." Postmodern "ontology" means "for the other" and "in relationship to the other." That is not some hip, psychological reading of the Scriptures. It is what the Scriptures themselves say. It is what God in the Scriptures says he is. The Trinity is the best theological model that one can

generate in a Hellenic environment from the relational language concerning
God that is essentially biblical. It is not some kind of Hellenic add-on. "This
dynamic conception of the *imago Dei* arising out of the relational model
launches us on the road toward an understanding of the self that can speak
within the postmodern context."[12]

In his book *The Second Reformation* William Beckham puts a practical
face on this new relational ontology. Beckham maintains that horizontal organization must be reinforced with "horizontal" or "lateral" thinking. Vertical
thinking, according to Beckham, tends to look for foundational warrants and
clear criteria of justification for concepts before giving them any kind of credence. Vertical thinking is the cognitive pattern of the modernist worldview.
It is wary of experimentation, impromptu initiatives, and entrepreneurship
in general. It wants to work out an entire theological ground plan before
the activity can actually begin. Vertical thinking also tends to be wedded to
clear and coherent concepts that certify themselves in the mind of whoever is
entertaining them. Beckham tells the story of the Swiss watchmaking industry,
which in the 1970s discovered that their preeminence in the world economy
had suddenly and unexpectedly been wrested away by American quartz
electronic manufacturers. The irony is that the Swiss themselves invented the
quartz watch. But they refused to bring the innovation to market because a
watch without moving, mechanical parts jarred with their ingrained presumption concerning what a watch is. So they discarded the invention, and other
nations and countries brought about a revolution in watchmaking.

TWO-WINGED CHURCHES

The same thing is happening in the church. Both mainline and evangelical church leaders have the ingrained habit of conceptualizing a church as
a vertical structure, with God at the top, the denominational administrative
hierarchy just below, the pastors and the individual church governing bodies
struck smack in the middle, and the congregation along with its outreach
programs at the lower tier. Both ecclesiastical authority and the ministrations
of the Holy Spirit are imagined to flow down from the heavens and reach
individual believers, whose lives are then altered and "sanctified" within the
familiar vertical matrix of top-down relationships. But vertical sanctification
is only one way in which God works with believers, according to Beckham.
A church that only concentrates on Sunday assembly and corporate worship
is like a great bird with only one wing. It takes two wings to soar. The other
wing is the horizontal dimension of corporate Christian life. In Beckham's

terms, a church that gives equal priority to the horizontal plane is a "two-winged church." Postmodern churches are two-winged. The Holy Spirit does not merely cascade down from above, but is the wind beneath their wings that provides uplift and supports the body in praise and adoration of God Almighty. Two-winged churches rely as much, if not more, on the horizontal thrust as on vertical oversight.

Beckham terms this design the "cell church." Cell churches—which usually have a corporate worship focus but rely on the vitality of small groups of believers ministering to each other and their immediate community—are the essential ingredient in the so-called postdenominational reformation. Cell groups do not congregate at a central location. They meet in people's living rooms, in coffee bars, in restaurants, and in serendipitous environments. The word "cell" is more than a homespun similitude. Because Christians believe that the living church is the body of Christ, the cell metaphor expresses the dynamism of all the fundamental units of life conspiring together. "The key to understanding the cell church is the cell itself," or the "'churchlike' character of base communities." For "everything that happens in a cell church—the weekly celebrations, harvest events, training and equipping retreats, camps, meetings for oversight—exists to support the cells. Everything relates out from, and back to, the base cell community."[13]

The theological template of the cell church is not just a religious application of nouveau organizational or management theory. Beckham contends that it springs forthwith from a close reading of Jesus' ministry and the Acts of the Apostles in the New Testament. "Every important event in Christ's life took place in some form of community. More often than not, it was in a small-group context. Jesus came down from heaven out of the Trinitarian community of the Father, Son, and Spirit—the original two or three gathered together."[14] In fact, the incarnate God redeems his creation not through the Old Testament assembly or *ekklēsia*—those who are "called"—but through the enfleshing of the triune Godhead. The New Testament is all about permanent incarnation. The Holy Spirit "descends" at Pentecost, but it forms and forges the scattered believers through active and intimate ministry into the kingdom that Jesus has established. The two-winged church looks upward toward the most holy and transcendent God, but it also looks outward toward community. It is founded on a relational ontology, the ontology of the Trinity.

The Reformation of the sixteenth century was a decentralizing of clerical authority, which ended much of the corruption and abuse of power against which Luther and Calvin had fulminated. But it did not, according to Beckham, bring about a true return to the primitive or first-century church, which the Reformers had set about to achieve. It consisted in a "reformation of doctrine," but not an ultimate spiritual reformation. "The New Testament cell design of the church promises to be the structure that will give the other elements the framework in which to become an explosive revolution. In the cell-church movement, God is providing the structure through which the church can be the catalyst for spiritual revolution."[15]

Half a millennium ago Luther himself had an intimation of what the two-winged church might turn out to be. Because he was fighting the Roman Catholic colossus of his time, he came up with a metaphor that "deconstructed" the entrenched model of hierarchical control prevalent at the time—the "priesthood of all believers," the third tenet of the Reformation. The phrase "priesthood of all believers" sounds like a contradiction in terms, because priests almost by definition are singular and special. They are mediators of God to their flock. If everyone is a priest, then no one is a priest. On the other hand, that is precisely what Luther had in mind. He took the phrase from the biblical idea of Israel as a "nation of priests"—in other words, a people in which the process of sanctification is internal, not external, to the life of the body. Faith, or belief, itself is what supplies the leaven for sanctification. Faith is the one, authentic vertical connection between Christians and their God, spilling over into a vibrant web of lateral relationships, including care, instruction, and evangelism. The church of the Next Reformation is grounded in faith alone. Yet this faith is not merely upward gazing. It is a faith that both seeks understanding and expresses itself in works of love. It is a faith that testifies to the Spirit coming down and spreading outward and returning back to the triune Godhead.

The postmodern church is not a church of pious and godly individuals. It is a Spirit-filled body. The modernist church may continue to grow, but it is not growing organically, as Christ intended. The dynamics of the modernist church are, in the phrasing of Christian Schwarz, not only vertically driven, but also captivated by rational strategies of technocratic engineering. "The psychological force behind the technocratic paradigm is a 'security mentality.'" How many Christian ministries and business enterprises primarily characterize themselves as "safe for the whole family," or something similar, rather than as risk-taking ventures of Spirit-led believers into the extreme and the unknown? Technocratic institutions "look for programs" that will ensure the "health" of the institution. In addition, "technocratic thinking is, at least in Western churches, the most widespread paradigm. It is their greatest liability—by the second generation if not sooner. Paradoxically, the intentions of people in these churches are in many cases good and spiritual," though "it can be shown how much this paradigm harms the organism church."[16]

Technocratic theories of church organization follow the social engineering paradigm that Foucault faults as the modernist-humanist conception of control through "surveillance." Technocratic ecclesiology assumes that the thoughts and behavior of increasingly large congregations must be "rationalized" through numerous demographically specific ministries and programs—professional family counseling, missions operations, community outreach, "accountability" sessions, "seeker-sensitive" services—all of which are customized and implemented according to the latest strategies for church "management and growth." The approach is what detractors have termed the "consumerist" approach to building bodies of faith. Personal desires of church members are carefully monitored and coordinated with marketing and financial strategies in a businesslike atmosphere. According to Foucault, every institution has its own "regime of truth," a system of discourses and nonverbal cues that regulate how people are feeling about themselves, or viewing others, and how they react, or do not react, to the signs and messages circulating in the broader culture. Regimes of truth can be cleverly orchestrated by social engineers, advertisers, and political communications experts. Churches also have their own regimes of truth as well as their own technocratic shepherds.

The modernist church is a managed "faith-body." There is a "reason" for everything it does, and these reasons are all part of the "plan." But the postmodern church does not simply actuate the game plan of the church-growth strategist. The postmodern church manifests the vital activity of the individual cells and their mutual "biochemistry." It is the kind of "asymmetrical horizontality" that deconstructs most paradigms of ecclesiology. The vital activity of the "self-organizing" (actually, *God-organizing*) church we can only say theologically is due to the "wind of the Spirit," and as Jesus said, "The wind [Spirit] blows where it wills."[17] The "power of the Spirit" does not fit well with modernist church doctrine. The concept and reality are too slippery, too imprecise, too unmanageable, too "irrational." That is why the charismatic movement in the churches, which we shall explore later, has become such a fly in the ointment for modernist evangelicalism. Charismatic Christianity is not modern, but instead thoroughly postmodern. It has what Max Weber called "charismatic" as contrasted with "rational" leadership.

Although large charismatic churches often run the risk of becoming staging areas for the showmanship of their charismatic leaders, many of the smaller ones are held together by the indwelling power of the Spirit and the life of the cell group. If the doctrine of the Second Person of the Trinity, an anonymous evangelist is reported to have said, signifies God's "entering into relation" with us, the doctrine of the Third Person connotes the growth of relation—a growing relationship for every believer to God and growing relationships to each other.

The modernist principle of social and political organization was encapsulated in Hegel's epigram that the "real is rational and the rational is real." Perhaps a postmodern, post-Hegelian, postrationalist rule of Christian corporate life could be summed up as follows: *the real is relational and the relational is real.* On this intuition the postmodern Christians take their stand.

7

Thoroughly Postmodern Ministry

Postmodern Revivalism

Baudrillard and the Ubiquity of Culture

"Almost all the religion in the world has been produced by revivals," declared the great nineteenth-century revival preacher Charles Finney. "God has found it necessary to take advantage of the excitability there is in mankind, to produce powerful excitements among them, before he can lead them to obey. Men are so spiritually sluggish, there are so many things to lead their minds off from religion, and to oppose the influence of the Gospel, that it is necessary to raise an excitement among them, till the tide rises so high as to sweep away the opposing obstacles." Finney was unapologetic about his ability as a revival preacher to bring the unsaved to Christ through what critics of such a methodology, today as well as yesterday, would contemptuously term "emotionalism." In order to be saved, lost souls "must be so excited that they will break over these counteracting influences, before they will obey God." Finney concluded: "Not that excited feeling is religion, for it is not; but it is excited desire, appetite, and feeling that prevents religion."[1]

Finney of course used the term "religion" with the contemptuous edge that it has in the rhetoric of contemporary youth-oriented Christianity. "Religion" implies doctrines, rules, and sobriety of worship. It is what Max Weber described as the "routinization" of charisma. Weber's theory was a more technical statement of Finney's dictum about the historic role of revivalism. According to Weber, "religion" is born with the fervent instruction of luminaries and prophets, so-called charismatic figures. Over time, the volcanic magma of these original inspirations cools and solidifies. Spiritual communities coalesce into churches, churches into complex organizations with their tiers of authority, hierarchical systems of administration, dogmas, canons, and legal and ceremonial strictures. The end product is "religion."

During three or more centuries of religious development in America, these revivalistic tsunamis have swelled, crashed, and receded. In early American history they were known as "Great Awakenings," which occurred in the early-eighteenth and nineteenth centuries. Finney was one of the motivating forces of the so-called Second Great Awakening. A native of New England, Finney grew up in western New York, which came to be known as the "burnt-over" district because of the firestorms of revivalism that raced through that region in the 1830s and 1840s. As a Presbyterian and a Calvinist by upbringing, Finney provoked the same kind of opposition and indignation that the new postmodern forms of worship and evangelism are stirring up nowadays.

Albert B. Dod of Princeton, a contemporary of Finney and a relentless critic of him, charged that his methods of bringing sinners to repentance and salvation undermined both the cogency and integrity of evangelical Christianity. Finney was dead wrong about the importance of "excitability" in promoting the gospel, Dod thundered, inasmuch as "it is impossible that our emotions should possess any moral character."[2] The times may have changed, but the arguments have not. Dod's attacks on Finney and revivalism are quite similar to the harangues of evangelical "foundationalists" against postmodernist styles and attitudes. Postmodernism promotes an irrational exuberance in worship and lifestyles, according to present-day hecklers, undermining the doctrinal and liturgical fundamentals of Christian corporate practice. The taunt that postmodernism is amoral and "nihilistic" also echoes the same erstwhile canard.

It is hardly a stretch to draw a comparison between earlier periods of revivalistic ardor and the current tilt toward offbeat and experimental forms of ministry, particularly among younger evangelical Christians. The origins of avant-garde evangelicalism are difficult to trace, but they seem to coincide with the explosion in popularity of Christian rock music during the 1990s. The hippie era of sex, drugs, and rock 'n' roll during the late 1960s passed over into the Jesus movement of the early 1970s, which in turn prefigured the evangelical resurgence later in that decade. By the same token, the Generation-X subculture of the 1990s, with its implicit revolt against the worldliness and success orientation of the baby boomers, has spawned a diffuse Christian counterculture that extols the heart over the head, has a passion for the unredeemed and unchurched, and affects styles of dress, behavior, and artistic expression that entirely belie the stereotype of the middle-class believer in America.

According to Robb Redman, who once taught ministry at Fuller Theological Seminary in Pasadena, California, we are at present witnessing what he terms a "worship awakening."[3] We might even go so far as to dub it the Third Great Awakening in this country. In many ways this awakening is unprecedented. To a large extent it has resulted from the growing ethnic and cultural diversity of America as a whole, but it is also the consequence of the reach of new media. What started as the so-called praise-and-worship movement in the late 1980s became a broadscale enterprise in its own right as it blurred the lines between what happens in church on Sunday morning, and onstage performances of youthful artists in various "Christian clubs" on any given Saturday night in trendy urban areas. The commercialization of the worship form itself through the expansion of the Nashville-based Christian music industry is highly significant as well, along with its tendency to mimic the promotional and entrepreneurial strategies of its secular counterpart, in a certain measure even outpacing the latter's growth and influence.

The pacesetters in the worship awakening and the new styles of postmodern ministry have been Brennan Manning, a writer, and Rich Mullins, a poet and musician. Manning and Mullins have been to the new Christian bohemians what Jack Kerouac and Bob Dylan were to the secular youth movement of the 1960s. Manning has played the role of Francis of Assisi, the preacher and reformer. Mullins has been the troubadour.

Like St. Francis, Manning has also advocated the life of utter simplicity and humility, a style of personal existence that is thoroughly contrary to the values of our acquisitive and competitive society. His message is one of unmitigated "grace," or what he terms "the ragamuffin gospel." The ragamuffin gospel "nullifies our adulation of televangelists, charismatic superstars, and local church heroes," Manning writes. "It obliterates the two-class citizenship theory operative in many American churches."[4] It is the simple gospel that "all is gift." Nothing is earned; everything is granted by God.

Manning refers to himself as a "vagabond evangelist" who preaches "madness" in his sermons. The madness is that of a totally gracious and forgiving lifestyle of outreach and engagement with sinners. "Something is radically wrong when the local church rejects a person accepted by Jesus: when a harsh, judgmental, and unforgiving sentence is passed on homosexuals; when a divorcée is denied communion; when the child of a prostitute is refused baptism; when an unlaicized priest is forbidden the sacraments. Jesus comes to the ungodly, even on Sunday morning."[5] The true saint, according to Manning, is Mary Magdalene, who would have died an insignificant hooker had it not been for the "fierce" and "transforming love" of Jesus Christ. She expected nothing and did nothing with her "religion." She merely had faith in the man who died for her and rose from the grave. "The confessing church of American ragamuffins needs to join Magdalene and Peter in witnessing that Christianity is not primarily a moral code but a grace-laden mystery; it is not essentially a philosophy of love but a love affair; it is not keeping rules with clenched fists but receiving a gift with open hands."[6]

Mullins, who died tragically in a late-night car accident in the fall of 1997, was Manning's friend and exemplar of the life according to grace. "He walked the way of the ragamuffin," Manning writes in the foreword to Mullins's biography. "His vivid awareness of his own brokenness made it existentially impossible to sit in judgment on the sins of others. Rich disdained money and material things and secretly gave away most of what he earned."[7] There is a tale about Mullins when he attended the Dove Awards—the Christian version of the Grammys—in Nashville and was seated along with other celebrities and dignitaries at dinner. Suddenly Mullins disappeared from his seat at the gathering and was nowhere to be found. Eventually he was located in the dining hall, working with the other busboys in clearing and stacking the plates from the table. Another anecdote relates how an employee for a recording studio sought eagerly to determine his whereabouts in order to inform him that one of his songs had topped the charts. Mullins was neither available nor interested. He had gone to Spain and was singing on street corners. Mullins was never comfortable with fortune and fame. He preferred the role of a lowly servant. In the biography Smith quotes one of Mullins's close friends, Beth Lutz, who says: "Rich put a face on grace."[8]

Mullins endeavored to emulate Francis of Assisi. Along with several college friends and musical associates, he actually tried to create something akin to a traveling Franciscan community, who took an unofficial vow of poverty, chastity, and obedience and regularly read from the writings of the saint.[9] Mullins believed in storing up treasures in heaven rather than on earth. In his personal relations as well as in his public statements and song lyrics, Mullins in the most radical way challenged both Christian literalism and legalism. He constantly stressed what the philosopher Kierkegaard had described as the task of "becoming" a Christian, as opposed to "being" a Christian. Becoming a Christian requires intense faith and spiritual discipline. It has little to do with intellectual conviction and even less with outward evidence of moral purity and perfection. Becoming a Christian, as Kierkegaard explained with irony, is not climbing a ladder of spiritual, let alone material, "success." It all comes down to submitting oneself constantly to God through confession of our failures and presumptions and in taking what Kierkegaard himself referred to as the "leap of faith," a leap into the fearful and unknown. Kierkegaard's paragon of faith was Abraham, who in hearing the morally incomprehensible demand of God to take his only son, Isaac, up to the summit of Mount Moriah and sacrifice him on an altar, did not flinch, but obeyed. For Kierkegaard, faith always requires what he called a "teleological suspension of the ethical," or a purposeful response to God's genuine demands in spite of what appears to us to be the theological norm. Kierkegaard, of course, is frequently the subject of commentary by postmodern philosophers.

RAGAMUFFIN MINISTRIES

Postmodern thinkers have adopted Kierkegaard as their prime mentor because of his abiding passion for truth and his realization, over a century before Derrida, that formal codes of argument and inference are innately incompatible with what he termed the "inwardness" of faith. Kierkegaard refused to call himself either a philosopher or a theologian. He called himself simply a writer. He regarded himself as a writer because all references to divine reality begin with the relationship between individuals and their God, in the struggle for self-revelation and personal authenticity, which the journey of faith entails. The life of sincere faith requires a profound humility and effacement of self exhibited in Manning's (and also Mullins's) "ragamuffin" lifestyle. Mullins testified that he was a Christian because he had "encountered God" in the many people who had "manifested (in many 'unreasonable' ways) His presence." He added: "I am a Christian, not because someone explained the nuts and bolts of Christianity to me, but because there were people who were willing to be nuts and bolts. Through their obedience to the truth and not necessarily through their explanation of it, they held it together so that I could experience it and be compelled to obey."[10]

Kierkegaard could not have phrased it better. *Postmodern ministry in large part is a ragamuffin ministry.* I myself have had the privilege of experiencing firsthand some real-life ragamuffin ventures of this ilk. One is a church comprised of twenty-somethings (and increasingly thirty-somethings, as time marches on) in Dallas, Texas. The other is a seminary in Seattle, Washington. Both have the same name, a New Testament name, which in a variety of senses has become a kind of emblem for postmodern ministry. The name is "Mars Hill," a reference to the site in Athens where the apostle Paul for the first time confronted the leading representatives of the cultural and intellectual elite of his day and sought to win them over to the gospel of Jesus Christ.

"Mars Hill" is an enduring symbol of both the clash of, and prospects of, rapprochement between faith and reason, or between the traditions of philosophy and the witness of the events of Easter morning. In the book of Acts we learn that Paul, while in Athens, was distressed by the prevalence of idol-worship in the city. So Paul regularly entered into the *agora,* or marketplace, on Mars' Hill and began debating with the Stoic and Epicurean philosophers who frequented the place. The philosophers accused him of proselytizing for "foreign divinities," an ancient expression for strange and barbarous forms of religious identification that the learned Greeks associated with anything other than the measured and skeptical discourse conforming to their cosmopolitan sensibilities. The notion of a resurrected Jewish messiah struck them not only as absurd, but as socially reprehensible. The Jews themselves had always been suspect because of their well-known "fanaticism." To maintain that someone be crucified and come to life again struck them as downright outrageous. They dismissed Paul as a "babbler," in other words, someone who just might have crossed the thin red line of dementia. But according to the author of Acts, they deigned to give Paul a polite audience because of their curiosity about what he might be saying. "Now the Athenians in general and the foreigners there had no time for anything but talking or hearing about the latest novelty."[11] In other words, they were willing to be entertained by an ancient showman for what today we might term "postmodernism."

Those of us who are conversant with Paul's speech at Mars' Hill know how he masterfully defused the anticipated assaults and cavils. "Men of Athens," Paul declaimed, "I see that in everything that concerns religion you are uncommonly scrupulous. For as I was going round looking at the objects of your worship, I noticed among other things an altar bearing the inscription—'To an Unknown God.' What you worship but do not know—that is what I now proclaim."[12] In other words, the "Unknown God" of the Greeks is in reality the living Creator and personal Savior who revealed himself to Abraham and Moses and became fully manifest in his Son Jesus.

The Mars Hill movement, as it may be loosely called, rides on the intuition that the unknown gods of contemporary culture do not have to be resisted so much as renamed, reclaimed, and redeemed. The putative nihilism of our post-Christian world cries out to be overcome by letting that world in on a little secret—the grandeur of a Christ who has hitherto remained unknown to Christians themselves, who is in Heidegger's words the quintessential "unthought thought."

The twentieth-century neoorthodox theologian H. Richard Niebuhr wrote an important book, quite influential in its day, entitled *Christ and Culture*.[13] In the book Niebuhr elaborated a historical typology of the varying relationships between Christ and culture that had been embraced by varying church figures and denominations in different eras. Niebuhr talked about "Christ against culture," the position of the early church father Tertullian, who perceived nothing good in anything that was Roman, pagan, or secular. He also described "Christ above culture"—the medieval view that art, morals, and philosophy are informed by a supernatural wisdom for which the church is the earthly custodian. The "Christ of culture" was instantiated in liberal Protestantism of the late-nineteenth century, he said, where the kingdom of God and Western middle-class society were pragmatically assimilated to each other. Niebuhr's final and normative category, however, was what he designated as "Christ the transformer of culture." On this model Christ is the principle that turns cultural dross into spiritual gold, the profane into the holy, the kingdom of this world into Christ's millennial reign.

Niebuhr's idea of Christ transforming culture conforms to none of the standard eschatologies that evangelicalism has embraced in the last few centuries. The concept can be characterized as neither premillennial, postmillennial, nor amillennial. It is simultaneously none and all of the above. Niebuhr tacitly identified the Christ of culture with postmillennialism. "Christ against culture" approximates premillennialism, which has been the dominant motif in evangelical theology for many generations now. But Niebuhr also gave short shrift to amillennialism (what Niebuhr dubbed "Christ and culture in paradox"), which in an important sense coincides with the older Reformation theology. Luther was basically unconcerned with end-of-the-world scenarios, as his disparagement of the importance of the book of Revelation indicates. Christ as the transformer of culture, nevertheless, indicates a kind of nonspecific eschatology in which the Holy Spirit is powerfully working in both private lives and corporate contexts, as both a prelude to, and a sign of, the return of the King of kings at an hour of which even the angels are unaware. Postmodern ministries and the Mars Hill movement, as we shall see, comport with this sort of soteriology. Christ does not renounce the fallen and chaotic culture of our times any more than he turned his back on the sinners, tax collectors, and profligates of his own day. But neither does he romanticize or acquiesce to it. The fluidity and rootlessness of postmodern culture is neither a curse nor a blessing. It is an opportunity unparalleled in history to boldly advance the gospel of grace.

A directory of churches on the World Wide Web offers as a simple caption for the Mars Hill Church in Dallas, Texas, the following three words—"coffee, couches, and conversation." For the most part the caption is accurate. The highlight of the church is its aisles of sofas, which function as pews during services and can be utilized for private conversations as well as beds for sleeping overnight on certain occasions. Mars Hill seeks to combine a casual, coffeehouse atmosphere with the feel of funky, bohemian-style hospitality. During the early years the church actually had a permanent live-in crew who slept there, cooked meals there, and ministered at times to homeless street people who would drop by to share their personal tragedies, talk about Jesus, and enjoy a hot meal. Mars Hill started in the late 1990s from a singles ministry called Fire by Night (FBN) at Metro Church in Garland, Texas—a typical large suburban congregation. According to former Mars Hill pastor David Anderson, the members of the singles ministry began to express themselves and their faith "a little differently":

> God led us to do art work, music, poems, and readings at our local Barnes and Noble. This gave us an opportunity to hang out and get to know individuals. As we used the arts to build common ground with people, God began to open the hearts of individuals to trust in Jesus. As people started their relationship with God, one of the things we tried to do is plug them into a local church near them. At the time one of the ideas was that we would do the outreach and the local church could carry the rest. Well, most of the individuals would come back to FBN saying this was their church. We had to adjust our ways so that we could start discipling individuals. As we made the adjustments, we felt the call to start a community, a community built on loving God and loving people.[14]

Why was the Mars Hill name selected? Anderson says:

> Of course Acts 17:16–34 is where we got the name. Our reason is, this is a generation that has it all. From palms to cars, books to movies. Everything and everyone has a reason for the season. We mix and pick what we want to believe. We can change who we want to look like. We can change how we are going to feel. In this environment we are called to be the church. Just as Paul says in Acts, this thing to the Unknown God, guess what, it's Jesus. All the things, experiences, and relationships—you still haven't found what you're looking for. It's Jesus. We identify with that, and we wanted a name that would identify us with that.

Anderson, who resigned in late 2003, does not envision what he calls "Mars" as a church. He sees it uniquely "as a family, . . . a community of individuals that understands what it means to love God. What it means to love people. What happens in family? Children grow up and go on their own and start their own family. Our vision is to be the church in the context of loving God and loving people. Some individuals will feel called to the mission fields, some to start a church, and some to grow old in this community. It's about Jesus and his love."[15]

At Mars Hill grace abounds, but it is not cheap grace. The church, large enough to be an established ministry and small enough to regard itself as a real extended family, accommodates itself readily to the bohemian lifestyles and unconventional dress of urban, and what a half century ago we casually referred to as "alienated," young adults. But it brooks no compromise with the self-destructive habits of those Generation-Xers who have been brought up to believe there are no standards to be respected, even from God's point of view.

Like the early church and later the Franciscans and the Salvation Army, who demanded that their followers be radically "in" but not "of" the world, the Mars Hill Church reaches out with open arms to street people, drug addicts, and the sexually promiscuous. But at the same time it insists upon the same kind of Christian virtues and self-discipline that the Franciscans were famous for. Anderson—who himself found Jesus at a moment of crisis after having been raised as a Buddhist (his mother's family is Korean) and then turning to the occult—knows how easy it is to succumb to the seductions of a pathologically tolerant contemporary society and tumble down the rabbit hole of addiction, libertinism, and self-loathing; thus he is probably more an advocate of personal holiness than were even the leading lights of the Holiness movement in the late-nineteenth century. The majority of Mars Hill members take part in weekly "accountability" sessions, where they disclose to each other, sometimes in emotional and poignant terms, their recent fears and failings while serving as a support circle for each other. "Accountability partners," as they characterize themselves, help each other to search their own consciences and offer encouragement in their walk with Christ.

The Mars Hill Graduate School is located twenty miles northeast of downtown Seattle, Washington, in a high-tech office park. Having begun in 1997 as a satellite campus of Western Theological Seminary in Portland, Oregon, the graduate department became an independent school in 2002 with a mission that is unparalleled not just among evangelical institutions, but in theological education overall. According to the catalog, "the mission of Mars Hill

Graduate School (MHGS) is to train people to be competent in the study of the Scriptures, the human soul, and the culture. To that end MHGS seeks to prepare professionals and others who desire to obey Christ's commission to serve in the fields of ministry, counseling, and spiritual direction and the arts."

MHGS views its mission as "unique in its emphasis and interdisciplinary study." The curriculum seeks to "equip future church leaders in their efforts to minister to a postmodern, post-Christian culture." If postmodernism has historically been associated with strange and even "heretical" formulations of the Christian message, MHGS defies that stereotype. Its statement of doctrine is about as orthodox as they come. According to the "teaching position" outlined in the catalog, Mars Hill affirms not only the wording of the Nicene and Chalcedonian creeds; it also adopts the classic stance of Reformed theology. "We believe that sinners are justified by the grace of God through faith alone in Christ alone, apart from works." The teaching position even takes a stance on the reality of the devil. "We believe in the personality of Satan, the true enemy and accuser of Christians, who was defeated at the cross and will one day be consigned to the lake of fire."

Dan Allender, president of Mars Hill and a well-known author and popular lecturer on Christian counseling, envisions MHGS as training clergy how to validate the power and truth of the gospel by deploying what they have learned in intense situations. The problem with evangelical Christianity, Allender insists, is not that it is too wedded to the traditional wording and communication of the "evangel"—the good news of Christ having died for us—or that the thrust of that "old-time religion" is inappropriate to "postmodern culture," as liberals often object. The difficulty resides in the fact that it does not recognize "how blended modernism is with evangelical Christianity."

According to Allender, modernism is deficient because of its preoccupation with self-certitude at the expense of deferral to otherness. As Heidegger has proposed, modernism actually turns Hellenic metaphysics upside down through the reification of the cognitive apparatus of the human self. Modernism dwells on the perdurance of the "substance" that is the rational ego. Modern evangelicalism has distorted the Reformation maxim of "faith alone" by transforming it into the self-referential notion of a logically consistent biblical text as the "metaphysical" scaffolding for a philosophically incontestable God. Such a rational "faith" is not really faith at all. Faith does not require any kind of unimpeachable demonstration. It is a passion for God amid the contingencies of experience and the messiness of life in general. The early

Christians did not sell all their possessions and set out along the highways and byways of the Roman Empire because they had acquired compelling and ample forensic evidence that Jesus had indeed overcome death and the grave. What the apostles proclaimed at the peril of torture and execution was in no way philosophically persuasive—it was intrinsically ridiculous. "A great portion of my faith," says Allender, "is built on breaking down Aristotle's notion of essential and accidental. The accidental is a louder voice of God. Postmodernism gives me a calling to see how God loves the bizarre. The incarnation is bizarre. The Lord's table is freaking bizarre."[16]

Mars Hill Graduate School is a "ragamuffin" institution, if the label "institution" sticks at all. The school is not about giving students the intellectual tools to develop a more "mature" and solid understanding of their faith. It is about putting faith to the test, about submitting oneself to deep doubts and anxieties that challenge those who have an all-too-comfortable faith. Allender says rather pointedly, "If hard questions are asked, inevitably you will enter into heartache. Academic institutions are fundamentally concerned with making sure students and professors do not have heartache." Ministerial education should be "porous," according to Allender. One's intellectual and religious presuppositions should be liquid and in continual flux, although faith should remain the true constant. God is revealed most dramatically and poignantly in the midst of confusion and personal breakdown. "He shows himself in the midst of heartache. If you want hope, it does not come through control but through dependence and fragmentation."

When one actually attempts "to teach that in an academic institution," one flies in the face of the "Aristotelian" paradigm. Theological education seeks to prevent fragmentation. It strives to mold and regiment learners into a culture of scholastic self-sufficiency. Athens and Jerusalem are inextricably entangled with each other, and fatefully confused. The gospel says that we should "lose" our lives and selves, that we should take up our crosses, that the last will be first, and the first will be last. But modernism, which historically represents the revival of Hellenism that began with the Renaissance, preaches the opposite. Higher education does not want students to be servants, but "masters." On the other hand, "it's really about being a servant in theology, but who wants a degree in servanthood?" Allender quips that when MHGS was formed, "We wanted a structure that could destructure itself ongoingly. We wanted an institution that did not take itself so seriously that the experts could train the naive ones to become masters. Our desire was to create an institution to honor truth by admitting it doesn't know much at all."[17]

THE NEW EVANGELICAL COUNTERCULTURE

The rhetoric is curiously reminiscent of the religious changes that many gurus of the 1960s described a generation ago. At that time the youthful baby boomers were rebelling against hierarchy, authoritarianism, denomination-alism, aridity in theology, and self-righteousness in Christian morality. The preoccupation with a Jesus who challenges authority, is hip and culturally radical, and hangs out with the wrong kinds of people was widespread in mainline Protestant seminaries, urban ministries, and pop cultural phenomena such as the musical *Jesus Christ Superstar.*

The long-term religious changes in baby-boomer religion have been chronicled and analyzed by Wade Roof, a historian of American social and religious history:

> The postwar generation grew up with pluralism of all forms—cultural, religious, lifestyle. Its members were not exposed, except possibly as young children, to the religious culture that the preceding generation of Americans had known as constituting the core of the American experience; instead, boomers came into adulthood at a time when the "mainline" Protestant churches were losing their hegemony over the culture and were competing with other faiths for a place in the sun. After the 1960s, and after Vietnam and Watergate in particular, the old normative faiths linking public and private piety had fallen upon hard times. Hence, as adults, the new generation has not known a strong religious center in American life. Religion was whatever one chose as one's own, whether of the denominational Protestant, Catholic, or Jewish variety.[18]

Writing a decade ago, Roof profiled changes in American religion itself that started in the 1960s but took almost thirty years to become a broader trend. A thorough reshaping of religious community is also underway. "It is these qualities that boomers look for—sharing, caring, accepting, belonging. The qualities themselves often are more important than the places where they find them: People find others with similar concerns while car pooling children to Sunday school, but also in Adult Children of Alcoholics meetings."[19]

Roof generalizes about the baby boomers, but Generation-Xers have taken what in the 1960s was simply called "the movement" into a new dimension. That new dimension is evangelical Christianity—not modernist evangelicalism with its insistence on cultural and intellectual "correctness," but postmodernist evangelicalism with its "ragamuffinness." Many of the baby boomers found their spirituality early on in drugs, sexual indulgence, and foreign or esoteric styles of religious practice, often branded "cults" a few years back; the Xers are turning to Jesus, and they are doing it in a serious way. The cultural and religious radicalism of the boomers has now ossified at many levels into the political correctness and neoliberal orthodoxies of the mainline Protestant churches. But young evangelical Christians with their third-world mission trips, interracial and multicultural music, and outreach to the poor and marginalized in America's cities, are readapting in a more serious spiritual way the "freak" ethic of the 1960s that the boomers with their "establishment" jobs and lifestyles have long abandoned. Is it generational change? Or is it the gospel? Not the theological gospel, but the ragamuffin one?

As scholars of American religion have noted, every wave of revivalism, or burnt-over district, engenders a new generation purposefully dedicated to cleaning up their act and adopting the opposite stride of their forebears. The 1960s may have been a time of moral and religious anarchy, but the kids who came of age in the 1990s often have seemed as ferociously bent on bringing back a hip and postmodern version of the old-time religion as their parents were on declaring God's death. Unlike their parents, they have been able to separate garden-variety Christian culture from the gospel of Christ. The nontraditional couture, music, and worship environments, although they can easily become as conventional as what was always associated in people's minds with "church" over a generation ago, actually are essential for clearing a wider and more informal space where new kinds of relationships, mutual honesty, and spiritual energy can be augmented.

Postmodernism, therefore, may at one level be regarded as an invitation to draw Christianity in general, and the church specifically, back to its beginnings. In the same way that the Reformation of the sixteenth century viewed itself as an effort toward recovering the mood and mind-set of the primitive church, so also the Next Reformation will focus on abolishing all the baroque trappings of the mode of Protestantism that moved into the breach after the call of Luther and Calvin for a less-worldly and culture-bound *ekklēsia* was coopted within a century by squires and princes.

In his book *A New Kind of Christian,* Brian D. McLaren argues that today's evangelicalism is dangerously and fatefully joined at the hip with the modernist worldview, or at least the world picture that became dominant and unassailable between the late-seventeenth and early-twentieth centuries. Churches are run like factory production facilities, churning out boilerplate Christian identities and personalities with efficiency and precision in response to the mass consumer demand for a safe, simple, and not-too-pricey faith product. Because the history of modernity has coincided with the age of book publishing and its bias toward linear thinking and logic, Protestant Christianity especially has tended toward bibliolatry, the worship of the holy and "iner-rant" book instead of the living Christ, whose life and presence the printed pages manifest.[20] The modernist Christ is as different from the postmodernist Christ as the Byzantine icon of *Christus Victor* enthroned on the rainbow was from the fifteenth-century depictions of the *Man of Sorrows*.

In another book subtitled *The Language of the Emerging Church*, which McLaren coauthored with Leonard Sweet and Jerry Haselmayer, McLaren maintains that the postmodern church needs more than a new image. It requires a whole different vocabulary. The authors employ the expressions "postmodern culture" and "emergent culture" equivalently. The emergent culture of the third millennium is what he terms "life on the edge." It is a fluid as well as an incessantly self-transforming and self-organizing entity. Ministering in the context of postmodern culture demands a flexibility and openness that Christian modernists have actively resisted.

Modernists seek solid and secure foundations for their deliberations in addition to clear and decisive options. Modern philosophical epistemology, inaugurated by Descartes, replaced classical authoritarianism with the ideal of "authorship." Deference to the unimpeachable will of God, the monarch, or the liege lord is replaced by the sovereignty of individual conscience and the preeminence of personal choice. As social and political historians have noted, the modern period is the advent of the idea of "inalienable rights" of the individual, including life, liberty, and property. The notion of "intel-lectual property" becomes increasingly important because it implies that the "author" of a text or an invention is the only true authority.

In the postmodern setting, however, individualism and *author-ity* become less significant than what Sweet, McLaren, and Haselmayer term "connectiv-ity." We experience the "self as a part of others." In the future the basic unit of human experience "is not the isolated individual, not the communal collective, but the interdependent collective. The more interdependent we become the more important our individual uniqueness becomes. The interplay of the individual and the interdependent yields a third entity: the connective self." They conclude: "Postmodern people seek new ways of fitting together, not of fitting in."[21]

In many ways the idiom is the sociology of the post-1960s counterculture applied to evangelical Christianity decades later. In the 1970s this kind of analysis found popular expression in such best-selling books as Theodore Roszak's *The Making of a Counterculture* and Alvin Toffler's *Future Shock*, in the early 1980s in Marilyn Ferguson's *The Aquarian Conspiracy* and John Naisbitt's *Megatrends,* and to a certain extent in what came to be called the New Age movement. The common thread that runs through all these popular writings is the dizzying pace of contemporary social and intellectual change, the erosion of traditional moral absolutes, the demise of organized religion as we know it, and the proliferation of consumer choices not just for material goods, but also for spiritual values, symbols, and ideas. Toffler and Ferguson, in particular, cited an ongoing shift in the operative paradigms of both physics and psychology to legitimize this new approach. The emphasis was always on the mobility of lifestyles and the preference for process over substance.

In cataloging what they regard as the ABCs of the "emerging church," Sweet, McLaren, and Haselmayer talk about the prevalence of "choice culture." Choice culture means that we are constantly in flux and self-transformation through an endless decision-making process. Choice culture is the nub of postmodernism. "Moderns," according to the authors, tend to say with Descartes, "I think, therefore I am." But "postmoderns" proclaim: "I choose, therefore I become." Postmodern culture is the same as choice culture. "You and I are the sum of our choices. The essence of the postmodern Renaissance [is] the right to define ourselves by the choices we make. We can choose what to put on our CDs. We can choose what to experience in life. We can choose what age we want to appear."[22]

There is no strategy or formula for postmodern ministry, the authors avow. One of the difficulties with their treatment of the topic is perhaps that it puts too much emphasis on faith as a form of cultural adaptation rather than as a form of cultural transformation. In that sense it plays into the clutches of some of postmodernism's most ferocious critics. Postmodern ministry makes an accession, albeit with an incisive spiritual awareness, to the endless surging of the tides of contemporary life that seem to propel us in countless directions and at times dash us against the seawall. We had better learn to swim, as the famous Dylan song of the 1960s exhorted us, or we will sink "like a stone." But the authors' hearts are in the right place. They stress that postmodern ministry does not amount to becoming postmodern, or converting everyone else to postmodernist styles of thought and speech. Postmodern ministry involves learning to be comfortable in preaching the gospel among the postmoderns, just as Paul was among the Cilicians, the Ephesians, the Corinthians, and the Romans.

Is postmodernism "amongness"? And, if so, what would that mean? Does it mean a totally immanent spirituality in which we all are somehow rewired to celebrate whatever, or whoever, we mean by God within the whirl and hubbub of a fast and furious world? Following the cue of the immensely popular movie (and now its sequels) by the same name, Sweet, McLaren, and Haselmayer describe postmodernism as a "matrix moment" for the church.

They cite Paul in 2 Corinthians as a theological uptake on what is happening around us. "Our eyes are fixed, not on the things that are seen, but on the things that are unseen: for what is seen passes away; what is unseen is eternal."[23] Postmodernity is the exposure of the flux that engulfs us, but it is also the realization that this vast panorama of fragmentation, instability, and discontinuity can be an opening to redemption. Postmodernity is all our doubts supersized, but it also is all the raw sinews of faith stretched out like a taut drum. At first glance the prospect appears both repugnant and frightening. Yet such recoil can become the true matrix moment. In the movie the main protagonist "had to decide whether to pledge allegiance to the world that was familiar and safe—a digitally simulated dream world called the matrix—or a scary, nonillusory real world that could only be met with courage and saving love."

The matrix moment is the choice of choices for the postmodern knight of faith, the new Christian spiritual adventurer in these putatively post-Christian times. It is akin, according to Sweet, McLaren, and Haselmayer, to the trek up Moriah. "Which power is your life and your church living out of—the power of the invisible or the power of the visible?"[24] The uncertainty of the visible, including our visible representations of the invisible, our modernist idolatries, is what draws us near into that invisible space. For indeed, "faith gives substance to our hopes, and makes us certain of realities we do not see."[25] *Postmodern ministry is about sheer, unconstrained faith-walking.*

One of the problems with the rising currency of the expression "postmodern ministry" in evangelical churches is that it often refers more to style than to substance. Postmodern ministry is a meaningless construct if it signifies little more than featuring youthful worship leaders with earrings and nose piercings who wear baggy pants on stage and dim the lights in the fellowship hall in order to replicate a coffeehouse ambience. That is simply one more up-to-date, flamboyant example of the Christ of culture. Postmodern ministry is the mobilization of the ragamuffin spirit that demands certainty in neither its concepts, its commitments, nor the outcome of its conversations. Postmodern ministry is reaching out, to modify slightly the old Star Trek motto, where no one has reached before.

THE NEW EVANGELICAL FRONTIER

Po'ministry (to coin a term for "postmodern ministry") occupies a space where—in the words of Sweet, McClaren, and Haselmayer—"boundaries have been replaced by frontiers." A frontier, of course, is not the same as a no-man's-land. Nor is it a twilight zone, as the antipomo (antipostmodern) crowd have often made it out to be. A frontier can be delimited, but it cannot be circumscribed. It has no fence, but it does have a perimeter. A frontier is on the edge, but it is not out of the end zone. The vigor of American evangelical Christianity was always to be confirmed on the frontier, as suggested by the memories of circuit riders and hilltop, on-the-verge-of-the-forest camp meetings in the early decades of the nation. No one could play it safe there. A journal entry by a Methodist bishop from the year 1811 describes with great empathy and clarity the frontier revival meeting:

> The glare of the blazing camp-fires falling on a dense assemblage . . . and reflected back from long ranges of tents upon every side; hundreds of candles and lamps suspended among the trees, together with numerous torches flashing to and fro, throwing an uncertain light upon the tremulous foliage, and giving the appearance of dim and indefinite extent to the depth of the forest; the solemn chanting of hymns swelling and falling on the night wind; the impassioned exhortations; the earnest prayers; the sobs, the shrieks, or shouts, bursting from persons under intense agitation of mind; the sudden spasms which seize upon scores, and unexpectedly dashed them to the ground; all conspired to invest the scene with terrific interest, and to work up the feelings to the highest pitch of excitement.[26]

Finney and the revivalists of his day understood that rhetorical intensity and the aesthetics of worship have a lot more to do with prompting conversion than the forcefulness of apologetics. This same spookiness the journalist conveys in sketching the night scene at the frontier camp meeting compares with what might be written today about postmodern worship and prayer assemblies.

When I laid eyes for the first time on the worship room of the Mars Hill Church, I thought for a second I had entered a time warp and blundered into some den of countercultural depravity such as I remembered from my student ministries days in San Francisco's Haight-Ashbury District. The darkened room was cluttered with all sorts of incongruous and unchurchlike paraphernalia, including a baseball bat, a folding Oriental screen, and low, battered wooden tables on which had been left half-consumed cups of coffee. There was no altar, only a lighted candelabra and an urn of smoking incense, which filled up the room with pungent odors of sandalwood. Above the screen were half-completed oil paintings on plywood with images that looked more like the lush graffiti slapped on New York City subway trains than any type of self-conscious art. The worshippers were praying silently in the candlelight. Every now and then one of the leaders would pluck a steel string on an electric guitar.

Then Pastor Dave, who had been sitting barefooted on the floor, quietly rose and began to comment earnestly on Paul's Epistle to the Ephesians. It was neither a sermon nor a Bible lesson. It was what Mars Hill calls "habitat," an impromptu but extended tête-à-tête between the church members and its leadership, which compassed meditation, confession, exposition of relevant scriptural passages, and personal revelation. It was "church," but it was not a "service." There was neither sermon nor liturgy. The focus was on the intensity of interpersonal communication, in which Pastor Dave is skilled in both formal and informal venues.

MESSAGE AND MEDIUM

As Robert Webber notes in his reflections on "postmodern worship," the underlying theme is the fusion of medium and message. Postmodern Christianity is ultimately about "communication," he says. In postmodern ministry "we are rediscovering the significance of oral forms of communication through the restoration of worship as a drama to be experienced, and we are drawing once again from the insights of medieval visual communication. We now live in an audiovisual age, a time when people want to 'see it,' 'taste it,' 'smell it,' 'touch it,' and 'feel it.'"[27]

The audiovisual age is at the same time the multisensory age. It is increasingly the age in which media and the real world are indistinguishable, and where human experience itself is routinely configured by what Mark C. Taylor terms "imagologies"—alluvial planes of sensory data that double as our daily thoughts and recall and have the semblance of patterns of thought, when in fact they are figments of electronic communications. Constantly we are bombarded with messages that induce us in the direction of other messages. We catch sight of billboards along the interstate, surf innumerable channels on television in our living room, listen to songs on the radio, watch music videos, play the VCR and flip through segments with our DVDs, turn on talk radio as we drive to work in the morning, learn how to garden or refinish furniture by inserting a CD in our computers. These visual signs and texts constantly override and seep into our cognitive activities.

Pundits of media culture from Marshall McLuhan to Neal Postman have made the point that media is no longer a secondary phenomenon to the "real world," if that ever was the situation. Media does not mirror reality. Nor does it necessarily "create" reality. More often than not it is reality. That is not necessarily as terrible as it sounds at first blush. The awe-inspiring vaults and flying buttresses of Gothic cathedrals were instrumental, not ancillary, to the propagation and reinforcement of belief in the High Middle Ages. The stained-glass windows were media, and they had an awesome effect on people's spirituality. They also inspired the metaphors for scholastic philosophy as a soaring architecture, like Coventry and Chartres, of "natural reason" pulling us upward to the majesty of God and the splendor of heaven.

The simplicity of books and other forms of print media along with the spread of literacy reversed this process and fostered the sentiment of democratic community and the importance of voluntary associations (in the churches that meant the multiplication of denominations) as the bulwark of modern civilization. Evangelical critics of postmodern ministry need to recognize that one can no longer evangelize through outdated means of communication and modes of association. Changing the medium in one sense does change the message, but Christ is both medium and message throughout the ages. He has always been. Modernists tend to hold on to the metaphysical supposition that the message is the medium. For postmodernists the medium is the message, because they discern that there is no real separation of medium and message, or message and medium. Medium and message comprise an ongoing historical two-step. *But Christ is the music.*

As the historian Jacques Barzun comments at the opening of his masterful history of the last five centuries *From Dawn to Decadence,* modernity began with a "revolution" that is "commonly called the Protestant Reformation."[28] Barzun reiterates the customary historical platitudes concerning what exactly was the Protestant Reformation. It was anticlerical. It was inspired by a stubborn and combative German monk who fanned the flames of Teutonic nationalism against a new Roman Empire that once again had grown absolutist and decadent at the same time. It would not have been possible without the invention of the printing press. It succeeded because the territorial sovereigns were at last confident enough to openly challenge the distant, imperial pretenders. But Barzun offers an insight that has rarely been urged as a summary judgment of the Reformation of the sixteenth century as a whole.

The Reformation began, according to Barzun, when Luther realized what the Word of God was really all about. Before Luther it had been about the authority of the "inerrant" church to interpret Scripture and to bestow the sacraments as the agency of salvation. But in rationalizing the entire administration of God in the personal, social, and moral spheres of life, the church had abandoned the mystery of Christ, which Christianity without qualification all boils down to. "The mystery was God's bestowal of grace."[29]

If the "revolution" of modernity began with such a singular recognition, cannot the shattering of the now sclerotic modern consciousness with the new postmodern sensitivity be about grace as well? Was Christ a "nihilist" because he unstintingly and heatedly attacked the Pharisees, trustees of the piety and probity of their day? Was he a "relativist" because he supped with sinners and tax collectors, or defended an adulteress who was about to be stoned according to the godly standards of first-century Judea? Jesus was accused of everything modernists accuse postmodernists of today—consorting with demons, being a drunkard and a party animal, behaving in an insane fashion, and having certain megalomaniacal fantasies about his "messianic" role as the Son of Man.

One needs "foundations" in order to uphold the law. But one requires the "shaking of foundations" in order to experience grace. For foundationalists and legalists, grace is a rather disturbing event. If Manning, Mullins, and McLaren are right on target, as I believe they are, then the Next Reformation, like the last one, is all about grace. It is *a revolution of grace*. Luther is reported to have exhorted his followers to "sin boldly." That attribution is generally taken out of context. But it emphasizes a discovery that Luther—who until his "revelation" of "grace" was completely obsessed like Paul with his inability to live the proper Christian life—tacitly made. We cannot know the power of grace until we truly understand the bondage of sin. We have to accept that our striving to be sinless (one may substitute here the expressions "morally pure" or "theologically correct") is what lays sin bare in the first place.

Sometimes we have to walk as far as the Lord will allow into the darkness of the world in order to experience the power of grace. The word "grace" comes from the Latin *gratia*, which means "gift," and is the equivalent of the Greek *charisma*. From that Greek term we derive a word that is often misunderstood in modernist Christianity—the word "charismatic."

8

DANCING WITH THE LORD

Charismatic Renewal and the Deconstruction of Worship

THE DANCE

There is a Methodist hymn about Jesus that goes: "I am the Lord of the dance, said he." In *Thus Spoke Zarathustra,* Nietzsche's own philosophical *Gesamtkunstwerk,* the theme of dancing is paramount. Zarathustra is not a prophet. Nor is he a teacher. He is a dancer. Nietzsche was ambivalent about the relationship of Jesus to Zarathustra. Nietzsche could only imagine the "Christian-moral view" of Jesus, which refused to dance, like Baptists for so long. Dancing is one of the root metaphors of postmodernity. It is not only an art form; it is also signification in motion. Music cannot be codified by Indo-European grammar; it cannot be "thought." But dancing is the sound of music combined with the performance and energy of the body. In the history of religion dancing has regularly been integrated into worship. It can be utilized for an expression of pagan and sensual rhythms, but it can also give form to the sensuous ecstasy of having come face-to-face with the most awesome God. When one is in the presence of the God of faith, one cannot easily sit still. Even at the risk of ridicule by his jealous wife, David danced before the Lord. The Scriptures indicate that Jesus might have danced. It appears that Paul did. Jews have never been ashamed of dancing. We can imagine what it means to dance "before" God. But what about "dancing with the Lord"?

It is the night of winter solstice in the late 1990s. I am in an abandoned movie theater in Grand Prairie, Texas. The metaphor of theater is telling. The theater serves as the regular gathering place for what I will call Eagles' Wings Church—a small band of Spirit-filled Christians, the majority of whom are African-American. They do not really know much about who I am. I have been invited to the meeting by one in the group who has come to know me. I am simply "Brother Carl." That is all that matters to them. Their hearts are open.

I have come to a gathering of the "church family," or simply "the body," as they call themselves. They are assembled in the pastor's office—a small, but brightly lit anteroom to this massive cathedral of the open heart. The name of the church is taken from an oft-recited passage in Isaiah. "They will soar on wings like eagles; they will run and not grow weary, they will walk and not be faint."[1] The inscription is embossed in silver lettering on the pastor's leather-bound Bible.

It is well below freezing on this North Texas night, and in the unheated auditorium where biweekly services are held, a chill enfolds the dimly lit seats and altar. Yet it is cheering and warm inside the office, where the body is gathered. This austere chamber bears comparison with the setting of an event known as the Azusa Street Revival, which took place in 1906 in Los Angeles, the City of the Angels. There an African-American preacher named C. H. Mason with no theological training began preaching that a "Second Pentecost" or "latter-day rain" of the Holy Spirit was suddenly about to descend, that a New Jerusalem was arising in the desert of Southern California. Mason, a minister of the Holiness denomination Church of God in Christ, was influenced by Apostle William Seymour, who began speaking in tongues on April 9 and ignited the revival.

By fifty years later in America, what happened on Azusa Street had ignited what came to be known first as "Pentecostalism" and later as "the charismatic movement." The movement initially swept through the lower social classes of the South and Midwest, gradually petered out, then revived in the aftermath of the Vietnam upheaval among middle-class Episcopalians, and suddenly emerged as a global force in third-world evangelism, particularly in Latin America. Statistically, Christianity today is the fastest growing religion in the world, having recently outpaced Islam. And charismatic Christianity—the Holy Spirit movement—is the fastest growing segment of Christianity. Currently there are over 400 million charismatics worldwide. In 1906, when the

Pentecostal revival first hit America, charismatics were less than 1 percent of the world's Christians. Today they are 25 percent.[2] The popularity of the motion picture *The Apostle*—which deals with the life of a white, Pentecostal preacher in East Texas and Louisiana—suggests a growing, mainstream interest in the topic. The movie is a quite authentic rendering of rural charismatic practices and points up the dramatic and intensely personal character of the religion's lifestyle.

The impact of charismatic Christianity, on the other hand, has been largely felt in the third world, and Latin America in particular. Like a prairie tornado spinning with immense force, it has torn through and shaken the foundations of Roman Catholicism. But the transformation of Catholicism has also swept into the United States on the crest of the new immigrant waves from Central and South America. Along the Gulf Coast Freeway in Houston, Texas—the port of entry for mass immigration from Spanish-speaking lands in the 1990s that can be compared only to New York City with its "huddled masses" a century ago—a megacenter for charismatic outreach to newcomers from the south has been established. Approximately eight hundred thousand people in Houston—a quarter of the city's population—are Catholic. Most immigrants in South Texas, however, do not attend church, but they do come regularly to the Catholic Charismatic Center, which is located near the University of Houston. "The Mass is the same; the people are different," says Richard Paulissen, a sixty-five-year-old priest who has been active for a quarter century in the Catholic charismatic renewal movement.[3]

But the movement has also sent tremors through the Protestant churches in America, especially across the Bible Belt. In the United States much of the so-called New Christianity has no denominational currency or structure of institutional authority and is charismatic. Peter Wagner, a former professor of church growth at Fuller Theological Seminary in Pasadena, California, coined the term "postdenominationalism" to typify what was happening. He also originated the term "third wave of the Holy Spirit" to describe the new charismatics. Wagner himself is a charismatic who was at one time a missionary to Bolivia and a dispensationalist. He has been instrumental in popularizing and providing a theological take on the new charismatics. The New Christian fellowships can be found sprouting up everywhere—in abandoned strip malls, in vacant warehouses, in roadside office suites, on docks and in shipping bays, wherever the gales of global commerce have spent their fury and the "new wind of the Spirit," as the prophets in the movement call it, is starting to blow. The new fellowships are no longer the bailiwick of the conventional Pentecostal churches, such as the Assemblies of God, the Church of God, or the Church of God in Christ, which came into existence (or were Pentecostalized) early in this century in the train of the Azusa Street phenomenon and drew predominantly white, blue-collar adherents. More often than not, these fellowships draw upon suburban and upscale evangelical Christians who have grown disaffected with both the moralism and the lockstep political preoccupations of mainstream conservative denominations.[4] The charismatic movement is not about politics, or theology for that matter, notes Harvard professor Harvey Cox, who has written one of the major sociological studies of the charismatic movement. It is about the "experience of God."[5]

Seated beside the pastor this evening is Brother Danny, a lanky, genial, and soft-spoken African-American who works in Grand Prairie as a coach and community sports director. On his right is Brother Gene, a diminutive black man with the gift of prophecy. And at his side is his wife Rosemarie, a well-dressed woman with a round face and an engulfing smile, who is always out front to greet newcomers to Eagles' Wings and to offer them Texas hospitality, whenever the occasion should arise. Finally, there is Brother P. T., the organist. If it were not for P. T.'s "celestial" touch on the ivory keys, the billows of praise and worship that roll through the sanctuary every Sunday and Wednesday would be far less awe-evoking and consequential.

When "God is moving in the service," according to the pastor, P. T.'s organ music—best described as a medley of Verdi's orchestra scores and New Orleans jazz—fills up the sanctuary like a cloud of glory. There have been times when I have witnessed P. T.'s fingers racing back and forth across the double-tiered keyboard in complete synchrony with the pastor's delivery. The action of the Holy Spirit within the body is like a complex ballet scene, according to the minister, whom I shall call Pastor Ferris. Each worshipper promenades with specific rhythms and routines to create an invisible cotillion of the spiritual life. Each day of worship is a new design script, a different "dance," from God's point of view. God gives silent direction to each participant and "deals with them," says Pastor Ferris, in deference to the longing of the hearts and their willingness to be "available" for whatever purpose the Holy One has in mind. The entire episode is one spare moment, one sliver of time, in a process that is increasingly repeated Sunday after Sunday in upstart congregations around the globe. Pastor Ferris terms it "the choreography of the Spirit." Each believer has his or her own steps to take, which are only the steps directed by the Lord of the dance himself. The Lord is the choreographer. He initiates the pattern of movement. Every worshipper must learn to be completely receptive to the Lord's promptings, to become "available" to go where God will take him or her on that day.

The metaphors are somatic, elusive, aesthetic. There is no liturgical formula or traditional theology to account for what is happening in the charismatic movement. According to sociologist of religion Thomas J. Csordas, "Charismatic religion as a religion is highly adaptable to postmodern forms."[6] We might take that observation one step further and assert that it is the essential nature of postmodern Christianity. Charismatic Christianity, like postmodern culture, is a dance of signs within the darkened amphitheater of migrant peoples we know as "global civilization." But it is an old-fashioned sort of dance, a dance that requires careful coordination between partners, a dance of delicate sensibilities and elegantly dressed performers, like the rondo, the waltz, or the samba. It is not a dance between equals. It is "dancing with the Lord."

BIBLICAL AND HISTORICAL BACKGROUND

> This is the testimony which John gave when the Jews of Jerusalem sent a deputation of priests and Levites to ask him who he was. He confessed without reserve and avowed, "I am not the Messiah." "What then? Are you Elijah?" "No," he replied. . . .
>
> "I baptize in water," John replied, "but among you, though you do not know him, stands the one who is to come after me. . . ."
>
> John testified further: "I saw the Spirit coming down from heaven like a dove and resting upon him. I did not know him, but he who sent me to baptize in water had told me, 'When you see the Spirit coming down upon someone and resting upon him, you will know that this is he who is to baptize in Holy Spirit.' I saw it myself, and I have borne witness. This is God's Chosen One."[7]

Few evangelical theologians have made much out of this Gospel's statement from John the Baptist that the Spirit "rested" on Jesus. Even fewer scholars have asked the question what such a statement means with respect to the unending controversy concerning who Jesus of Nazareth was, and in what sense he was, and is, and will be forever "divine." This omission is not in any way indicative of the failures of the church or of Christian theology. On the contrary, it may be a true indicator of "the end," a chasm that cannot be bridged until the close of days, a blind spot in the vision of believers that hides the fullness of God's presence, to be revealed only with the grand flash of eschatological lightning.

Or perhaps it is a simple matter of not having entertained until now the thought of the "power" of the Holy Spirit. In early church doctrine the Holy Spirit was always a source of perplexity. The church fathers identified the Holy Spirit as the "third person" of the Trinity at the Council of Nicaea, but that development did little to clarify what believers at the time really meant by the term. Most theological reflection in the ancient Greco-Roman world centered on the relationship between Jesus the man and Jesus as "God's Son." The peoples of the Mediterranean basin could understand very well the paradoxical notion of the Word made flesh. They had a more difficult time grasping what the Latin church called *Spiritus Creator:* the idea that the incarnation of God continued beyond the disciples' sighting of Jesus after the resurrection, that the word was becoming ever more present in the world and in the flesh as time wore on, and that new followers were being baptized into Christ.

What must have baffled the early theologians was the biblical treatment of the Spirit as God's elusive presence. Pagan thought struggled with the iconoclastic, or nonpictorial, character of Christian spirituality. To the heathen mind God always had form—whether it be a statue of Zeus or the vision of a goddess in the secret, nocturnal ceremonies of the time known as the mystery religions. The notion that Jesus, as the church officially put it, was both "fully God and fully man" was easy to accept. The ancient Greeks had long believed in divine, or semidivine, heroes who were simultaneously deity and humanity. Since the days of the poet Homer, who lived about 850 B.C., the Greeks had perceived "divinity" as a play of ethereal images and forms, as an exchange of visible signs and invisible realities.[8] In his musings on the "paradox" of the incarnation, Kierkegaard rightly discerned that the union of divine and human was logically impossible. He also recognized that the inner core of Christian faith was thoroughly alien to the pagan mind. In *The Sickness unto Death* Kierkegaard declared that it is the "Spirit" who conjoins, even if it does not unite, the opposite poles of time and eternity. It is noteworthy, however, that Kierkegaard did not come anywhere close to discerning the Holy Spirit that John the evangelist's Jesus describes: "A little while, and you will not see me; again a little while, and you will see me."[9]

Charismatic theology teaches that the "early rain" of the Spirit took place during the first century. The "latter rain" is now beginning to fall from the heavens, an indicator that the harvest is ready and that Christ's return is imminent. The "Christian era" that began with the conversion of the emperor Constantine in the fourth century, in which the church militant became the "church triumphant," has actually been a long dry time, according to charismatic theologians. While the church experienced a millennium and a half of worldly dominion, its spiritual roots withered and its fruit dried on the vine.

The Choreography of Spirit

Worship in the Spirit is not the same as "practicing religion." The choreography of the Spirit is as free-form as the music played at Eagles' Wings. There is no selection of hymns, no specific "order of worship." The difference between the dance of the Spirit and standard worship is akin to the distinction between Brubeck and Haydn. It is a total difference. That is why "harkening to the voice" constitutes the core of the service. In every service the Lord is said to "have a word" for different individuals. Sometimes the pastor imparts the word to the participants. The pastor then calls the participants forward toward the altar and announces what has been spoken by the Lord before the congregation.

Sometimes the word is received by one member of the body in silent prayer and after the service conveyed confidentially to whomever it was intended. Sometimes it is simply the "still, small voice" that one hears in prayer. When one hearkens to God's word, it is up to the believer to decide whether it is truly God's word that has been heard. A "word," of course, can be misunderstood by the hearer. Or it can be an errant voice, the voice of one's own "carnal-mindedness." But those kinds of situations are rare, and it behooves other members of the congregation to confide with the believer when he or she has doubts about what has been spoken or heard. The Spirit, as John tells us, is always the Spirit of "truth."

Brother P. T. stands up from the organ. Any member of the congregation may speak when the Spirit moves, and he begins a discourse on what is entailed in hearing the word. His sentences are clipped, his voice deep with the sonorous drawl of the southern Arkansas backlands, where he has lived most of his life. The story of Jesus' ascent into the clouds, followed by the descent of the Spirit upon the disciples, is a story that is often too lackadaisically told, P. T. begins. His countenance draws taut with conviction, his eyes flash with wonder. It is a story without parallel, a tale stranger than fiction, a recounting more marvelous and eerie than any story told around a campfire. It is a genuine "Ghost story," says P. T. It is about the Holy Ghost, "Jesus' Ghost."

"So, when they were all together, they asked him, 'Lord, is this the time when you are to establish once again the sovereignty of Israel?' He answered,

'It is not for you to know about dates or times, which the Father has set within his own control. But you will receive power when the Holy Spirit comes upon you; and you will bear witness for me in Jerusalem, and all over Judea and Samaria, and away to the ends of the earth.'"[10] When the disciples asked about the restoration of Israel, Jesus instead spoke of Pentecost.

During Jesus' era Pentecost was a harvest festival at which the establishment of God's covenant with Israel was celebrated. In the ancient festival described in the book of Leviticus, the people of Israel were bidden to offer the "firstfruits" of the harvest.[11] The symbolic meaning of Pentecost, therefore, is quite telling. The advent of the Holy Spirit at Pentecost confirms the "new covenant" Jesus made with his disciples the night before his arrest, which Christians affirm regularly at communion.

The Spirit-filled Christians, whom the author of Acts describes in the second chapter, are the firstfruits of the harvest in the new aeon. "When the Day of Pentecost was running its course they were all together in one place, when suddenly there came from the sky a noise like that of a strong driving wind, which filled the whole house where they were sitting. And there appeared to them tongues like flames of fire, dispersed among them and resting on each one. And they were all filled with the Holy Spirit and began to talk in other tongues, as the Spirit gave them power of utterance."[12] They are the "new wine" of the Spirit prefigured in Jesus' first miracle, narrated by the evangelist John during the wedding at Cana. Furthermore, in Leviticus the Pentecost festival serves as a remembrance of the Lord having given the people the new land and blessing them with the first harvest. The firstfruits are offered fifty days after the giving, or sacrifice, of "the sheaf as a special gift."[13]

The descent of the Spirit at Pentecost is testimony to the "firstfruits" of the harvest of those reborn in Christ. The new land is now the "new body," or "new Israel." The Spirit manifests exactly fifty days after the giving of the "special gift," which corresponds to Christ's death on the cross and resurrection. The importance of Pentecost for an understanding of early Christianity cannot be underestimated. Following the descent of the Spirit and the appearance of tongues of fire, the apostle Peter explains the event as the fulfillment of the prophecy of Joel: "This is what the prophet spoke of: 'God says, "This will happen in the last days: I will pour out upon everyone a portion of my spirit; and your sons and daughters shall prophesy; your young men shall see visions, and your old men shall dream dreams."'"[14]

Just as the Spirit is to be poured out upon all Israel, according to Joel, in Acts it falls upon the figurative congregation of all peoples and all nations. That is what speaking in tongues truly means in the biblical context. "We hear them telling in our own tongues the great things God has done."[15] Therefore, the incident of Pentecost really is an account of God's founding of the church, and the manifesting of its mission. The speaking with tongues in all languages signifies the unification of the faithful from all backgrounds and all cultures. It is not the "restoration" of the kingdom of Israel, as the disciples expected, but the establishment of a new, universal kingdom, Christ's kingdom on earth.

PENTECOSTALS AND CHARISMATICS

The image of a Pentecostal among mainstream Christians, and even evangelical Christians, carries a somewhat derogatory connotation. It needs redefinition. While most discussions of twentieth-century Pentecostalism have focused on the individual psychology of the believer, there has been much less attention to the Holy Spirit movement as a whole. It is clear from the New Testament itself that the workings of the Spirit were the decisive factor in promoting church unity, and that the influence of "Jesus' Ghost" counted far more than any touchstone of doctrine, discipline, or governance. Paul's consistent identification of the Spirit with Christ's body emphasizes this point. For a theologian, the Holy Spirit movement is something far more significant than some vague "revitalization movement" in the churches, as sociologists would call it. The "resting" of the Holy Spirit on Jesus—as the fourth evangelist has John the Baptist report—has always been the sign that the man from Nazareth was anointed with God's heretofore undisclosed power, the power to run over and subject all agents or forces arrayed in opposition to his kingdom. The receipt of this power is what the New Testament means by the "baptism of spirit." John could merely baptize with water. The one to come after him will be God's Chosen One, the one to "baptize in Holy Spirit."[16]

Today the Holy Spirit movement is not simply an index of revival, as evangelists have commonly proclaimed for generations. As in John the Baptist's day, it is something much more momentous. It was, as in the vision of the prophet Joel, the epiphany of the "day of the Lord." It is a sign of the end times.

It is a Sunday morning at the Glory of Zion fellowship in Denton, Texas, the last weekend in August 1997. The services are held in what appears to be a remodeled storefront or showroom, packed from wall to wall in semicircular arrangement with hardback chairs. There is no altar. The congregation is predominantly white, youthful, suburban, and female. A five-piece orchestra, outfitted with guitars, flute, violin, and percussion, inaugurates the regular worship service, which can last from two to three hours.

The songs are contemporary and compelling, belonging to the genre routinely termed "praise and worship." Many of the same numbers can be heard today on major Christian radio stations—KBIG in Los Angeles, KFISH in Anaheim, KLTY in Dallas, or the national K-LOVE network. If the lyrics did not have biblical or devotional themes, most of the songs could not be distinguished by the untrained ear from secular "soft rock." The lyrics flash on a large screen at the front of the congregation. A young woman with cascading, nut-brown hair places black-and-white slides containing the lyrics on an overhead projector, as the orchestra glides from number to number.

That morning the worshippers have received a simple gold flyer announcing a "100-Day Prayer Thrust":

> Overall Battle Plan. 21 Days "Preparing the Way." 40 Days to Break Desolation. 40 Days for Empowerment. . . . On September 1, our 100 days prayer focus enters its second phase: 40 days of prayer and fasting to break desolation. This corresponds with O.T. calendar established by God to prepare His people for His presence. In the Bible, the 30 days preceding the Feast of Trumpets (Sept. 1–30 this year) are days of prayer and preparation. It was a time for early morning prayers and personal repentance. The next 11 days—from Trumpets to the Day of Atonement (which begins Oct. 10 this year)—are called the "Days of Awe." It is a season to SEEK THE LORD INTENTLY, to "be right with God" and "be right with man." The days of awe end with the Day of Atonement, the Holiest Day of the year. It's a day for corporate fasting and seeking the Lord with all your heart.

Glory of Zion has made informal alliances with the Messianic Jewish movement, both in this country and in Russia. Messianic Judaism retains many of the traditions and practices of conventional Judaism while revering Jesus—or Yeshua, as he is called in Hebrew—as the Messiah. Jesus is sometimes addressed as Yeshua in the praise and discourse carried forward in the Glory of Zion. Some worshippers occasionally wear Jewish prayer shawls. One of the most striking elements common to both Glory of Zion and Messianic Judaism is the practice of dancing in front of the congregation during the praise music. Dancing itself, let alone at a service, is forbidden in much of the "old-time religion" of Christianity. Yet David did dance before the Lord.

There are apparently different shades and styles of Messianic Judaism. Some congregations are essentially Christian fellowships that adopt many of the trappings and ceremonies of Judaism. Others are largely Jewish organizations that have moved theologically in the direction of New Testament Christianity. Other Jews tend, as would be expected, to scorn Messianic assemblies. Mainline Christian denominations will normally have no part with them. Glory of Zion is not interested, however, in the politics of what is authentically "Jewish" and what is genuinely "Christian." The work of the Holy Spirit, if one reads the Bible in even a casual fashion, embraces both the so-called Old Testament and the New.

As some biblical exegetes have observed, the difference between the Old Testament and the New Testament is fundamentally a difference in the operation of the Spirit. In the Old Testament the Spirit manifests itself in the deeds and utterances of certain religious authorities. The Spirit—*ruakh* in Hebrew—is bestowed upon kings to rule wisely and to vanquish their enemies. Or it is withdrawn from them if they disobey the command of God, as in the tale of David and Saul. The Spirit falls upon prophets, enabling them to proclaim what God is saying to his people. Or it is given to judges to perform their task of discernment in settling difficult matters.

In the new aeon that follows Easter morning, however, the Spirit is manifestly conferred on *all* believers. That is the decisive meaning of Pentecost. In Jesus' life the Spirit rests upon him all the days of his ministry. After his death and resurrection the Spirit is shed abroad in order to propel the spread of the gospel to all the ends of the earth. Unlike the services at Eagles' Wings, worship at Glory of Zion does not concentrate on what the Spirit is doing at a single moment in each person's life. The focus is on the way in which corporate praise and worship reflects God's plan for the "end times," for these dramatic last days of history.

It is the morning Princess Diana has died in a car crash in a Paris traffic tunnel. Attendance has burgeoned that day because of a visit by Chuck Pierce, the fellowship's chief prophet and "apostle." Chuck is regarded as the apostle because it was through his influence that Glory of Zion—formerly Believers' Fellowship—was transfigured into a dynamic ministry after nearly two decades of glacial growth and relative stagnation. Just as the apostle Paul entered Jewish synagogues from one end of the Mediterranean to the other during the first century, preached the gospel, and converted them into the first Christian "churches," so Chuck came to Glory of Zion and turned it charismatic.

From its outset the Holy Spirit movement, according to historian of Christianity Martin Marty, saw itself as "nothing less than God's providential restoration of the 'apostolic faith.'"[17] Chuck calls it the Messianic Church. "In this age," he writes in one of his newsletters, "the Church will be made

known to the powers and principalities that have withheld spiritual blessings
through the Ages. The power of a resurrected Christ is being released in His
Children. This is occurring throughout the earth."[18] Originally a local Bible
church regarded for its strict moralism and fundamentalism, Glory of Zion
shambled along until, as the story runs, the Holy Spirit came down. The
change was so staggering that in both sermons and informal remarks Pastor
Robert regularly renounced everything that went on in the past, including
what he publicly termed the "false teachings" embraced by the congregation.
Several Sundays later Pastor Robert would "repent" of the church's former
practices and beliefs.

But on this occasion the call is to hearken to God's special call to the assembly. Diana's death underscores how we as individuals have no control
over our destinies, Chuck declares. The dread finale can come at any moment. It is essential that we become right with God in order that we are not
caught, like the foolish virgins in the parable, unprepared and unaware.
The congregation must be ready for God's Spirit to act in and through it.
In the book of Acts it is the direct action and power of the Holy Spirit that
transforms the early Christian community from an obscure Jewish sect into
a "light to the Gentiles."

The process is described quite sensationally in chapters 14 and 15 of Acts.
Paul and Barnabas perform a healing at the city of Lystra. The pagan resi-
dents of Lystra are so impressed that they hail Barnabas as the Roman god
Jupiter and Paul as Mercury, then summon the local priest to offer sacrifices
to them. A group of neighboring Jews are enraged at what is happening
and persuade the crowds to stone Paul and drag him from the city. But the
author of Acts notes that a breakthrough has occurred. "They reported all
that God had done through them, and how he had thrown open the gates
of faith to the Gentiles."[19]

The growing number of Gentile converts, however, causes a backlash among
certain members of the Jewish leadership of the infant church. The author
of Acts refers to these individuals as "certain persons who had come down
from Judaea" and who "began to teach the brotherhood that those who were
not circumcised in accordance with Mosaic practice could not be saved."[20]
The book of Acts notes that as a result "fierce dissension and controversy"
broke out. But eventually the "Judaizers" lose the struggle. James, who is the
head of the church in Jerusalem, quotes the prophet Amos that God "will
. . . rebuild the fallen house of David" after the exile of the Jews in Babylon,
so that "all the rest of mankind" may "seek the Lord." These Gentiles, says
the Lord, "I have claimed for my own."[21]

James determines that there should be no inhibitions placed on "those of the Gentiles who are turning to God."[22] He declares that such a radical move is not his own choice, but a "decision of the Holy Spirit."[23] Paul himself emphasizes this point in his letter to the Galatians. Paul's diatribe against James and Cephas in the second chapter throws into question whether, and to what degree, the elders in Jerusalem ever really let go of requiring observance of the Mosaic law for participation in the church. On the other hand, it is clear Paul has adopted the notion that the Holy Spirit has brought an end to "Judaism" as we know it. "Answer me one question," Paul demands of his Galatian readers rhetorically. "Did you receive the Spirit by keeping the law or by believing the gospel message?"[24] The answer is so obvious that Paul asks contemptuously of the Galatians: "Can it be that you are so stupid?"[25] The blessing of Abraham is not through the Mosaic law, but through the work of the resurrected Christ. "The purpose of it all was that the blessing of Abraham should in Jesus Christ be extended to the Gentiles, so that we might receive the promised Spirit through faith."[26]

For Paul, therefore, the Spirit is truly eschatological. It is the fullness of God's grace present in the life of the body. Indeed, the Spirit and the Christian body are one and the same, as Paul declares in both Romans and Corinthians. The Spirit is "living water," the power of the resurrection itself.[27] "If the Spirit of him who raised Jesus from the dead dwells within you, then the God who raised Christ Jesus from the dead will also give new life to your mortal bodies through his indwelling Spirit."[28] In Ephesians Paul asserts that it is the "secret of Christ" that the Spirit through the Gospel has made the Gentiles "joint heirs with the Jews, part of the same body, sharers together in the promise made in Christ Jesus."[29] The Spirit is the sign of the fulfillment of the ages. It is the reality of the new corporate existence in Christ. It is "given as firstfruits of the harvest to come."[30]

Throughout the middle chapters of Romans it is evident that Paul views the Spirit as the force that dissolves Jewish legalism and constitutes a new community of faith. It is what shapes us "to the likeness of [God's] Son."[31] The question in the early church concerning who is the true Israel can only be answered by understanding how the Spirit operates in Jewish history, how the promise of God is revealed. The promise is the Spirit itself. "It is not those born in the course of nature who are children of God; it is the children born through God's promise who are reckoned as Abraham's descendants."[32] The Spirit, therefore, is a critical theological concept in the New Testament. It is far more critical than either traditional Catholic or Protestant thought has granted.

Theologians have largely ignored the issue of how an obscure form of messianic Judaism was able to take over the Gentile world. Both Paul and the writer of Luke-Acts ascribe the cause to the Holy Spirit, the same Spirit that in the Gospels anoints Jesus and "rests on" him throughout his ministry, culminating in the cross and Easter morning. With Pentecost the Spirit as "Jesus' Ghost" reactivates the secret plan God had built into both the awaiting of the Messiah and Jesus' life and death. The anointing passes from the king to the multitude of believers, from the head to the body. The "indwelling" of God is in all who are joined in faith. The Holy Spirit, or "charismatic," movement has too long been dismissed by theologians and religion teachers as a psychological or sociological oddity rather than as a key to understanding God's action in the world. Much of evangelical Christianity has been hobbled by the so-called dispensationalist doctrine, which holds among other things that the Holy Spirit no longer is present in this day and age. But classic critics of charismatic Christianity miss what is happening at the heart of the Holy Spirit movement. Much of the misunderstanding arises from the history of Pentecostal Christianity, which must be distinguished from the charismatic movement in general.

Throughout this century Pentecostal Christianity has centered on the phenomenon of speaking in tongues, or what the New Testament calls "ecstatic utterance." The common stereotype of the Holy Roller owes to this legacy. The Bible, on the other hand, does not give the same privilege to speaking in tongues that Pentecostal Christianity has done. In his first letter to the Corinthians Paul addresses the issue of spiritual gifts, and he insists that speaking in tongues is only one charismatic form among others. The term "charismatic" comes from the Greek word for "gift." "There are varieties of gifts, but the same Spirit," Paul writes. "In each of us the Spirit is manifested in one particular way, for some useful purpose."[33] In 1 Corinthians 14 Paul lists speaking in tongues as subordinate first to the gift of love and second to prophecy. Speaking in tongues is "talking with God, not with men," according to Paul. "The language of ecstasy is good for the speaker himself, but it is prophecy that builds up a Christian community."[34] Love is the sinews that solidify the congregation. Prophecy is the people's gift of vision.[35]

"HE'S UNDER MY FEET"

The third wave of charismatic Christianity that began for the most part in the late 1970s has not been coupled with any fixed tradition about the role, or meaning, of tongues. Speaking in tongues—or *glossolalia,* as it is

called in Greek—has always been an important feature of Christian revivalism, as well as what scholars of religion term "revitalization" movements.
According to Morton Kelsey, "Glossolalia can be a regenerative influence
with relatively few dangers when it occurs within a Christian community in
which there is understanding of the mysterious spiritual levels of the human
psyche and of the God which touches men at those levels." Furthermore, "it
forces us to reexamine some of our basic Western theology, our presuppositions, indeed our certainty that there is nothing worth reaching for beyond
the practical, sensory world. Any practice which encourages such reevalua-
tion is valuable."[36]

But among the new charismatics the tongues of ecstasy come intermit-
tently in the service, or in private prayer. The gift of prophecy dominates. At
Eagles' Wings the service revolves around the reading and exposition of "the
Word." There is no set text, or texts, to be studied on any given day. Either
the preacher or a participant in the service chooses a selection, sometimes
on the spur of the moment, according to the "movement" of the Spirit. That
is the Spirit's "choreography." To follow along with the service is to flow
with the signals, gestures, and invisible promptings of worship in the Spirit.
It is driven by rhetoric, by music, with a language of total engagement, a
pattern rather than a protocol. Here is what we might call a theology of
performance. The service is spirituality that has become high art form. It is
truly dancing with the Lord.

"First Friday," they call it. It is the first Friday evening in October. Among
new charismatics the traditional Sunday morning service has given place to
the "gathering" on any weekend evening. North Church in Dallas—another
storefront ministry—has mushroomed into a sprawling complex of conference rooms, child facilities, and worship space. The church has spent large
amounts of dollars for radio advertising to launch its First Friday. There are
at least a thousand people assembled in the expensively decorated, capacious
sanctuary. The tiny choir is clapping and swaying to a seven-piece orchestra.
After delivering a twenty-minute message on the power of the Holy Spirit
to transfigure one's personal life and to vanquish demons, the evangelist has
stepped over and joined the musicians. He is up on the dais, rocking backward
and forward on his saxophone, as if performing a parody of a Little Richard
concert from the 1950s. But in this instance it is no parody. "He's under my
feet. Satan is under my feet."

The crowd is on their feet, dancing, leaping, and undulating with a mes-
merizing cadence. Frenzied shouts go up as the evangelist bends and blares
a solo. Then he digs his heel into the stage and yells, "He's under our feet.

Satan is under our feet." The people imitate his gesture en masse, stomping rhythmically and squashing their heels into the floor. The scene recalls the delirium of a metal concert. It is what the new charismatics call spiritual warfare. The idea of spiritual warfare is as old as the first generation of the church. Paul's injunction to the Ephesians is perhaps the classic text. "Find your strength in the Lord, in his mighty power. Put on all the armour which God provides, so that you may be able to stand firm against the devices of the devil. For our fight is not against human foes, but against cosmic powers, against the authorities and potentates of this dark world, against the superhuman forces of evil in the heavens."[37]

It is noteworthy that this passage is the one which Saint Augustine read after hearing the voice of a child in the garden, and which led to his celebrated conversion to Christianity. That conversion, in turn, brought about the so-called Augustinian turn in Christian thought, culminating in the modern Protestant tradition. Paul offers this advice at the end of a long discussion on Christian conduct: We must behave like "sensible [people], not like simpletons," he says, "for these are evil days."[38] Life is a constant battle not just between our better aspirations and our worse desires. We are also under constant assault by what the early church distinctly understood to be encircling forces of wickedness and destruction. Paul compares the Spirit to the sword by which one slays spiritual adversaries. No matter how hard one tries, it is impossible to psychologize what is said in Ephesians. "The dark world" was very much a reality not just to the primitive church, but to the pagan culture as well. It is still a reality today.

"When Adam and Eve yielded to Satan's temptation in the garden of Eden, they submitted to his rule," writes Pastor Heidler in his book on spiritual warfare. "As Christians, we are living in enemy territory. This world is held by rebel forces; dominated by an evil tyrant who desires to kill and destroy his subjects."[39] The notion of "territory" is crucial to the charismatic doctrine of spiritual warfare. The territory can be the "turf" of one's own personality, or it can be actual physical terrain.

The primary battlefield, according to charismatic teaching, is the mind itself. The pastor at Eagles' Wings calls the mind the "everyday Armageddon." Charismatics have frequently been accused of "anti-intellectualism," and in a strict sense the allegation is apt. The intellect is the source of rationalizations and excuses by which the power of the Spirit is thwarted. The intellect can justify any action or form of sin. Because the intellect is the faculty that makes critical distinctions, it is also able to oppress the mind with negative thoughts about oneself, or about one's capacity to accomplish certain things.

These oppressive structures of the mind and of the emotions are what charismatics term "strongholds."

One evening during one of my first services at Eagles' Wings a woman began shouting, "The strongholds are coming down, the strongholds are coming down!" I was not sure what she was talking about, but it was clear she was referring to something that seemed both tangible and intangible at the same time. Her tone was triumphant, and I realized that in her spirit she had experienced something dramatic, if not extraordinary. The woman had been a childhood victim of chronic sexual abuse, I later learned, and what apparently went on inside her was a sudden sense of having let go of the awesome weight of a painful past, and the self-hate and futility that kind of personal history carries with it. Because she did not identify her own intensely negative self-image with something which she personally was responsible for overcoming but as a "stronghold of Satan" that could only be demolished with the power of the Holy Spirit, she had succeeded in dealing with an affliction that has challenged conventional psychotherapy.

The term "strongholds" is used by Paul. "Weak men we may be, but it is not as such that we fight our battles. The weapons we wield are not merely human, but divinely potent to demolish strongholds; we demolish sophistries and all that rears its proud head against the knowledge of God."[40] The Greek word that is translated in this passage as "sophistries" is *logismous*. It also means "arguments" or "speculations." The technical meaning of the term would be "false assumptions." The ancient sophists were wordsmiths, virtuosos in crafting convincing arguments, regardless of whether the conclusions might be true. Sophists were philosophers for hire. They were rhetorical magicians who did not care whether there was any substance to what they said or taught. Sophists could rarely be challenged on the formal consistency of the argument they offered. They tricked people, however, by convincing them to start off with certain presuppositions that appeared valid, but in fact were untrue. The expression "sophistry" came to signify a type of reasoning that appears to be unassailable, but in actuality is a deceit.

Steeped in Greek oratory, Paul knew well how to commandeer words. He also grasped the way in which words enforce certain patterns of thought. During most of his ministry Paul was engaged in ferocious controversy with opponents—Greek and Jewish. He was laying siege to the conceptual strongholds that held sway over ordinary discourse, to habits of communication and webworks of assumptions that were not easily impugned. The battering ram to shatter the stronghold was not a more pungent argument. The secret lay in shifting the ground from which all conversation or reflection might begin.

"We compel every human thought to surrender in obedience to Christ."[41] Paul makes it clear that life "in Christ" and life "in the Spirit" are well-nigh one and the same.

To abide in the Spirit is to have the "mind of Christ." But acquiring the mind of Christ does not come from some mysterious elevation into a supernatural cloudland. It stems from what charismatics term "saturation in the Word." Protestant Christianity as a rule has maintained that salvation comes from the hearing and reception of God's Word as contained in Holy Scripture. The Protestant Reformers also declared that the Spirit offers illumination to the believer. Yet in charismatic Christianity the theme persists that the Word has a kind of effective power in itself. The extreme version of this outlook is the so-called Word of Faith movement, represented in such figures as Robert Tilton, Kenneth Hagland, and Kenneth Copeland. The basic premise of the movement is that the faith itself activates the power of God, and that the believer can therefore share in the abundant riches and blessings of the divine.

Certain critics have claimed that the Word of Faith movement is archetypal of the charismatic revival, which in turn amounts to nothing more than a Christian subset of New Age thinking with its emphasis on "becoming God." But that is sheer calumny. Charismatic experience and teaching harks back to Wesley. In his description of the Aldersgate experience in which he discovered that all religion is of the "heart," Wesley says that "none hath any faith till the law of the Spirit of life has made him wholly free from the law of sin and death."[42] In other words, there is no such thing without the empowerment that comes through the Holy Spirit. Having the power of the Word is taking authority over demonic entities.

As Heidler says, "If you are seated with Jesus in the place He is sitting, and He is seated in the place of authority over all the forces of the enemy, where does that put you in relation to the forces of Satan? You are also in a position of authority over Satan!"[43] Heidler even instructs the reader how to cast out demons by the authority of the Word. "If demons resist you, take up the Sword of the Spirit. Stand on the Word. That's what Jesus did when he confronted the devil. Over and over he said, 'It is written!' That's a good example to follow. Speak to the demon and say, 'It is written, "Resist the devil and he will flee from you!" On the basis of God's Word, I resist you and command you to flee.'"[44]

In mass culture the prevailing image of spiritual warfare is that of the exorcist. The perception became prominent over two decades ago when the motion picture *The Exorcist* captivated the fantasies of American audiences and fomented the impression that satanic powers and influences were skulking in the shadows and crevices of the average American's psyche. The popular script is dramatic enough. The demon manifests in a gross, corporeal manner, seizing control of the victim's entire body and consciousness. A courageous priest confronts the evil entity with stalwart faith and a liturgical formula that has been tested down through the ages. The outcome always hangs in the balance, with magic pitched against magic. In the Hollywood version it is frequently the demon that has the final say.

Spiritual warfare in actual practice has none of these theatrics. It depends on earnest, corporate prayer. The reason the twentieth-century mind falters in the face of such a concept as spiritual warfare is that it is unable to compass what goes beyond its own meager sense of the real and the intelligible. It can neither fathom the depth of darkness nor the immensity of what lies heavenward. When Jesus taught us to pray the Lord's Prayer, he was teaching the form of all prayer. "Thy kingdom come" is inseparable from "deliver us from evil." Jesus did not confront Satan in the wilderness as some species of spiritual vermin. He met him as the Adversary, the tempter, as a real and daunting power. Jesus, whom Luke says was "full of the Holy Spirit," rebuked Satan with the phrase "it is written."[45]

In recent years certain "modernist" evangelical rationalists have gone on a campaign to discredit the practice of spiritual warfare as both unbiblical and unchristian, tarring it as a covert form of New Age religion and spirituality.[46] But that view is not only unbiblical itself; by its slandering it also perhaps borders on the unchristian. Spiritual warfare is not supernatural sumo wrestling. It is a struggle for truth over the lie within the secret chambers of the heart. Before undertaking his ministry Jesus' own spiritual battle with Satan conforms to what Heidler has been teaching. It was also a key part of the spiritual discipline of the early church fathers. Augustine wrote about the importance of spiritual warfare in *The City of God*, which according to the subtitle is "against the pagans." "It is by true piety that the men of God cast out this power of the air, the enemy and adversary of piety; it is by exorcising, not by appeasing them, and they triumph over all temptations of that hostile power not by praying to the enemy but by praying to their God against the enemy."[47]

The crucial section in the whole of the New Testament that underscores this fact is the Gospel of John 15–16. The fifteenth chapter is a complicated and remarkable segment of the broader biblical text. But in many ways it represents the notion of what spiritual warfare is essentially all about. John 15 begins with Jesus' discourse on the vineyard. Jesus proclaims, "I am the

real vine." In different prophecies and oracles in Isaiah, Jeremiah, and Eze-
kiel, Israel is described as a wasted and desolate vineyard. God had planted
it and watered it, but Israel was not fruitful.[48] Jesus is embodied, however,
as both the true vine and the true Israel. "He who dwells in me, as I dwell
in him, bears much fruit. . . . He who does not dwell in me is thrown away
like a withered branch."[49]

Recognizing by faith that Jesus is the true Israel means the order of the
world is upended. In the last verses of the preceding chapter Jesus warns
his disciples that he must leave them because "the Prince of this world approaches."[50] The lines convey the sense that Jesus has come into this world
almost like a sovereign who has sneaked behind enemy lines into the domain
of his antagonist. His full-scale and frontal attack on Satan and his imperial
storm troopers will come in the final days. But meanwhile those who know
Jesus and have intimate fellowship with him—true "Christians," or the ones
Jesus calls "friends"[51]—will know him as "Jesus' Ghost," as the "Paraclete"
or "Advocate," who is "the Spirit of truth that issues from the Father," who
bears witness to all that Jesus has said and done.[52] The Spirit as Advocate
"when he comes" will "confute the world," revealing where "wrong and
right judgement lie." He will show that "the Prince of this world stands
condemned."[53]

If we blow away the fog of centuries of pious theological speculation and
silence the prattle of Pentecostalism itself, we catch an astonishing glimpse
from the standpoint of Jesus' disciples in his lifetime, a glimpse of what the
Holy Spirit movement actually consists. John 15 concerns the coming bitter
conflict between the followers of the dedicated sect that its Judean foes called
the "the Way" or "the Nazarenes," and the Jewish establishment itself. Despite everything promoters of "Jewish-Christian dialogue" might offer, John
is clear about the immensity of the struggle. "They will ban you from the
synagogue," Jesus tells his disciples. "Indeed, the time is coming when anyone
who kills you will suppose that he is performing a religious duty. They will
do these things because they do not know either the Father or me."[54]

The language in John departs from the metaphors of the Old Testament.
The figure of Satan, who is always the Adversary in spiritual warfare, does
not appear in the Bible as either a Goliath-like bully or a helmeted captain
of a rival army. He is a crafty prosecutor, as portrayed in Job, or a honey-
tongued supersalesman, as in the Gospel account of Jesus' temptations. Few
biblical commentators have noted the way in which the Holy Spirit in John
functions as foil to Satan in the "courtroom" of history. If Satan is prosecutor,
the "Paraclete" is the defense attorney. Indeed, the term "*paraclētos* (advo-

cate)" is just that—a counsel for the defense! One thought that comes from a close reading of John 15–16 is that the coming of the Holy Spirit involves, above all, the discernment of truth from the lie: "When he comes who is the Spirit of truth, he will guide you into all the truth."[55] If we read this passage in close context, we discover that the Holy Spirit serves to dispel the false claims and accusations that Satan makes. The Holy Spirit does not have "his own authority," but makes manifest the authority that Jesus gained at the resurrection. The Spirit shows that the "historical Christ" is also the "suprahistorical" Lord, the risen Savior, the alpha and the omega.[56] "Everything that he makes known to you he will draw from what is mine."[57]

On a personal level spiritual warfare is the struggle to hear the word of redemption in distinction from the condemnation conjured in our minds by what charismatics term "religion" or the "religious spirit." They also call such negative internal messages—psychologists would call them "personal tapes"—the "voice" of Satan. Charismatics tend to employ the term "religion" in the fashion Paul used the expression "the Law." Religion, as contrasted with being "Spirit-filled," or having "life in the Spirit," is letting preconceived beliefs or moral fixities dictate what God expects of us. While charismatics on the whole are as strict about private morality as other evangelicals—and are often more comfortable citing Deuteronomy than Galatians, with its affirmation of "Christian freedom,"—there is an inherent suspicion of all rules and rituals.

Unlike Baptists or Holiness sects, charismatics do not talk about "the Ten Commandments" or "God's law" per se. Instead, they speak more as Paul did about the way in which the Spirit makes us "new persons" in Christ. The Spirit is corporate, but it is fundamentally "indwelling." Having the Spirit dwell inside us makes "following the law" superfluous. The Spirit gives us "new hearts," which by the same token revives and sanctifies us as we grow in Christ. The same precept, of course, was at the center of John Wesley's teaching and was the motivating force behind historic Methodism. In an important sense the new charismatics are psychologically the old Methodists, even while being the children of the postmodern in theology, music, and style.

The acquisition of a new heart, however, requires a sacrifice of the old self. The notion of letting go not only of one's past, but also of the whole negative configuration of self—fears, desires, resentments, obsessions—is integral to the charismatic experience. Many evangelical congregations conclude their worship services with what is called an "altar call." In mainline evangelicalism the altar call is for those who have been "convicted" in the Spirit during the service, urging them to accept Christ, step forward, and make some kind of public gesture or profession. In the charismatic service the altar call varies with the promptings of the Spirit. It is usually an opportunity for the believer to yield up in his or her own spirit what is most painful or troubling. It is never a public confession. It is a silent surrender. At Eagles' Wings the preacher repeatedly would refer to the surrendered soul as an "empty storehouse." The lead singer in the choir would break into a haunting solo: "My storehouse is empty, and I am available." Then Pastor King would intone, "God wants people who are available." To be available means to let the Spirit work in the way the Spirit directs, to give up all one's own aims or projects, and to allow oneself to be totally "Spirit-led."

There is a tendency to misunderstand spiritual warfare as endless combat between the "spirit man" and the "man of flesh." But the combat is merely prelude to surrender. In charismatic preaching there is a constant emphasis on "dying" as the importance of the cross—not physical death, but spiritual death. In pop psychology this concept often comes to be expressed as "letting go." But the charismatic notion of dying is far more radical. Dying "gives Satan no longer any opportunity." It means throwing away every feeling of hurt or remorse to which one is attached. It means confronting these destructive thoughts or emotions and casting them away. During one altar call at Glory of Zion, members of the congregation were invited to step forward and make the gesture of surrendering one's private anguish "to the heart of God." One by one many of them did exactly that. The solemn folks filed toward the front of the church, opened their palms, and engaged in the pantomime of casting "oneself" onto the altar. The sentiment occurs in Augustine. "Let me not be my own life! I lived evilly of myself; I have been death to myself; I come back to life in you. Teach and instruct me!"[58]

There was the moment when at Eagles' Wings I "crucified myself" before the Lord. Such a moment is not something that can be communicated easily or sensibly in the idiom of doctrinal or analytical religious thought. It was certainly not an "emotional" moment in my life. The common canard persisting over the centuries that charismatic religion is "emotional" religion for the most part misses the point. Philosophically and psychologically speaking, the emotions are reactive to stimuli. Neuropsychologists tell us they derive from the structure of the mammalian or "limbic" brain. A threatening pose by an antagonist stimulates anger. A friendly face stirs affection. That is not what happened.

THE DOUBLE KNOWLEDGE OF GOD

The moment that changed my life came several weeks after I had begun attending regular services at Eagles' Wings. It was not anything that could reasonably or intelligibly be termed a "feeling." It was more a transforming realization. The experience happened after I had been for months in turmoil over an unexpected separation in my previous marriage and an impending divorce. I had little idea what charismatic Christianity was all about and had gone to the church for completely unrelated reasons. At that time I was invited to worship, and during the first hour of the service I recognized in a strange and almost unaccountable way that something was happening to me that I had never confronted in my more than fifty years.

My first sensation in that darkened, empty theater was that of having been penetrated by my own thoughts. The best way to describe the experience is simply a concentrated "self-knowledge" rebounding from a sense of overwhelming divine presence. It is akin to what Calvin describes at the opening of his *Institutes* as the *"duplex cognition Dei* (double knowledge of God)." The more we know the limitlessness of God, the more we know the limitations of ourselves, our abject state.

In the charismatic service the worshipper's self-awareness is circumscribed by the sense that he or she is in the presence of Something or Someone awesome and immeasurable. As a matter of course charismatic ministers welcome God into the house of worship with the same reverence as one would show to every honored guest. This "invocation" is not in any way rote or strictly liturgical, as is the case in most mainline churches. Either the invocation is through rousing music, or it is through shouts of adoration. "Blessed be your name, O Lord. Blessed be your name," the worshippers would intone at Eagles' Wings.

The overwhelming sense that "God is in the house" strips away all illusions of self-importance, all chunks and shards of ego-armor. On that Sunday evening in September I found myself with few defenses. The self is like a once-proud stack of cards that suddenly is swept away in a precipitous gale. The wind of Spirit blows it down. It makes one poignantly aware of the pettiness and inconsequence of all one's accomplishments. They became truly like "stubble." Pastor King kept dwelling on the fact that the mind of flesh must be "broken" to be restored by the power of the Spirit. On that day I did not have to be forced to surrender myself. I was already shattered to the core. I went to the front of the church and fell on my face before the maroon and green vestments that are standard issue on most charismatic altars. My storehouse was empty, and I became "available" for the Spirit to work within me. I was never the same after that moment. I had been, as charismatics say, "slain in the Spirit." Rosemarie helped me up. "You are blessed, Brother Carl," she said. We hugged each other. Most charismatics hug each other during services. I stood up straight. I was reborn.

It is midmorning on a Sunday at the Church of Marshall in Marshall, Texas. The church, a refurbished warehouse on the edge of town, is completely packed. The walls of the sanctuary are embellished with a kind of surrealistic graphics that appears a cross between Salvador Dali and Indian temple art. The most intriguing piece is a large fresco entitled *The Two Witnesses*. The two witnesses are mentioned in the eleventh chapter of the book of Revelation. They are an enigmatic pair that for a season hold off Satan's assaults on the earth. The faces of the two witnesses in the fresco are imperceptible. Only their eyes remain visible, staring out lionlike from behind an oil lamp that signifies the endurance of faith in this world.

The service begins in a most unusual fashion. A single note from one of the electric guitars in the orchestra is sustained until the entire room is charged with anticipation. The rest of the orchestra holds the sound in suspense. There is no movement toward resolution. In the charismatic experience the music is the cipher. In fact, from a human point of view, it is everything. It is what makes possible the choreography. Through the music the unseen acquires a "voice" this day. The choreography of pure sound is transmuted into articulate speech through a ritual-less set of cues that do not obey any kind of score. The vocabulary of this "language" is not a grammatical one. It is akin to the kind of nonverbal intercommunication that musicians for ages past have shared in ecstasies of performance. The preacher knows precisely when to preach. The choir, or orchestra, knows precisely when to accompany the speaker. Nothing is said. It is simply done.

Brother Randy, the chief elder for the Church of Marshall, rises. The church has no pastor. It is more like what one would call the original apostolic church, where elders were called to minister. Brother Randy's message this day is on "deep-sea diving," but it is better described as a homily on spiritual warfare. He talks about the need to have an air hose when one plunges into the murky deep. He uses the metaphor of scuba exploration to characterize the relationship between human existence and the lifeline offered by the Spirit. If someone gets caught in kelp, a supply of oxygen is what will keep him or her alive. Kelp is something that looks harmless when one approaches it, but its coils and oily tentacles can be lethal to the unsuspecting swimmer. Once an ankle is ensnared, the kelp envelops and drags the diver to his demise. Beware of the "kelp," which we know as the devious delights of the world around us. If you go down, wear an air hose.

Charismatic Christianity is distinctively "postmodern" in many ways. At one level it is simply the "old-time religion" in a rock 'n' roll format. There was a sizable span of time from the Great Awakenings in America during the eighteenth and early-nineteenth centuries, when the seeds for the later Pentecostal revival were first sown, until the crop appeared. But from a theological standpoint the gulf is not that wide. The experience I underwent at Eagles' Wings—in which for the first time in my own life and academic career I had a profound intuition of what Christians in an often rote fashion term "the glory of God"—does not depart much from what Jonathan Edwards, America's greatest theologian and interpreter of the Great Awakening, referred to as "spiritual knowledge" or "the sense of the heart." For Edwards, spiritual knowledge is the kind of "sensual spirituality" that comes with the experience of conversion and "regeneration," through which the Holy Spirit is consistently and detectably operative. Edwards's unique, systematic explication of the experience of the Holy Spirit in the revivalist context laid the conceptual groundwork for the so-called New Divinity movement, which in turn supplied the rhetoric for the rural revivalism that over two centuries engendered American evangelicalism and the distinctive culture of the Bible Belt.[59]

But the contemporary charismatic movement is neither rural nor tradition-bound. The Church in Marshall, while situated in a bucolic and faintly redneck environment, has a decidedly suburban feel. The "storefront" or "warehouse" church, for example, is quite a familiar feature of charismatic worship. While mainline churches, including evangelical ones, usually undertake building campaigns as soon as financially feasible, charismatic congregations usually put their money into outreach and the capital such ventures require—printing, audio tapes, and the rental of conference centers and revival facilities. To understand modern Pentecostalism we have to go back to John Wesley, Jonathan Edwards, and the Great Awakening. Similarly, to comprehend the new charismatics we must hark back to the Jesus movement of the early 1970s. Many of the new charismatic leaders are veterans of the Jesus movement. The refusal of the new charismatics to "settle down" in recognizable church buildings and their penchant for informal, small-group ministries known as cells is part of the legacy of the movement.

THE THIRD WAVE OF CHARISMATIC CHRISTIANITY

The Jesus movement began in the late 1970s as an antiestablishment, antidenominational type of countercultural revivalism that assumed many forms and guises. Common to all the different strands and factions within the Jesus movement, however, was an emphasis on the Jesus "experience." At the time this experience took on the sundry camouflage and colorations of the counterculture itself, with its endless chemical and psychospiritual experimentation. And in a number of cases it resulted in the formation of what we now know as aberrant cults.[60] Yet it also dissolved many denomination barriers and fractured the rationalistic shielding of mainline Christianity. The contemporary charismatic movement, one may argue, is the third wave of postmodern spirituality, although increasingly in proper doctrinal surroundings.

The first wave was the Jesus movement and the "spiritual supermarket" of 1960s-style religious innovation. It was characterized largely by offbeat, hippie-style religious experientialism, often involving drugs and communal living. The second wave was the so-called charismatic revival of the 1970s and the New Age religiosity that peaked in the late 1980s. The second wave consisted of ecstatic and intense experiences that were usually played out within a more traditional, bourgeois lifestyle. The third wave represents a maturing of the trends that started over a generation ago. It compasses the experimentalism of the 1960s and the antitraditionalism of the 1970s and 1980s. But it has now become normative. The forms of worship—such as the "Top 40" musical sound and the peculiar "art deco" imagery that has become stock in trade for charismatic churches, together with the informal habits of dress—are more in keeping with the tastes and conventions of citizens of the 1990s than with the subtle Victorianism of the so-called mainline denominations. It is not the charismatic churches that are culturally outré at the turn of the millennium; it is the denominations that are outré.

In many respects charismatic revivalism has followed the functional dualism of contemporary American society. The dadaism and decadence of pop culture, which usually results in anti-Christian and sacreligious messages, has been coopted by contemporary religious evangelism, brandishing everything from black leather jackets stenciled on the back with "Only He can save" to so-called Christian heavy metal, which with the exception of the words sounds hardly any different from its raunchy counterparts. The Church at Marshall is no exception. When one enters its worship space, one does not have the feeling of involvement in what academic specialists might call a religious event. Every service has its own flow and energy. Brother Randy quotes Scripture readily, often with an incisiveness of scholastics. Charismatic preachers frequently know their Greek and Hebrew very well. But the scriptural citations belong to a dramatic narrative that weaves the speaker's own experiences into the culminating language of the worship itself.

Charismatic Christianity *is emblematic* of the new, postmodern evangelicalism. It is multicultural, global in its scope, and interracial. It is postdenominational, not simply nondenominational. It is also postpropositional and posttheological. For the most part it is more biblically oriented than many of today's so-called Bible churches. The dance with the Lord is the dance of the believer in the full presence of, and in full relationship with, the Lord of heaven and earth, who is Lord of the dance. Dancing, like genuine faith, is an *intimate experience.*

Much of the hostility between conventional, or what we have dubbed modernist, evangelicalism and the charismatic revival may have far more to do with cultural style than biblical teaching. The styles once defined an ethnic divide, which was also a religious divide in America. That is no longer the case. Despite the hermeneutical machinations of the anticharismatics to proof-text the reasons why the Holy Spirit cannot be doing in today's environment what charismatics say the Spirit is doing, their arguments are scripturally weak. The power and centrality of the Spirit is unmistakable in the New Testament, and it is the very definition of evangelical faith to seek models, precedents, and lifeways that emulate as much as possible the early church. Critics often go even further to connect the use of tongues with psychological disorder and condemn it as divisive in the church body. But that would lead us to conclude that the history of the church after Jesus' ascension was itself founded on a psychological disorder. As for tongues-speaking or glossolalia, Morton Kelsey, a scholar of historical Christianity, observes that "glossolalia in its fullest range and depth surely has been no more divisive in Christian history than other doctrines such as predestination or other practices such as baptism and the Eucharist, and it should not therefore be singled out for special opprobrium."[61] After all, many evangelical Christians have thought dancing in itself was a sin.

9

THE END OF THEOLOGY

The Next Reformation

THE THIRD MILLENNIUM IS DAWNING with pallid sun and mixed clouds. In retrospect we can recognize the past century of unprecedented material and technological advance, but at the same time it was a century of profound spiritual darkness and moral bewilderment. People suffered two catastrophic World Wars, a half century of Cold War with the unremitting threat of nuclear holocaust, spasms of economic calamity and social anarchy, the shattering of the West's theological and intellectual bedrock that had seemed impregnable. Periods of darkness are not immediately followed by intense light. There is the decisive moment of daybreak when the eastern horizon is beginning to brighten and the impalpable pinks and blue-grays of sunup gather and swirl at all the corners of the sky. It is a time for both awe and preparation as well as pondering. We are in such a time.

There was a similar time about half a millennium ago. Like ours, it was a time of transition from dark to light. It was the early 1500s, and Western civilization was just emerging from two centuries of disillusionment and disaster. The Black Plague had wiped out almost a third of Europe's population, and devastating and protracted wars had done the rest. No throne was stable or could command authority for very long. The church had been fractured and divided. For a spell there were even two rival popes, backed by warring monarchs, one in Rome and the other in Avignon. The Italian Renaissance was in full swing, however, and the "humanistic" spirit was spreading out of Venice and Florence into Central Europe and France.

The discovery of America and the invention of the printing press had rekindled economic growth. The revival of learning was pleasing to various church reformers, who believed that the spread of the new knowledge would mitigate the moral excesses and unbelief of the Roman clergy and inspire a return to classical piety. Western culture was becoming increasingly rowdy and not a little corrupt, but at least it was on the move. New artistic and intellectual fashions, such as various types of antirealist philosophy, the occult interest in Hermetic magic, the use of perspective in painting, and the celebration of pagan symbols and imagery—these were widespread and well received. The Age of Faith, whatever that might have entailed, was over. The modern epoch was rapidly supplanting the medieval era.

Into this theater strode a monk named Martin Luther. He did not quite fit into any of the mentalities or cultural contexts of the early-sixteenth century. Luther was neither a scholastic—an academic theologian steeped in Aristotelian philosophy—nor a humanist enamored with Greek and Latin literature. His forte was the study of the Bible, which the church of his time took seriously, but not as seriously as Luther believed it should. Moreover, he was from German peasant stock and lacked the civility or polish of the Renaissance men of his generation. Finally, he was obsessed with his own individual salvation.

Luther would have been regarded as a postmodernist by the standards of his day. For instance, he did something with Scripture that raised suspicion among his contemporaries. He was interested not so much in what Scripture said in some sort of doctrinal or objective manner as how it spoke to him personally. Luther was not concerned with the fine points of technical exegesis of Scripture, although he certainly had the background and training to be a humanist like the great Erasmus of Rotterdam. Nor was he a clear strategist of church reform, even though history has now enshrined him as the father of the Reformation. He had immersed himself for a time in the writings of the German theology of Meister Eckehart, which stressed the mystical infinitude of the experience of God, although Luther was by no means a mystic in the standard sense of the word. He was irreverent and not a bit uncouth in his manner of speech and his style of writing. He was popular with his students but had the reputation of being quite bull-headed and impatient. Finally, he had a very weird approach to the Bible. He was slightly suspicious of the way in which the different books of the Bible had been canonized. He distinguished between the traditions of the church about what the Bible said and what the Bible actually said. That appeared to most of his contemporaries as prideful nit-picking. He placed undue emphasis on the Pauline writings and the teaching of justification by faith, which everyone knew was only a portion, not the whole, of the scriptural message.

When Luther posted his 95 Theses in 1517, no one in their wildest imagination could have expected the move to touch off a veritable religious, political, and social revolution. The 95 Theses were a tiny spark that fell into powder-dry tinder, and the rest is history. But what ensuing events showed is that Luther's somewhat eccentric ideas about religious authority and the importance of the Bible had touched a deep spiritual nerve in the Western outlook. What before had seemed outrageous and nonsensical suddenly made sense. As historians have long been fond of reminding us, the precursors of the Reformation went back more than a century. The disaffection with the Roman Church and the theological radicalism that went with such criticism had been mounting for a long time; it all represented a final rejection of Constantine's imperial solution to the tension between Christian faith and state power that had been imposed over a millennium earlier.

The trifold Protestant doctrines of *sola fide, sola scriptura,* and *communio sanctorum* were not simply a Christian version of the "return to basics." They were not the fundamentals of a sixteenth-century fundamentalism. They articulated a thesis that had been integral to Christian thought and practice from the first century. Although Christian historians and historical theologians over the years have attempted, by various probes and gambits, to uncover what in the nineteenth century was called the essence of Christianity, one filament of this search has remained constant.

According to historian Justo L. González, that constant is the distinctive Christian concept of truth, which is not at all as Nietzsche understood it. *It is the Incarnation.*

González writes: "Christian truth is such that it is not lost or distorted upon uniting itself with the concrete, the limited, and the transitory. On the contrary, the truth—or at least that truth which is given to men—is given precisely there when the eternal unites with the historical; where God became flesh; where a specific man, in a specific situation, is able to say: 'I am the truth.'"[1]

Christian truth is not, never was, and never will be propositional truth. Propositional, or purely philosophical, truth is conditional truth, even if it claims to be about what is unconditional. It can never be made into the touchstone of Christian truth, which is always *personal* and *relational.* Propositional truth statements cannot accommodate paradoxes. By its very definition a paradox resists propositional rationality. As Kierkegaard and his postmodernist successors continue to remind us, the Incarnation *is* a paradox, and one that can never be resolved in thought. The Bible is not a system of arguable and debatable propositions. A genuine systematic theology forged from the Bible is impossible. The *sola* in *sola fide* and *sola scriptura* is not a qualifiable adverb. As Kierkegaard says, the paradox of the Incarnation demands faith more than assent. For faith is the total surrender of one's heart, mind, and body to the infinite and Almighty God, who calls us into relation. Scripture is the voice that calls us into that relation.

Postmodern thought in its religious as well as its nonreligious variants is not a surrogate for faith. There is nothing preferential, let alone spiritual, or even crypto-Christian, concerning the postmodern outlook. Postmodernism simply encapsulates a sense of our times. We have gone beyond the modern. The worst-case scenario is that the postmodernist revolution in culture and letters is comparable to the plagues of Egypt. They are instrumental in forcing the "pharaoh" of Enlightenment philosophy to let the Israelites go. The best rendering is that postmodernism offers a different sort of parlance that can revitalize Christian reflection and communication in a way that modern philosophy could not do. It may be that the postmodernist vocabulary will ultimately reconfigure how we naturally and normally express our faith, and not just conceptually, just as the marriage of Platonism and personal confession early in the formation of the tradition contributed extensively to the stuff of familiar Christian doctrine.

Postmodernism is not a subterfuge for undermining the coherence of Western thought any more than the writings of the apologists of the second century were efforts to subvert classical learning. After all, many of the pagans' accusations at the time against Christians, which prompted the rise of apologetics, are eerily similar to what many evangelicals say about postmodern Christianity. According to the respected pagan authorities of the day, Christians were "atheists," their statements were illogical and "contradictory," they were disrespectful of authority, they were overly sympathetic with popular culture.[2] Classical learning in its pagan form was in decay and would soon be superseded by the new "Christian" synthesis. Enlightenment modernism—what the famous historian Peter Gay has called "modern paganism"—has the same destiny.[3]

The calumny of the Hellenists against the early Christians should give us pause. Perhaps what Derrida has called the "Jew-Greek" amalgam of Christianity has swung in five hundred years too far in the wrong direction.

Athens has indeed overrun Jerusalem. However, postmodernist philosophy, particularly in the case of Derrida and Lévinas, favors Jerusalem. The implicit question is Kierkegaard's, as it was Luther's. *Has Christianity silently and inexorably become paganized?* What remains that is truly evangelical in evangelical Christianity?

We cannot, and do not really need to, answer these sorts of questions. But we can pose ourselves a far more incisive question: *What does it signify to entertain the prospect of a postmodern Christian faith?* In what measure can we give a theological accounting of this faith? In what argot will it speak? Is it a recognizably biblical faith, and if so, what would that mean? Does the appropriation of that faith have consequences—even serious consequences—for the organization of Christian life? Is the term "Reformation" more than an oratorical device?

The Next Reformation, like the Reformation of the sixteenth century, can be anticipated, but it cannot be foreglimpsed in any significant detail. History does not work that way. And the sovereign God of our faith who is in charge of human history would not give us a detailed topographical map. If he did, we would not need faith.

After Theology

When I introduced the expression "the end of theology" into philosophical and religious discourse years ago, the intent was not only to cause a stir. It was to provoke the sort of thought about the character of thought and language that postmodern philosophy during that interval has overwhelmingly and astutely introduced. The aim was to point out that one does need theology necessarily to support faith. The modern assumption has always been that faith needs a powerful protector. Yet, as always happens with feudal arrangements, the provisions for protection become methods of domination and suppression.

At the same time, the "end of theology" implies a Copernican revolution in a provisional sense of the word with regard to language. "Overcoming metaphysics" involves more than "thinking the unthought" (Heidegger), or outgrowing representationalism (Derrida), or rediscovering immanence (Deleuze). At its very core postmodernism is a *theory of language,* and these particular philosophical theories serve mainly as critiques of the covert Aristotelianism that has crept into philosophy in almost every generation. In that respect the "post-" in postmodernism marks little more than the disruption of, or transition beyond, what has gone before. The abolition of reason has made a wide berth for faith, but again, what faith? A language of faith in the age of the hyphen must reconsider the very theory of language. If the last stage of philosophical modernism was the "linguistic turn" that spanned a sizable portion of the twentieth century, then we are on the verge of something unprecedented, and perhaps unwarranted, in the legacy of philosophico-theological thinking. We are witnessing the makings of what we shall call the dialogical turn.

The dialogical turn is the genuine revolution that has been generically appraised as postmodernism. The philosophical apparatus, cumbersome as it may be, can be found in the writings of Lévinas. The richness and complexity of Lévinas's thought cannot be either summarized or explored in a few paragraphs. Like all postmodern writings, a certain technical jargon needs to be mastered if one is to appreciate thoroughly and consistently what Lévinas is saying. A certain amount of the opacity of Lévinas's language arises from the translation of certain key terms of German philosophy into French. But one can begin to grasp the importance of Lévinas's undertakings for faith—and their long-term and powerful implications for evangelical faith—if one painstakingly appraises the shift not just within the philosophy of language, but in postmodern philosophy itself, which Lévinas embodies.

Like Heidegger, Lévinas understood that the history of metaphysics as ontotheology had come to an end. Modernity completes and closes the book on philosophical thought as the representation of being. This eventuates in a twilight moment in the experience of the West when, in Heidegger's poetic phrase, "The old gods have fled"—particularly the Greek "gods" of form, proportion, rational symmetry, and predicative consistency—and nihilism in Nietzsche's sense "stands at the door." Heidegger sought to hear the "voice" of Being, as Nietzsche thought it had been heard during the tragic age of the Greeks, and render it as a new "fundamental ontology." But Lévinas sought a way of letting the God of Abraham, Isaac, and Jacob speak in a "dialect" never spoken—*philosophically.*

Lévinas's philosophy supplies a Hebraic, or biblical, critique of the paganism of Greek metaphysics and redirects it toward the One who speaks all languages and gives all names. The overcoming of metaphysics entails more than the reduction of the representation to the sign and the repudiation of linguistic foundationalism. Iconoclasm only lays the groundwork for true worship. In order to worship and adore God philosophically, we must enter into relationship with him. And to enter into relationship with him we must set aside the dualism of subject and object that has overshadowed the tradition of Western thinking.

Both ancients and moderns took as their metaphysical point of departure the binary distinction between subject and object, or subject and predicate. The ancient, or classical, position was that thought is a "seeing" or inspection *(theoria)* of the object. The goal of thought is to obtain a clear and precise picture of what one is viewing. The correspondence, or representationalist, theory of truth derives from this particular trope. With Descartes modernism capsizes the relationship and asserts the primacy of the subject: *ego sum.* The structure of consciousness now determines the makeup of the object. Kant and Hegel codified the new Cartesian foundationalism.

The phenomenological movement gave it a kind of precision that opened the road for Heidegger to launch his assault on ontotheology. Yet, for Lévinas phenomenology also brought into the open what he calls the "sociality" of ontology itself. The "I" of the "I think" speaks a common language. It thinks what it thinks, or says what it says, as part of a community of interpretation. The "intersubjectivity" of being is confirmed by this interpretative matrix, a point which the American philosopher Charles S. Peirce underscored in his effort to transform the science of logic into "semiotics," the science of signs and their relationships to each other. When one cognizes a truth within the intersubjective matrix, one's knowledge is no longer constituted by the simple dyad of subject and object.

The Matrix and Mystery of Otherness

In that matrix the "other" and all his or her mystery intrudes. "To put an end to the conception that thought and the subject-object relation are coextensive," Lévinas writes, "is to offer a glimpse of a relationship with the other that is neither an intolerable limitation of the thinker, nor a simple absorption of this other into an ego, in the form of a content. Where all *Sinngebung* [making sense] was the work of a sovereign ego, the other could in fact only be absorbed in a representation."[4] But, on the contrary, the other makes a "claim" on the subject, or ego. Otherness, or alterity, is a jagged and spreading fissure within the foundations of Western metaphysical thought; it reveals the pure infinity that inaugurates all finite differences and connections. The difference of otherness is different from the difference of Derrida's *différance.* It is a difference that smashes through the stone walls of selfhood and the sufficiency of rational self-consciousness. It is the final challenge to predicative logic, because it is God's challenge. That is who God is. God is *tout autre,* wholly other.

God's holiness is his *wholly* otherness. Paganism experiences the indeterminacy of the world—the tragic vision—without this sense of radical alterity. It is the latter that distinguishes Judaism and Christianity from pagan culture. What makes Christianity fundamentally distinct from paganism—including the paganism of modernist rationalism and postmodern forms of paganism—is that it is much more than profound monologue. It has the sense of a difference that addresses us, not merely Heidegger's "*Es spricht* (it speaks)," but the sense that we are speaking to Someone, and being spoken to. When we speak to Someone, we do not merely say "it"; we say "You."

For Lévinas, inside the fractures and heterogeneity of being that otherness discloses, there arises an irrepressible feeling of relationality and responsibility. The presence of the other makes a demand on my subjectivity to be patient toward the other, to care, to extend a hand, to give of myself, to *love*. The first commandment of the Decalogue is the warrant of this relationality. Responsibility is integral to any description of being, yet the metaphysical tradition has not been able to give an account of it. "All ontology," Lévinas declares, "is really *ethics*." What Lévinas means by such a suggestion is that relationality—not logical but personal relationality—is at the heart of all existence. Indeed, it marks in bright highlights the difference between theology and ontotheology, or between faith-based theological reflection and metaphysics. It decides the difference between being and creation, between the philosopher's God and a personal God.

"Responsibility for the other to the point of dying for the other! This is how the alterity of the other—distant and near—affects, through my responsibility as an *I*, the utmost present, which, for the identity of my 'I think,' still gathers itself together . . . into presence or representation, but which is also the end of [allegorical] attribution of meaning by intentional thought."[5] Responsibility is the way beings, particularly human beings, are. Responsibility and "ethical" relation are the mode in which being manifests itself. To be is to be what Lévinas calls "one-for-the-other." One-for-otherness cannot be redescribed in any manner other than God's own presence, the "glory of the infinite." God's presence as the One who is always for us, as the Other who is in his nature one-for-the-other, is impossible to inscribe within the structure of logic and metaphysics.

> Representation does not integrate the responsibility for the other inscribed in human fraternity; human fraternity does not arise out of any commitment, any principle, that is, any recallable present. The order that orders me to the other does not show itself to me, save through the trace of its reclusion, as a face of a neighbor. There is the trace of a withdrawal which no actuality had

preceded, and which becomes present only in my own voice, already obedient in the harsh present of offerings and gifts.[6]

This site of God breaking through as other Lévinas calls "anarchy"—it has no "rule" other than God's rule. It is a "beginninglessness" that is "otherwise than being." It opens itself up in dialogue to us through the "diachrony of transcendence."

God is not *prima ousia,* first cause or principal being. God is Creator and Savior. God may be characterized as pure being, as the impersonal ground of things in metaphysical philosophies, but he is ultimately described as Father, friend, or Savior. "The face of the Other, irreducible difference, bursting into all that gives itself to me, all that is understood by men and belongs to my world; an appearance in the world which un-makes and dis-orders the world, worries me and keeps me awake."[7] For "the idea of infinity, occurs in the relationship with the Other. The idea of infinity is the social relationship. This relationship consists in approaching an absolutely exterior being. . . . The exteriority of the infinite being is manifested in the absolute resistance which by its apparition, its epiphany, it opposes to all of my powers. . . . Its *logos* is: 'You shall not kill.'"[8]

The commandment not to kill—that is, not to murder, not to take a life willfully for the sake of one's own aggrandizement—grounds ethics because it is the ultimate call of the Infinite One, who summons us created, finite beings into his presence for a frank talk, for a dialogue. Ontotheology is eminently monologue. The end of theology makes it possible finally to dialogue with God, just as Luther did through Scripture. The end of theology is not by any conceivability an invitation to a-theology. The very notion of a-theology is modernistic to the core. A-theology denies the power of otherness, and thereby of infinity. It denies the sign of Sinai. Even though it denies theology, it is still theology. The end of theology is saying an *adieu* to theology in the most literal sense of the word. To say *adieu* to theology is to "say it like it is" (in French)—literally, *to God.* It is the power of God liberating evangelical, if not the whole of Christian thought and theology from its long captivity in the Egypt of metaphysics and the Babylon of modernism and drawing it back "to God," of "letting God be God," in the face-to-face relationship of faith and worship.

After theology we must all get on our faces.

Notes

Chapter 1: Postmodernism and the Crisis of Evangelical Thought

1. Frederic Jameson, *Postmodernism, Or, the Cultural Logic of Late Capitalism* (Durham, N.C.: Duke University Press, 1992).

2. Douglas Groothuis, *Truth Decay: Defending Christianity against the Challenges of Postmodernism* (Downers Grove, Ill.: InterVarsity, 2000), 22.

3. Ibid., 20.

4. "Fighting Truth Decay: An Interview with Doug Groothuis," *Antithesis,* http://www.antithesis.com/conversations/groothuis_01.html.

5. Bertrand Russell, *Why I Am Not a Christian, and Other Essays on Religion and Related Subjects* (New York: Simon & Schuster, 1957).

6. Graeme Codrington, "Postmodernism," http://www.geocities.com/athens/pantheon/3675/graeme.html. See also Graeme Codrington, "Postmodernism—the Future's Not What It Used to Be," http://tomorrowtoday.biz/generations/genxthesis/ch2.htm.

7. Stan Wallace, "The Real Issue: Discerning and Defining the Essentials of Postmodernism," http://www.leaderu.com/real/ri9802/wallace.html.

8. Daniel Ryan Street, "Faith without Foundations: Christian Epistemology and Apologetics after Modernity," http://www.faithmaps.org/faithwoutfoundations.htm.

9. Groothuis, *Truth Decay*, 175–76.

10. Excerpts from Groothuis, *Truth Decay,* 175–76. The theory of minimal foundationalism does not originate by any means with Groothuis. It is one of the key arguments in twentieth-century epistemology. For an application of the argument to contemporary philosophy of religion, see Matthew C. Bagger, *Religious Experience, Justification, and History* (Cambridge: Cambridge University Press, 1999).

11. Bruce Ellis Benson, *Graven Ideologies: Nietzsche, Derrida and Marion on Modern Idolatry* (Downers Grove, Ill.: InterVarsity, 2002), 42.

12. Rom. 4:13.

13. Rom. 1:18–25 (NEB, with alternate reading in footnote).

14. John Locke, *An Essay concerning Human Understanding,* abridged and edited by Maurice Cranston (London: Collier-Macmillan, 1965), 61.

15. Harriet A. Harris, *Fundamentalism and Evangelicals* (Oxford: Oxford University Press, 1998), 100.

16. Ibid., 121.

17. Ibid., 316.

18. See Dave Tomlinson, *The Post-Evangelical* (London: Triangle, 1995).

217

Chapter 2: The New French Revolution

1. Charles Jencks, *The New Paradigm in Architecture: The Language of Postmodernism* (New Haven: Yale University Press, 2002).

2. Friedrich Nietzsche, *The Gay Science*, trans. Walter Kaufmann (New York: Random House, 1974), 181–82.

3. An excellent and classical study of the philosophical problem of nihilism, which Nietzsche inaugurated, can be found in Stanley Rosen, *Nihilism: A Philosophical Essay* (New Haven: Yale University Press, 1969).

4. Friedrich Nietzsche, *The Will to Power*, trans. Walter Kaufmann and R. J. Hollingdale (New York: Vintage Books, 1967), 3.

5. Ibid., 7.

6. Friedrich Nietzsche, *Beyond Good and Evil: Prelude to a Philosophy of the Future*, trans. Walter Kaufmann (New York: Random House, 1966), 60.

7. Nietzsche, *Will to Power*, 13.

8. Ibid., 9.

9. David B. Allison, ed., *The New Nietzsche: Contemporary Styles of Interpretation* (Cambridge: MIT Press, 1985).

10. Exod. 20:3.

11. Martin Heidegger, *Essays in Metaphysics: Identity and Difference*, trans. Kurt Leidecker (New York: Philosophical Library, 1960), 64–65.

12. Jean-Luc Marion, *God without Being*, trans. Thomas A. Carlson (Chicago: University of Chicago Press, 1991), 52.

13. Jacques Derrida, *Of Grammatology*, trans. Gayatri Chakravorty Spivak (Baltimore: Johns Hopkins University Press, 1974), 61.

14. Ibid., 62.

15. Jacques Derrida, *Margins of Philosophy*, trans. Alan Bass (Chicago: University of Chicago Press, 1982), 3.

16. Ibid., 11.

17. Ibid., 67.

18. Jacques Derrida, *Writing and Difference*, trans. Alan Bass (Chicago: University of Chicago Press, 1978), 196–97.

19. Ibid., 9.

20. Ibid., 76.

21. This argument can be found in Jonathan Z. Smith, *Imagining Religion: From Babylon to Jonestown* (Chicago: University of Chicago Press, 1988).

22. Derrida, *Margins of Philosophy*, 71.

23. Jacques Derrida, *Acts of Religion* (London: Routledge, 2002), 88.

24. Ibid., 100.

25. Ibid., 56–57.

26. Ibid., 57.

27. Jacques Derrida, *On the Name*, ed. Thomas Dutoit (Stanford: Stanford University Press, 1995), 54.

28. Ibid., 35.

29. Ibid., 120.

30. Gilles Deleuze, *Nietzsche et la philosophie* (Paris: Presses universitaries de France, 1962); idem, *Nietzsche and Philosophy*, trans. Hugh Tomlinson (New York: Columbia University Press, 1983).

31. Ronald Bogue, *Deleuze and Guattari* (London: Routledge, 1989), 37.

32. See Gilles Deleuze and Félix Guattari, *L'anti-Oedipe* (Paris: Éditions de minuit, 1972); idem, *Anti-Oedipus: Capitalism and Schizophrenia*, trans. Helen R. Lane et al. (New York: Viking, 1972).

33. R. D. Laing, *The Politics of Experience* (New York: Vintage Books, 1983); Herbert Marcuse, *Eros and Civilization: A Philosophical Inquiry into Freud* (Boston: Beacon, 1974).

34. Bogue, *Deleuze and Guattari*, 65.

35. Carl A. Raschke, *Fire and Roses: Postmodernity and the Thought of the Body* (Albany: State University Press of New York, 1996), 7.

36. Gilles Deleuze, *Difference and Repetition*, trans. Paul Patton (New York: Columbia University Press, 1994), 10. For their most important works, see Laing, *Politics of Experience*; Marcuse, *Eros and Civilization*.

37. Deleuze, *Difference and Repetition*, 1.

38. Ibid., 301.

39. Gilles Deleuze, *Pure Immanence: Essays on a Life* (New York: Zone Books, 2001), 31.

40. Deleuze, *Difference and Repetition*, 272.

41. Ibid., 273.

42. Deleuze, *Pure Immanence*, 15.

43. Gilles Deleuze and Félix Guattari, *What Is Philosophy?* trans. Hugh Tomlinson and Graham Burchell (New York: Columbia University Press, 1994), 50.

44. Ibid., 77.

Chapter 3: The Religious Left Bank

1. See Carl Raschke, *The End of Theology* (Aurora, Colo.: Davies Group, 2000); originally published as *The Alchemy of the Word: Language and the End of Theology* (Missoula, Mont.: Scholars Press, 1979).

2. Immanuel Kant, *The Critique of Pure Reason*, trans. F. Max Müller (Garden City, N.Y.: Doubleday, 1966), xxxix.

3. Augustine, *Confessions*, 1.1.

4. Raschke, *End of Theology*, 91.

5. Mark C. Taylor, "Gnicart Tracing," in *New Dimensions in Philosophical Theology*, ed. Carl A. Raschke (Missoula, Mont.: American Academy of Religion, 1982), 85, 108.

6. Mark C. Taylor, *Deconstructing Theology* (Chico, Calif.: Crossroad Publishing & Scholars Press, 1982), 107–29.

7. Ibid., 126.

8. G. W. H. Hegel, *Hegel's Philosophy of Right*, trans. T. M. Knox (New York: Oxford University Press, 1967), 19: "What is rational is actual and what is actual is rational. On this conviction the plain man like the philosopher takes his stand."

9. Taylor, *Deconstructing Theology*, 113.

10. Ibid., 108.

11. At this point the most notable of Mark C. Taylor's works are *Hiding* (Chicago: University of Chicago Press, 1997); and *Disfiguring: Art, Architecture, and Religion* (Chicago: University of Chicago Press, 1994).

12. In Thomas J. J. Altizer et al., *Deconstruction and Theology* (New York: Crossroads, 1982), 73.

13. Thomas J. J. Altizer, *The Gospel of Christian Atheism* (Philadelphia: Westminster, 1966).

14. Mark C. Taylor, *Erring: A Postmodern A/theology* (Chicago: University of Chicago Press, 1984), 15.

15. Ibid., 113.

16. Ibid., 117.

17. Ibid., 174–75.

18. Ibid., 175.

19. Jean Baudrillard, *Simulacra and Simulation*, trans. Sheila Faria Glaser (Ann Arbor: University of Michigan Press, 1999), 43.

20. Charles Winquist's most important work is *Epiphanies of Darkness: Deconstruction in Theology* (Philadelphia: Fortress, 1986;

reprinted, Aurora, Colo.: Davies Group, 1999). See also idem, *The Surface of the Deep* (Aurora, Colo.: Davies Group, 2003).

21. John Milbank, *The Word Made Strange: Theology, Language, Culture* (Oxford: Blackwell, 1997), 112.

22. John Milbank makes this sort of argument in a book coauthored with Catherine Pickstock, *Truth in Aquinas* (London: Routledge, 2000).

23. Paul Lakeland, *Postmodernity: Christian Identity in a Fragmented Age* (Minneapolis: Fortress, 1997), 72.

24. Milbank, *Word Made Strange*, 279–80; italics added.

25. Ibid., 280.

26. Peter Viereck, *Metapolitics: The Roots of the Nazi Mind*, rev. ed. (New York: Capricorn Books, 1965).

Chapter 4: *Sola Fide*

1. Harriet A. Harris, *Fundamentalism and Evangelicals* (Oxford: Oxford University Press, 1998), 210.

2. Francis A. Schaeffer, *The God Who Is There*, in *The Complete Works of Francis A. Schaeffer: A Christian Worldview*, 5 vols. (Westchester, Ill.: Crossway Books, 1982), 1:12.

3. Francis A. Schaeffer, *How Should We Then Live?* in *Complete Works*, 5:84.

4. Ibid., 5:83.

5. Francis A. Schaeffer, *Back to Freedom and Dignity* (Downers Grove, Ill.: InterVarsity, 1985), 103.

6. Schaeffer, *How Should We Then Live?* in *Complete Works*, 5:123.

7. Rebecca Ritzel, "Francis Schaeffer's Relevance to Contemporary Epistemology," *World Journalism Institute*, March 3, 2000.

8. For a discussion of "revolutionary Calvinism," see Michael Walzer, *The Revolution of the Saints: A Study in the Origins of Radical Politics* (Cambridge: Atheneum, 1974).

9. "Heidelberg Disputation," *Selected Writings of Martin Luther*, ed. Theodore C. Tappert, 4 vols. (Philadelphia: Fortress, 1967), 1:78.

10. Ibid., 1:78–79.

11. Ibid., 1:79.

12. Ibid., 1:83.

13. Alister E. McGrath, *Reformation Thought: An Introduction* (Oxford: Blackwell, 1988), 58. For a more detailed explanation of the principle of *facere quod in se est*, see Heiko A. Oberman, *The Harvest of Medieval Theology: Gabriel Biel and Late Medieval Nominalism* (Grand Rapids: Eerdmans, 1967), 132.

14. McGrath, *Reformation Thought,* 76.

15. John D. Caputo, *The Prayers and Tears of Jacques Derrida: Religion without Religion* (Bloomington: Indiana University Press, 1997), 5.

16. Ibid., 6.

17. Ibid., 15.

18. Jacques Derrida, *Acts of Religion* (New York: Routledge, 2002), 40–101.

19. Ibid., 59.

20. Ibid., 105.

Chapter 5: *Sola Scriptura*

1. Emmanuel Lévinas, *Totality and Infinity: An Essay on Exteriority*, trans. Alphonso Lingis (Pittsburgh: Duquesne University Press, 1969), 67.

2. Ibid., 187.

3. The International Council on Biblical Inerrancy (ICBI) produced three critical statements, on three topics: biblical inerrancy (1978), biblical hermeneutics (1982), and biblical application (1986). The following text—containing the "Preface" by the ICBI draft committee, plus the "Short Statement," an "Exposition" of the articles (propositions) on inerrancy—appears in Carl F. H. Henry's *God, Revelation, and Authority*, 6 vols. (Waco: Word Books, 1976–83), vol. 4: *God Who Speaks and Shows (15 Theses, Part 3)* (1979), 211–19. A commentary on the articles is in R. C. Sproul's *Explaining Inerrancy: A Commentary* (Oakland, Calif.: ICBI, 1980). See also a collection of essays by many of these authors, Francis Schaeffer et al., in *The Foundation of Biblical Authority*, ed. James Montgomery Boice (Grand Rapids: Zondervan, 1978).

4. Sproul, *Explaining Inerrancy,* 41, in the appendix.

5. Ibid., 42.

6. For a good historical overview of these issues, see R. Laird Harris, *Inspiration and Canonicity of the Bible* (Grand Rapids: Zondervan, 1969). See also Rupert E. Davies, *The Problem of Authority in the Continental Reformers: A Study in Luther, Zwingli, and Calvin* (Westport, Conn.: Greenwood, 1946).

7. Charles Hodge, *Systematic Theology,* 3 vols. (London: James Clarke, 1960), 1:152.

8. Ibid., 1:163.

9. Kevin Vanhoozer, "The Inerrancy of Scripture" (Oxford: Latimer House; republished online), http://www.episcopalian.org/efac/articles/inerncy.htm.

10. Martin Luther, *Commentary on the Epistle to the Galatians* (1535), trans. Theodore Graebner (Grand Rapids: Zondervan, 1949), 49.

11. Paul D. Feinberg, "The Meaning of Inerrancy," in *Inerrancy,* ed. Norman L. Geisler (Grand Rapids: Zondervan, 1980), 294.

12. Harold Lindsell, *The Battle for the Bible* (Grand Rapids: Zondervan, 1976); idem, *The Bible in Balance* (Grand Rapids: Zondervan, 1979). See also J. I. Packer, *God Has Spoken* (Grand Rapids: Baker, 1993); Harold Dayton, "The Battle for the Bible Rages On," *Theology Today* 37 (1980): 79–84.

13. "Sendbrief von Dolmetschen," trans. Gary Mann, from *Dr. Martin Luthers Werke* (Weimar: Hermann Boehlaus Nachfolger, 1909), Band 30, Teil II, 634f.

14. Charles Hodge, *Systematic Theology,* Introduction, ch. 6, §1, electronic version: http://www.dabar.org/Theology/Hodge/HodgeV1/Int_C06.htm.

15. Harold Bloom, *The American Religion: The Emergence of the Post-Christian Nation* (New York: Simon & Schuster, 1992), 264.

16. Alister E. McGrath, *Reformation Thought: An Introduction* (Oxford: Blackwell, 1988), 107.

17. John H. Gerstner, "The Church's Doctrine of Biblical Inspiration," in *Foundation of Biblical Authority,* ed. Boice, 34.

18. Jean-Luc Marion, *God without Being,* trans. Thomas A. Carlson (Chicago: University of Chicago Press, 1991), 53.

19. Rev. 22:6.

20. Emmanuel Lévinas, *Otherwise Than Being or Beyond Essence,* trans. Alphonso

Lingis (The Hague: Martinus Nijhoff, 1981), 10.

21. Emmanuel Lévinas, *Alterity and Transcendence*, trans. Michael B. Smith (New York: Columbia University Press, 1999), 104.

22. Emmanuel Lévinas, *In the Time of the Nations*, trans. Michael B. Smith (Bloomington: Indiana University Press, 1994), 110.

23. Ibid., 110–11.

24. Gordon R. Lewis, "The Niebuhrs' Relativism, Relationalism, Contextualization, and Revelation," in *Challenges to Inerrancy: A Theological Response,* ed. Gordon R. Lewis and Bruce Demarest (Chicago: Moody, 1984), 173.

25. G. R. Evans, *The Language and Logic of the Bible: The Road to Reformation* (Cambridge: Cambridge University Press, 1985), 114–15.

26. Heb. 3:7–8.

27. Moisés Silva, *Has the Church Misread the Bible? The History of Interpretation in Light of Current Issues* (Grand Rapids: Zondervan, 1987), 118.

Chapter 6: The Priesthood of All Worshippers

1. Jean Baudrillard, *The Transparency of Evil: Essays on Extreme Phenomena*, trans. James Benedict (London: Verso, 1993), 11.

2. Ibid., 17.

3. Ibid.

4. Jean Baudrillard, *Simulacra and Simulation*, trans. Sheila Faria Glaser (Ann Arbor: University of Michigan Press, 1999), 81–82.

5. Michel Foucault, *Power/Knowledge: Selected Interviews and Other Writings, 1972–77*, trans. Colin Gordon et al. (New York: Pantheon Books, 1980), 142.

6. Michel Foucault, *The Order of Things: An Archaeology of the Human Sciences* (New York: Random House, 1994), 59.

7. Mark C. Taylor, *Deconstructing Theology* (Chico, Calif.: Crossroad Publishing & Scholars Press, 1982), 53.

8. Ibid., 56.

9. Stanley J. Grenz and John R. Franke, *Beyond Foundationalism: Shaping Theology in a Postmodern Context* (Louisville: Westminster John Knox, 2001), 193.

10. Ibid., 195.

11. Ibid., 197.

12. Ibid., 198.

13. William A. Beckham, *The Second Reformation: Reshaping the Church for the Twenty-First Century* (Houston: Touch Publications, 1995), 31.

14. Ibid., 135.

15. Ibid., 235.

16. Christian A. Schwarz, *Natural Church Development: A Guide to Eight Essential Qualities of Healthy Churches*, 3d ed. (Carol Stream, Ill.: ChurchSmart Resources, 1996), 89.

17. John 3:8.

Chapter 7: Thoroughly Postmodern Ministry

1. Charles G. Finney, "What a Revival of Religion Is," *Lectures on Revivals of Religion* (1835; Orange, Calif.: Gospel Truth Ministries, 2000), lecture I, http://www.gospeltruth.net/1868Lect_on_Rev_of_Rel/68revlec01.htm.

2. Albert B. Dod, *On Revivals of Religion: Review of Charles G. Finney* (1835; reprinted, Naphtali Press, 1997; online release, 1998), part I, http://www.graceonlinelibrary.org/full.asp?ID=573.

3. Robb Redman, *The Great Worship Awakening: Singing a New Song in the Postmodern Church* (San Francisco: Jossey-Bass, 2002).

4. Brennan Manning, *The Ragamuffin Gospel* (Sisters, Ore.: Multnomah, 1990), 26.

5. Ibid., 30.

6. Ibid., 204.

7. Brennan Manning, foreword to James Bryan Smith, *Rich Mullins: An Arrow Pointing to Heaven* (Nashville: Broadman & Holman, 2000), xi.

8. Ibid., 63.

9. Ibid., 140.

10. Ibid., 170, quoting Rich Mullins, "Joking Matters," *Release* magazine, January/February 1996.

11. Acts 17:21.

12. Acts 17:22–23, with "Mars' Hill" in NEB footnote to 17:22.

13. H. Richard Niebuhr, *Christ and Culture* (New York: Harper, 1951).

14. E-mail exchange with David Anderson, July 2, 2003.

15. Ibid., July 3, 2003.

16. Telephone conversation with Dan Allender, July 16, 2003.

17. Ibid., July 16, 2003.

18. Wade Clark Roof, *A Generation of Seekers* (San Francisco: HarperSanFrancisco, 1994), 244.

19. Ibid., 252.

20. Brian D. McLaren, *A New Kind of Christian: A Tale of Two Friends on a Spiritual Journey* (San Francisco: Jossey-Bass, 2002).

21. Leonard Sweet, Brian D. McLaren, and Jerry Haselmayer, *A Is for Abductive: The Language of the Emerging Church* (Grand Rapids: Zondervan, 2003), 72–73.

22. Ibid., 62.

23. 2 Cor. 4:17–18.

24. Sweet et al., *A Is for Abductive*, 192.

25. Heb. 11:1.

26. Quoted in William Warren Sweet, *The Story of Religion in America* (Grand Rapids: Baker, 1973), 229.

27. Robert Webber, "What Postmodernity Means to the Church," *Worship Leader* (March–April 1999); http://www.resource foundation.org/Current/PostMod/articles/web ber.shtml.

28. Jacques Barzun, *From Dawn to Decadence: 500 Years of Western Cultural Life* (New York: Harper Collins, 2000), 3.

29. Ibid., 6.

Chapter 8: Dancing with the Lord

1. Isa. 40:31 NIV.

2. Ian Cotton, *The Hallelujah Revolution: The Rise of the New Charismatics* (London: Little, Brown, and Company, 1995), 2.

3. Nancy Wark Cook, "Catholic Megacenter Services Houston's Charismatics," *Charisma* (Oct. 1997), 38–40.

4. The difference in political leanings between mainline conservative evangelicals and charismatics, or "neo-Pentecostals," as they are sometimes (wrongly) called, is summarized by Diane Winston, "One Spirit, Many Faces," *Dallas Morning News,* August 27, 1997, G1: "The overall political stance of Spirit-filled

people is quite diverse and can include many liberals and even social activists."

5. Harvey Cox, *Fire from Heaven: The Rise of Pentecostal Spirituality and the Reshaping of Religion in the Twenty-First Century* (New York: Addison-Wesley, 1995).

6. Thomas J. Csordas, *Language, Charisma, and Creativity: The Ritual Life of a Religious Movement* (Berkeley: University of California Press, 1997), 57.

7. John 1:19–34.

8. See Curtis Bennett, *God as Form: Essays in Greek Theology* (Albany: State University of New York Press, 1976).

9. John 16:16.

10. Acts 1:6–8.

11. Lev. 23:15–18 and Num. 28:26.

12. Acts 2:1–4.

13. Lev. 23:15–18 and Num. 28:26.

14. Acts 2:15–17.

15. Acts 2:11.

16. John 1:34.

17. Martin Marty, *Theological Roots of Pentecostalism* (Grand Rapids: Francis Asbury, 1997), 35.

18. Chuck D. Pierce, "God's Heart for Israel," *Pray for the Peace of Jerusalem* (ca. 1997), 1:1.

19. Acts 14:27.

20. Acts 15:1.

21. Acts 15:2, 16–17.

22. Acts 15:19.

23. Acts 15:28.

24. Gal. 3:2.

25. Gal. 3:3.

26. Gal. 3:14.

27. John 7:37–39.

28. Rom. 8:11.

29. Eph. 3:4, 6.

30. Rom. 8:23.

31. Rom. 8:29.

32. Rom. 9:8.

33. 1 Cor. 12:4–6.

34. 1 Cor. 14:1–4.

35. Col. 3:14.

36. Morton T. Kelsey, *Tongue Speaking: The History and Meaning of Charismatic Experience* (New York: Crossroad, 1981), 232.

37. Eph. 6:10–17.

38. Eph. 5:15–16.

39. Robert Heidler, *The Art of Spiritual Warfare* (Denton, Tex.: Believers' Fellowship, 1994), 16.

40. 2 Cor. 10:3–5.

41. 2 Cor. 10:5.

42. Albert C. Outler, *John Wesley* (New York: Oxford University Press, 1964), 69.

43. Heidler, *Art of Spiritual Warfare,* 60.

44. Ibid., 66.

45. Luke 4:1–11 NRSV.

46. See, for example, Hank Hanegraaff, *The Covering: God's Plan to Protect You from Evil* (Nashville: W Publishing, 2002); idem, *Counterfeit Revival* (Nashville: W Publishing 2002); and John F. MacArthur Jr., *Charismatic Chaos* (Grand Rapids: Zondervan, 1993).

47. Augustine, *Concerning the City of God against the Pagans,* trans. Henry Bettenson (New York: Penguin Books, 1972), 402 (10.22).

48. See Isa. 5:1–7; Jer. 2:21; Ezek. 19:10–14.

49. John 15:5–6.

50. John 14:30.

51. John 15:15.

52. John 15:26; 16:14–15.

53. John 16:8–11.

54. John 16:1–3.

55. John 16:13.

56. Hans Windisch, *The Spirit-Paraclete in the Fourth Gospel,* trans. James W. Cox (Philadelphia: Fortress, 1968), 38.

57. John 16:15.

58. *The Confessions of Saint Augustine,* trans. Rex Warner (New York: New American Library, 1963), 290 (2.10).

59. For an excellent historical analysis of Edwards and the New Divinity movement, see David W. Kling, *A Field of Divine Wonders: The New Divinity and Village Revivals in Northwestern Connecticut, 1772–1822* (University Park, Pa.: Pennsylvania State University Press, 1993).

60. The beginnings of many of these groups are mentioned by Erling Jorstad, *That Newtime Religion: The Jesus Revival in America* (Minneapolis: Augsburg, 1972), 99ff.

61. George H. Williams and Edith Waldvogel, "A History of Speaking in Tongues and Related Gifts," in *The Charismatic Movement,* ed. Michael P. Hamilton (Grand Rapids: Eerdmans, 1975), 105.

Chapter 9: The End of Theology

1. Justo L. González, *A History of Christian Thought,* vol. 1 (Nashville: Abingdon, 1970), 21–22.

2. Ibid., 100.

3. Peter Gay, *The Enlightenment: The Rise of Modern Paganism* (New York: Norton, 1995).

4. Emmanuel Lévinas, *Discovering Existence with Husserl,* trans. Richard A. Cohen and Michael B. Smith (Evanston, Ill.: Northwestern University Press, 1998), 121.

5. Emmanuel Lévinas, *Entre Nous: On Thinking-of-the-Other,* trans. Michael B. Smith and Barbara Harshav (New York: Columbia University Press, 1998), 173.

6. Emmanuel Lévinas, *Otherwise Than Being or Beyond Essence,* trans. Alphonso Lingis (The Hague: Martinus Nijhoff, 1981), 140.

7. Emmanuel Lévinas, *Beyond the Verse: Talmudic Readings and Lectures,* trans. Gary D. Mole (Bloomington: Indiana University Press, 1994), 112.

8. Emmanuel Lévinas, *Collected Philosophical Papers,* trans. Alphonso Lingis (Dordrecht: Martinus Nijhoff, 1987), 55.

INDEX